D1443191

THE
LAST DAYS OF
MARIE ANTOINETTE
AND
LOUIS XVI

THE
LAST DAYS
OF
MARIE
ANTOINETTE
AND
LOUIS
XVI

Rupert Furneaux

DORSET PRESS • NEW YORK

This edition published by Dorset Press
a division of Marboro Books Corporation,
by arrangement with
Harper & Row, Publishers
1990 Dorset Press

ISBN 0-88029-458-2

Printed in the United States of America

M 9 8 7 6 5 4 3 2 1

CONTENTS

CONTENTS

THE
LAST DAYS OF
MARIE ANTOINETTE
AND
LOUIS XVI

I

THE TOCSIN

Worn by weeks of anxiety and exhausted by the fatigue of the night's vigil, the women clustered at the open windows of the Council Chamber, listening to the clamour of the tocsins. As suddenly as they had begun the bells fell silent; the last echoes of their peals died away. For an hour and a half the silence was unbroken; then, at 3 a.m., came the dull beat of drums and muffled boom of cannon. Below, in the courtyard of the palace, a musket fired. 'That is the first shot, it will not be the last,' exclaimed the Queen in her agony, unaware that it had gone off accidentally. Surrounded by her ladies, Marie Antoinette listened to the rising clamour of the city. Into the room burst her husband, his clothes in disarray, his wig awry, his pendulous lower lip trembling. The gunfire had aroused Louis from fitful sleep.

A streak of red in the sky heralded the dawn, the presage of another hot, stifling August day. 'Come, see the sun rise,' called Madame Elizabeth, the King's sister. The Queen shuddered. The eastern sun glowed blood-red. From the city came the roar of gathering tumult. An officer, M. de la Chenaye, burst into the room. 'This is your last day. The people have proved the strongest,' he cried, adding in a hoarse whisper, 'What carnage there will be.'

Shrilly, stridently the tocsin of the Cordeliers clanged the alarm. 'To arms, to arms', it called. Section by section the forty-eight city bells echoed the summons. Their clamour swept Paris, arousing its citizens. Seizing their weapons, the *sans-culottes* poured from their homes and marched on the Tuileries. To the anxious listeners, faintly at first but swelling in volume, was carried the sound of tramping feet and the strains of the Marseillaise, the marching song of the Revolution. The months of uncertainty are over; king and people stand face to face in their final trial of strength.

It is August 10, 1792, the day upon which the French people finally repudiated the absolute despotism that had held them in thrall for a thousand years. The Americans had shown the way to popular sovereignty; the spark of liberty had been carried back across the Atlantic by the volunteers who had gone to the aid of the repressed colonists. In France the Revolution became dominated by the Terror and by the guillotine.

It seemed at first that the French would gain their objectives peacefully. When the wind of change first blew, Louis XVI bent before the storm. He bowed to the clamour for reform, and he accepted the role of constitutional king; the monarchy survived the first clash with the people. *'Rien'*, Louis wrote in his diary on July 14, 1789. The fall of the Bastille, the symbol of *ancien régime*, was 'nothing', yet it heralded the end of the old order of aristocratic privilege and corruption. The tragic events that followed were not inevitable. The Revolution triumphed because at every stage Louis took the wrong decisions; in the end it failed because the revolutionaries were as weak as he.

The French people did not desire to abolish the monarchy, which they held in almost religious veneration, and they did not hate Louis XVI. Fat, gluttonous, awkward, pious, shy, gentle, kindly, conscientious, unambitious, ineffective, he lacked the vices of his predecessors; they had supported parasitic noblemen and kept expensive women; Louis was a keen amateur locksmith and he failed to consummate his marriage for seven years. When he declared, or rather stuttered, that he 'loved the people', he was sincere. He was sympathetic to the cry for change and the need for reform, and he accepted that the day of the absolute monarchy and of the autocratic kings was over.

By accepting the Constitution forced upon him by the Assembly on October 10, 1789, Louis became the representative and no longer the master of the French people: it reduced his status to that of a salaried state functionary, responsible for his actions to the Assembly which could depose him if he committed treason or quitted the kingdom without permission. Louis was King of France by the will of the nation, the figurehead of a bourgeois republic, and he retained only the right of suspensive veto by which he could delay legislation for two sessions. He retained his dignity, but he felt humiliated. The spectre of

Charles I haunted him and he intrigued weakly against the new regime.

The Revolution was middle-class in origin and it depended for survival on the co-operation of the King who alone might have controlled the dangerous forces lurking in the background, the half-starved city proletariat, an incalculable weapon in the hands of a few ruthless men, and the disgruntled *émigrés*. In 1790 20,000 nobles withdrew across the French frontiers and lodged themselves chiefly in the German states of Mainz and Coblenz where, led by the King's brothers, the Comte de Provence and the Comte d'Artois, they intrigued with the rulers of Europe, and recruited soldiers in order to stage a counter-revolution. Their actions discredited the monarchy and created the suspicion that Louis was plotting to regain absolute power. 'The Constitution was a veritable monster,' declared Dumont, Mirabeau's pupil; 'there was too much republic for a monarchy and too much monarchy for a republic; the King was an hors d'oeuvre'.

In her fear, the Queen, the Austrian princess whom Louis had married at fifteen in 1700, exercised a malign influence over her husband. Marie Antoinette has suffered from the verdict of history which portrays her as a wilful, heartless woman who, when the starving people of France asked for bread, offered them cake. She was uncomprehending, rather than unsympathetic. Steeped in monarchical tradition, she believed that the King of France had been accorded the divine right to rule, and she rejected all compromise with that principle. She goaded her easily influenced husband to stand up for his rights, but she failed to impregnate him with her own strength of will; yet she was the only man at his side. Marie Antoinette was picturesquely beautiful, extravagant, haughty, reckless and indiscreet. The people hated her as an Austrian and as the symbol of the *ancien régime*. She manoeuvred clumsily to revive the absolute monarchy.

Encouraged by his strong-willed wife, Louis sought to escape from the hateful restraint imposed on him by the Constitution. On June 20, 1791, the Royal Family made a dash for the frontier, intending to galvanize the *émigrés* and to solicit the help of the Great Powers, whose hereditary rulers viewed the establishment of people's sovereignty with alarm. Detected almost within reach of their goal, Louis and Marie Antoinette were brought back to Paris in ignominy. He became a prisoner in the Tuileries, a hostage against foreign intervention. The wealthy middle-classes still needed Louis but the people had lost faith in him. 'We have need of some great treachery,' declared Brissot, a member of the Assembly.

The Emperor of Austria, Marie Antoinette's brother Leopold, and the King of Prussia threatened to intervene, to crush the Revolution and rescue the Royal Family, and the French took the threat more seriously than it was intended. Both parties, the Constitutionalists and the Royalists, believed they could benefit by a preventive war; the popular party hoped it would strengthen internal loyalties and rally the nation to their side, and the King's supporters hoped for an early French defeat. The Assembly forced Louis to declare war against the potential aggressors. He did what he was ordered, and he imposed his veto on two popular measures: the laws requiring priests to take an oath to the Constitution and *émigrés* to return or be treated as traitors. Believing that the King was lukewarm to the Constitution, treacherous to the nation, and responsible for military reverses, the mob invaded the Tuileries on June 20, 1792. Louis faced the people calmly and bloodshed was avoided. The extremists determined to abolish the monarchy and they made no secret of their plans. The palace would be defended, announced the government.

Events moved quickly but obscurely. On July 30th 516 volunteers from Marseilles, all fervent republicans, dragging their cannon and singing their revolutionary hymn, invaded Paris bent upon the deposition of the King. Two days later Parisians learned of the Declaration of Pillnitz, where the Duke of Brunswick, the Commander of the Allied armies massed on the frontier, threatened them with 'an exemplary and unforgettable vengeance, by delivering up Paris to military execution and complete destruction', if they again insulted the King. Suspicion that Louis was plotting to overthrow the Revolution increased and it galvanized the resolute minority who were determined to abolish the monarchy and to liquidate the Legislative Assembly, the symbol and strength of the sovereignty of middle-class wealth. These men turned for support to the hitherto untapped strength of the city proletariat, the small tradesmen and artisans, the *sans-culottes* of Paris, who were so termed because they lacked the breeches of the aristocrats and wealthy bourgeois. These 60,000 part-time and partly-armed soldiers who formed the

National Guard recruited from the city's forty-eight sections were controlled by the municipality, the Commune as it was named.

Its elected representatives and its guardsmen contained all shades of political opinion, with a predominance towards republicanism, and they were not far separated in their common aims from many of the delegates to the Assembly, the Jacobins (the members of the political club of that name) and the Girondists (the political faction which had originated as a geographical expression). Now, while the majority vacillated, the minority (as has become the rule in successful revolutions) acted. During the night of August 9th, the extremists, the leaders of the Parisian sections, overthrew the municipality and established the Insurrection Commune, an organization lacking legality but which, as the night progressed, seized control of the National Guardsmen. These shadowy figures set out to dethrone the King and render futile the government represented by the King's Ministers and the Assembly, and to seize the reins of power, if not its semblance. The elected officers of the municipality bent before the storm. The Insurrectionists organized the attack on the Tuileries; the officials disorganized its defence.

The alarm gun, fired from the Pont Neuf at 1 a.m., called the people of the sections to assemble. Half an hour later the tocsins pealed; thousands of armed men, carpenters, clerks, wine-merchants, lawyers, shoe-makers, labourers and workmen, massed on the Place de Grève. The Marseillais came with their cannon.

2

THE TUILERIES

The Royal Family had been expecting attack for days, and in the words of the American Ambassador, Gouvernor Morris, 'sat up all night expecting to be murdered'. The ministers and officers of the municipality had agreed that an assault on the monarchy must be resisted and troops had been sent to defend the Tuileries, to support the Swiss mercenaries, the traditional bodyguards of French royalty who numbered 900 men. But the loyalty of these 2400 National Guardsmen and 1000 mounted policemen was doubtful; many had become infected by revolutionary ideas and the position of their Commander, Captain Mandat, was equivocal. An honourable man and a staunch 'Constitutionalist', he had been appointed by the municipality which was now about to be superseded by the Insurrectionary Commune. To sustain the monarchy at its hour of peril, these men needed the inspiration of a determined and courageous leader, and he was lacking. Louis XVI was terrified of bloodshed and incapable of inspiring loyalty. 'Ah, if I had been in command', lamented an eye-witness of the debacle of August 10th, a young lieutenant of artillery who became its only beneficiary.

Napoleon Bonaparte played no part in that day's events. The men who sowed the wind and who reaped the whirlwind are shadowy figures, the self-appointed committee of the Commune, who as the night progressed seized power at the Hôtel de Ville. Like the Bolsheviks at St Petersburg in 1917, they were resolute and determined men.

The Assembly, the elected representatives of the people of France, meeting in the Riding School behind the Tuileries, had no executive power, for the French had adopted the American constitutional system whereby the deputies were merely legislators. The King was the executive and he appointed the ministers whose responsibility it was to enforce the law. But they were as weak as he and they spent the night of August 9th–10th scurrying to and from the Assembly, seeking decisions that no one had the power to make. The real power lay in the hands of the Commune, for they alone controlled a resolute and armed force, the troops of the city's forty-eight sections.

Louis allowed himself to be swept from the throne without a fight. 'If,' wrote twenty-three-year-old Lieutenant Bonaparte next day in a letter to his brother Joseph, 'Louis XVI had shown himself on horseback, the victory would have been his.' Alas, Louis was irresolute and at the hour of crisis the strength of monarchical tradition was too strong for the Queen to take command. Her husband was the King. To protect their sovereign in the hour of danger, 300 elderly noblemen had rallied the *chevaliers du poignard*, the noblesse of the sword. But their weapons were no more than tiny ceremonial swords, and they were commanded by the eighty-six-year-old Maréchal de Mailly.

The soldiers were deployed to guard the Tuileries, the ancient château built in 1564 by Catherine de Medici; it comprised an irregular mass of buildings, encircled by walls, and backing on the Place du Carrousel, from which it was divided by three courts, each separated from the other by high walls and iron railings. Behind the main buildings lay extensive gardens. Early on the evening of August 9th, Captain Mandat made a strategic move; he sent detachments of the National Guard, each equipped with cannon, to seize and hold the bridges crossing the Seine; as long as these bridges were held, the troops of the Commune were prevented from converging.

The month of August came, ushered in by days of gasping, tropical heat and by sultry, airless nights. Beneath the burnished sky lurked the hint of autumn. The leaves fell early that year, laying a rustling, golden-brown carpet in the streets, that accentuated the uncanny silence into which the city fell, for they deadened the sounds of traffic and disguised the rising tide of anger of the people who believed that the King had betrayed them to their enemies. As day succeeded day the Royal Family became more and more isolated. Their visitors, other than the ministers and courtiers who fussed around them, became fewer and on the afternoon of the ninth only one friend called to see Marie Antoinette. Lady Gower, the wife of the British Ambassador, defied the angry mutters and glowering stares of the crowds who thronged the narrow streets leading to the Carrousel to spend an hour with the unhappy Queen. Behind the palace, in the Riding School, the Assembly met in continuous session to debate the abolition of Negro slavery in the French overseas colonies. While its deputies argued the rights and wrongs of servitude in an egalitarian society, their equalitarian world was crashing about their ears. Others were to prove more equal than they.

When Lady Gower's carriage rattled away, the guards clanged to the gates of the palace, and within the Royal Family, with its few devoted servants and friends, settled down to endure another anxious, uneasy night of vigil that was made more fearful by the rumour that the Insurrectionists had selected August 10th for the day of decision. Louis had not undressed for weeks and streaks of grey were beginning to fleck Marie Antoinette's auburn hair, yet she was only thirty-seven years of age. The Royal Family stood in mortal danger; repeatedly the King had retreated, and now he had his back to the wall. Louis and Marie Antoinette were the parents of young children whose lives were in peril. To safeguard their thirteen-year-old daughter, Madame Royale, and their seven-year-old son, the Dauphin Louis Charles, they were prepared to undergo any humiliation, to lay down their own lives. By his vacillation, Louis brought about his own death, and that of his wife and sister, and maybe that of his son. The experiences she underwent turned Madame Royale into a bitter woman who nursed her hatred to the grave.

That night, when she put her son to bed, the Queen's face was streaked by tears. 'Maman, why are you weeping?' cried Louis Charles. 'Be calm, I shall not be far from you,' replied the distraught mother, leaving her son in the care of his governess, Madame de Tourzel and her daughter, Pauline. While these devoted attendants watched, the child fell into a peaceful sleep. Of all the people in the palace, only Louis Charles slept that night, the last of the ancient monarchy.

The events that took place that night and next day have been described by an historian[1] who made an exhaustive study of the records, as 'the most obscure and uncertain in the whole course of the Revolution', and several modern historians have remarked

[1] A. Tuetey, *Repetoire* V.

how little we really know of the motivations behind the final acts of the French Revolution.

Several eye-witnesses have described what they saw and heard on August 10th; they do not always agree and they are imprecise about time and places. The central figures of the drama move about within the royal apartments at the Tuileries, but we do not always know which room they are in, or the exact times at which the acts of the drama unfold. Nevertheless a picture emerges; a portrait of the irresolute King and the nerve-racked Queen; around them circulate a host of lesser figures, courtiers, servants, ministers, officers of the municipality, guards and noblemen, the devoted *chevaliers du poignard*. It is a picture of heroism, perfidy and vacillation.

That the night of August 9th was different from other nights became evident when after supper the King announced that he would retire to his bedroom. The court functionaries made ready to enact the traditional ceremony of unrobing the King, an ancient rite attended by carefully defined etiquette. Louis shut the door in the face of the courtiers. It was the first time for centuries that any change had been made in the rigid court ceremonial, and it troubled the functionaries. Louis threw himself on the bed, fully clothed.

No one else went to bed. After bidding her son goodnight the Queen rejoined her ladies in the great Council Chamber on the first floor of the palace, a large room overlooking the courts at the back of the building. The aged de Malesherbes, his tiny ceremonial sword in his hand, stood guard at the door leading to the royal apartments. The 300 elderly noblemen patrolled the long gallery, leading from the grand staircase, in which milled a throng of courtiers and ministers, who strode up and down, for strict etiquette forbade that even the most noble should sit in the royal apartments. Many became weary and several of the boldest stopped to lean against tables and chairs; some even lay on the floor, defying the horrified remonstrances of the ushers who tried to preserve the traditional customs. Almost imperceptibly, the old order passed away.

Up the grand staircase and along the crowded long gallery came Pétion, the Mayor of Paris, the executive officer of the municipality whose functions were at the point of being usurped by the Insurrectionary Commune. Pétion was playing it safe; his duty required his presence at the palace, for its guards came under the jurisdiction of the municipality; he was determined to avoid compromising himself with either side, the Constitutionalists of the Assembly or the Insurrectionists at the Hôtel de Ville. He was circumspect even in his progress along the gallery; he avoided brushing against anyone as he walked to the door of the royal apartments.

Pétion was taken to the Council Chamber where he joined the Queen and the King, who had been roused by the news of the Mayor's arrival. With them also was Pierre Louis Roederer, the Attorney General, who tells the story of the interview at which he needed to tread as softly as Pétion, and Captain Mandat, the Commander of the palace guards. He had come to allay the agitation against the King, announced Pétion. 'No, Monsieur, it is under your eyes that it is being organized,' Marie Antoinette told him, and she insisted that the Mayor should sign an order giving authority to Captain Mandat to repel force by force. Reluctantly Pétion signed the paper and gave it to Mandat, who reported that many of his soldiers had only three rounds of gunpowder each and some had none at all. 'You have no right to any more,' retorted Pétion and, on the pretext that he needed to inspect the defences of the palace, he descended into the gardens and slipped through a gate, leaving his coach standing in the courtyard. He reached the Hôtel de Ville at midnight to find that the Commune had seized control from the elected deputies. Pétion claimed that he had been forced to sign the order under duress, and he was allowed to retain his office.

The information brought by Pétion, that Captain Mandat had been authorized to order the National Guardsmen, the soldiers of the municipality, to defend the monarchy, precipitated the crisis. Mandat held the whip-hand, for, as long as he held the Mayor's order, the National Guardsmen would obey his commands. For the insurrection to succeed, the Mayor's authorization to Mandat had to be withdrawn, and he had to be eliminated.

We know nothing about the deliberations of the Commune that night and the order of events is doubtful. The tocsin bells, calling the people of Paris to arms, rang at 1.30 a.m. and quickly the armed *sans-culottes*, the petty bourgeois of the nearby sections, gathered in the Place de Grève, where they were joined by the 516 men of Marseilles and Brest, the spear-head of the Revolution.

Next, and apparently in that order, the leaders of the Commune despatched a messenger to the Tuileries, summoning Captain Mandat to their presence. When the man brought the order, Mandat said that his sworn duty was to defend the constitutional King. When a second messenger arrived, he turned pale and obeyed. 'I shall never return,' he told the King. At the Hôtel de Ville, Mandat was accused of planning to attack the sovereign people and he was sentenced to be imprisoned. As he was removed under guard a bullet crashed into his skull. The mob tore his body to pieces and threw it into the Seine. The only man capable of defending the palace was gone. The Commune sent their emissaries to the bridges ordering the guardsmen to remove their cannon. They obeyed, and several contingents joined the Insurrectionists, bringing their cannon. Blooded by the murder of Mandat, the armed section guards surged through the dark narrow streets leading to the Carrousel. At their head marched the men of Marseilles, dragging their cannon.

An English visitor, John Moore, who had gone to bed early that night, was aroused by the clamour of the tocsins and by the beating of drums and by shouting. The people of Paris, he was told by other guests in the hotel, were marching on the Tuileries but, despite this alarming news, Moore returned to bed, where he fell asleep again. He did not rouse until 9 a.m. Another Englishman was equally slothful; both men made up for their tardiness later.

The noise of gathering tumult swept across Paris and penetrated the Tuileries. To the anxious listeners it sounded like the roar of an angry sea. Above the tramp of feet and the beat of drums arose the strains of the Marseillaise. The occasional boom of cannon dispelled any doubts; the sans-culottes were on the march, their objective the Tuileries; their intention, the dethronement of the King.

About 4 a.m., Madame de Tourzel, the Dauphin's governess, left the peacefully sleeping boy in the care of her daughter Pauline and went to the Council Chamber to see what was going on. Everyone, she says, was anxiously awaiting the upshot of the day; the Queen spoke to everyone in the most affectionate manner, encouraging their zeal. One of the noblemen, M.

d'Hervilly told Madame de Tourzel, 'I have the worst possible opinion about today; the worst thing is to do nothing and nothing is being done.' Her son on the other hand, according to another source, thought that nothing of importance was afoot; he and another young officer, François de la Rochefoucauld, who had returned to the palace after an evening at the Comédie-Française, had missed their supper and they sat up and drank punch instead.

Madame Campan, the Queen's First Lady-in-Waiting and an inveterate and generally unreliable gossip, was also about. Earlier in the night she had come upon two sentinels fighting at the door of the royal apartments: one said he was hearty in the cause of the Constitution and would defend it at the peril of his life; the other declared that the King was an encumbrance to the Constitution. They were ready to cut each other's throats. Madame Campan's face betrayed her fears, and the King asked the reasons for her emotion. When she recalled what she had heard, the Queen said she was not surprised, for more than half of the National Guardsmen belonged to the extreme party, the Jacobins. When the tocsins sounded Madame Campan watched the soldiers, to catch their reactions; the Swiss mercenaries stood like walls, in marked contrast, she thought, to the guardsmen who kept up a continual din. One of their officers whispered to her, 'Put your jewels and money in your pocket; our dangers are unavoidable and the means of defence are nil.' Madame Campan returned to the royal apartments; the Queen emerged from the King's room and told her 'there is no longer any hope'; Captain Mandat had been assassinated and the people were carrying his head through the streets on a pike.

Two men who will play a more conspicuous part later flit across the scene. J. Hanet-Cléry, the King's valet (more a confidential servant than a menial), made two excursions into the streets to learn what was going on, and François Hue, one of the Officers of the King's Chamber, says that between four and five in the morning he found the Queen in tears. To an officer she cried, 'Save the King; save my children,' and she ran to the Dauphin's room, where Hue followed. He heard the boy exclaim, 'Maman, why should they hurt Papa? He is so good.' The Queen dressed her son and carried him into the Council Chamber where he was joined by a little girl, the companion of his games, the daughter perhaps of one of the courtiers. 'Here, Josephine,' cried Louis Charles, 'take this lock of my hair and promise to wear it as long as I am in danger.'

Pierre Louis Roederer, the Attorney General, spent the night at the palace. A man of icy temperament and legal exactitude who owed loyalty neither to the Constitutionalists nor to the Insurrectionists; he was concerned to keep his job. Shortly after the tocsins sounded Roederer received a note from his department which warned him that 1500 to 2000 rioters had collected in the Faubourg Saint-Antoine and that the section was in 'commotion'. He read the letter to the ministers present and to the King and Queen, and he was asked if he could proclaim martial law. 'We have something quite different from a simple disturbance of public order,' he explained, 'we have an insurrection.' Under the circumstances it would be absolutely useless to proclaim martial law. Nor did he know who could proclaim it. He retired to a lamp to study the law in the three large volumes he carried. 'What are you trying to find out?' enquired Madame Elizabeth, the King's sister. 'I am trying to learn whether my department has the power,' replied the precise M. Roederer. 'Well, has it?' she asked. 'I don't think so, Madame,' the Attorney General cautiously replied.

Roederer sat himself on a stool near the door of the bedchamber. There was no formality, he says. The Queen, Madame Elizabeth and several other women sat on stools in line with his. A second message was brought to Roederer. It stated that the Commune was having difficulty in getting the people to assemble and that many of those who had collected were growing tired; it looked as though they would refuse to march on the palace. When Roederer read out this reassuring news, a wit remarked 'the tocsin doesn't pay'. A further message stated that the guns on the Pont Neuf had been withdrawn; ominous news indeed. The Assembly, Roederer was informed, had recommenced its session at 2 a.m. and the eighty deputies present were debating the order of the day, the question of Negro slavery.

A few minutes later, we find Roederer in the room of the King's valet where the Queen was seated by the fireplace with her back to the windows. 'What should be done?' she asked and she said in a very downright manner, 'Monsieur, there is a conflict of forces. We have come to the point where we must know which is going to prevail—the King and the Constitution, or the rebels.' M. Lachesnaye, the officer commanding in succession to Captain Mandat, was sent for. When he came to the room, Roederer asked what measures had been taken to prevent the demonstrators from reaching the palace. The Carrousel was guarded, replied Lachesnaye, and turning to the Queen he said that the National Guardsmen were objecting to the presence outside the royal apartments of the *chevaliers du poignard*, 'persons of all sorts', as he called them, who were usurping the guardsmen's functions. Marie Antoinette quickly settled the demarcation dispute. The elderly noblemen, she explained, were civilians and they were brave men who would share the guardsmen's danger to the last. 'I will answer for them,' she said and she told Lachesnaye, 'You can rely on them fully and dispose of them as you wish.' She went to the door where a group of young guardsmen were standing. 'Our interests are one,' she told them. 'All that you hold dear, your wives and children, depend upon our existence.' Whereby she meant that they were safe only if they upheld the Constitution. Marie Antoinette's impromptu little speech moved the men to tears and they declared that they would die if necessary, in defence of the King and Queen. Alas, when the King had a similar opportunity to rouse the loyalty of his defenders, he failed to take it.

The Queen's words convinced Roederer that within the palace there was a strong determination to fight and that this faction, as he calls it, had promised the Queen a victory. It filled him with the fear of a bloody but useless resistance that might lead to an attack on the Assembly after the troops guarding the palace had been defeated. He insisted that the Assembly should be consulted and two commissioners were sent to the Riding School. This discussion had blinded the participants to what was going on outside the palace. Boos and cries from the courtyard alerted the Queen and the Ministers, and they craned their heads out of the windows. 'Good God, it is the King they are booing. What the devil is he doing down there?' exclaimed one of the Ministers. The Queen began to weep.

Louis had made another of his fatal decisions. He had decided at 6 a.m. personally to review the troops guarding the palace. François Hue was watching from a window. When the King first appeared he was greeted by a general acclamation and by shouts of 'Vive le roi', but they soon turned to 'Vive la nation', and 'Down with the tyrant'. In vain, the little knot of courtiers, who tried to form a chain around the King, chanted, 'Messieurs, vive le roi.' The threats swelled in volume. Many of the guardsmen broke their ranks, surrounding the King. Madame Campan, who was watching, saw some of the gunners quit their posts, go up to the King and thrust their fists in his face, insulting him in the most brutal language and calling him 'Cochon'. To a member of the National Guard, Frenilly, the King appeared to be a tired, dishevelled man, a pathetic figure; 'What a distressing review for men who asked only a master and a leader. I can still see him, the unhappy Prince, passing before us, silent, troubled, slouching and seeming to say to us "all is lost".' Dressed in a purple coat, breeches and white stockings, with his hat held under his arm, Louis ambled along the lines; 'We must defend ourselves, don't you think?' he stuttered, and he told those who would listen, 'They are certainly "coming". What do they want? I will not separate myself from good citizens; my cause is theirs.'

'All is lost', cried the Queen through her tears. On his return journey through the palace, Louis was greeted by the elderly noblemen guarding the royal apartments. Bending his knee, Maréchal de Mailly cried, 'Here are the faithful nobles who have hastened to re-establish your Majesty on the throne of your ancestors.' 'We will perish or save ourselves together,' replied Louis, and he raised the Dauphin, who had been brought by the Queen, to his shoulder. 'Long live the King of our forefathers,' exclaimed one old man; another went one better; 'Long live the King of our children,' he emphasized.

The King was out of breath and very hot from the effort of running, says Roederer, but he did not seem upset by his experience. Nevertheless, the last opportunity to resist the attack had been lost. Barbaroux, one of the leaders of the men from Marseilles, said afterwards that if the King had mounted a horse and ridden among the soldiers as a commanding presence, 'the very great majority of the National Guards would have declared for him.'

Roederer withdrew to a small room to discuss the situation with the other Ministers. A police officer reported that the whole of Paris was up in arms; the battalion of the Cordeliers and the men of Marseilles were on the march and the people of the outer districts were coming with their cannon. The Commune had issued 50,000 cartridges. Roederer set off to go to the Assembly, to 'learn its wisdom'. On the way, he saw crowds surging out of the narrow streets surrounding the Tuileries, and an artillery man to whom he spoke asked in a distressed voice, 'Will we be obliged to fire on our brothers?' 'You will not have to fire if no one fires on you,' Roederer told the man. He made a little speech to the men. 'Show a bold front and be strong in defence,' he urged. To a gunner's question, 'If they fire on us will you be there?' he replied, 'Yes, and not behind the guns, but in front of them.' And pointing to his colleagues, he said, 'We shall be the first to go.' Without replying, the gunner unloaded his cannon, threw the ball on the ground and put his foot on the lighted match. Roederer, having been told that only eighty deputies were present in the Assembly, an insufficient number to decide anything of importance, withdrew to the palace.

The civilian army, the mob, reached the outskirts of the Tuileries about 7.30 a.m., led by the contingent from Marseilles marching in fine order, dragging their cannon and with matches lighted. Entering upon the Carrousel, they swivelled the guns round and trained them on the palace. They were followed by thousands of men, carrying pikes, cutlasses and muskets. François Hue relates that when a municipal officer tried to stem the ferment, he was dragged from the stand on to which he had mounted. His place was taken by Theroigne de Mericourt, a noted feminist whom the royalists called a 'notorious prostitute', who was dressed like a man with a sword at her side. 'Her eyes, gestures and words, everything about her, was expressive of fury,' states a scandalized adherent of the *ancien régime*.

The appearance of the rioters was sufficient for most of the National Guardsmen. Three-quarters of them deserted and joined the Insurrectionists. Not more than four to five hundred remained at their posts around the palace, records Cléry. Maréchal de Mailly assumed command and the remaining guardsmen and the Swiss were brigaded together. Cléry walked among them and on hearing that none had eaten for hours he organized the supply of loaves of bread and bottles of wine. The noblesse guarding the royal apartments drew themselves into two lines. 'Many others,' states Madame Campan, 'members of the Court, some of whom had no technical right among what was called the *noblesse*, but

26

whose self-devotion ennobled them at once, joined them. One of the King's equerries and a page broke and divided a pair of tongs which they carried on their shoulders instead of muskets. Another page produced a pistol which he stuck against the person who stood next to him, and who begged him to be good enough to rest it elsewhere.

'What do they want?' asked Louis when he was told that thousands of angry rioters were pouring into the Carrousel. 'Your deposition,' replied the municipal officer who led a deputation from the Hôtel de Ville. 'What will become of the King?' asked the Queen. The officer made no answer and he withdrew, walking backwards and punctiliously observing the ancient customs in the presence of royalty.

Roederer reappeared, wearing the tricolor sash, his badge of office, and accompanied by several members of his department. In after years he remarked that Marie Antoinette was not the heroic woman that legend had made her out to be. She was a woman in despair, a mother, a wife in peril. Nevertheless, it was to the Queen that Roederer addressed his remarks. Defence was impossible. He advised the Royal Family to take refuge in the Assembly. 'Leave the palace, there is not a moment to be lost,' he urged. From outside came the crash of splintering wood and the clang of iron upon iron, and the cries of furious panting voices. Louis went to the window and looked out. 'I don't see a very large crowd,' he remarked. 'Sirs, they have twelve cannon and a large multitude is streaming in from the *faubourgs*,' cried Roederer.

A member of the municipal deputation, whom Roederer describes as a 'zealous patriot', a small tradesman named Gerdret from whom the Queen used to buy lace, began to speak in support of the Attorney General. 'Silence, Gerdret; it is not for such as you to raise your voice here,' stormed the outraged Queen. Turning to Roederer she exclaimed, 'But, you know, we have a defence here.' There were insufficient men to defend the courtyards, and they were not well disposed, remarked Roederer, and he emphasized, 'All Paris is on the march, Madam.' 'Are we totally deserted?' asked the Queen. 'Will no one act in our favour?' Roederer repeated his advice, 'resistance is impossible', and he asked the Queen. 'Do you wish to make yourself responsible for the massacre of the King, of your children, of yourself, of the faithful servitors who surround you?' 'God forbid!' exclaimed the Queen, 'Would that I could be the only victim.' Only a few minutes before she had told two of the noblemen that she would rather be nailed to the walls of the palace than go to the Assembly. Turning again to the King, Roederer said with great emphasis, 'Time presses, Sire.'

Thrusting herself forward, Madame Elizabeth asked, 'Monsieur Roederer, will you answer for the life of the King?' He would answer for it with his own life, replied Roederer according to his own version of the events of the day. Another Minister who was present, M. de Joly, says that Roederer replied, 'Madame, we will answer for dying at your side; that is all we can promise.' 'Let us be going,' the King interrupted, and walking over to the assembled noblesse he said, 'Gentlemen, I beg you to withdraw and abandon a useless defence. There is nothing to be done here for you or for me.' Abruptly, he uttered one final word, '*Marchons*'.

The royal party assembled about 8 a.m. According to one version of the story, Louis, before leaving the palace, shut himself up with his confessor, the venerable Abbé Herbert, and besought from Heaven the resignation and courage he needed.

Roederer went to the door of the royal apartments and announced in a very loud voice, 'The King and his family are going to the Assembly, alone, with no other escort than the representatives of the department and the ministers and a guard of soldiers. Be good enough to allow us to pass.' He called the officer commanding the guard, telling him, 'You must bring up some men of the National Guard to march on either side of the King's party. This is the King's wish.' 'That will be done,' the officer replied.

When the guard had assembled, Roederer led the way. Louis came next. Beside him walked M. Bigot de Sainte Croix, the Foreign Minister. The Queen followed on the arm of M. Dubouchage, the Minister of the Marine, holding one hand of the Dauphin, while Madame de Tourzel held the other. Finally came Madame Elizabeth arm-in-arm with Madame Royale and the Princess de Lamballe, the Superintendent of the Queen's Household. On either side marched a double row of Swiss and National Guardsmen, the Grenadiers of the Filles Saint Thomas and of the Petits Pères sections. 'The King,' says young La

Rochefoucauld, a member of the guard, 'walked straight ahead, his face calm but engraved by misfortune.' The Queen was in tears, dabbing her eyes with her handkerchief. For a moment she leaned on La Rochefoucauld's arm and he felt her trembling. To her ladies she called, 'We shall see you again.' Princess de Lamballe whispered, 'We shall never return.' Several other Ministers and a number of courtiers attached themselves to the rear of the procession.

It was half past eight o'clock on a glorious summer morning. The birds sang, the sun shone brilliantly, the ornamental pools glittered, the neatly scythed lawns shimmered in the heat, the gardens were gay with flowers; nature was at her most radiant. The sad procession wended its way beneath the chestnut trees shading the path. Behind rose the splendid palace of the Kings of France; ahead lay uncertainty. Only the Dauphin was carefree; he amused himself kicking at the heaps of dry leaves that had been swept into neat piles by the diligent gardeners. 'How many leaves there are,' remarked Louis, recalling perhaps the prophecy of one of his opponents, the writer Manuel, who had declared in his newspaper that the monarchy would not survive the fall of the leaf. The King stretched out his arm and took the red bonnet from the head of the guardsman walking at his side, placing it on his head and giving his own hat in return. The man looked surprised and put the hat under his arm.

The procession reached the gate leading from the Tuileries to the Riding School. A jeering mass of humanity barred the way. 'Death to the tyrant,' the people chanted. Vainly, Roederer begged them to give way. The people shouted, screamed threats and brandished weapons. Howls of fury rose. 'Death, death, we want no more tyrants,' screamed the demonstrators. 'Send your wife away. It is she who has brought misfortune to the French,' shouted a woman. 'Let not Your Majesty be afraid,' said the guard at the Queen's side. Unconscious of the irony of his remark, he added, 'She is surrounded by good citizens.' 'I am not afraid, but what will become of my children?' replied Marie Antoinette. 'These people have been led astray,' whispered Madame Elizabeth to her companion.

The crowd pressed forward, surging upon the Royal Family. In the crush the Queen's watch and purse were stolen. A huge guardsman, a man of enormous height and of repellent countenance, seized the Dauphin. The Queen gave a cry of terror, then to her relief, the man raised her son to his shoulder and carried him above the heads of the crowd. A deputation arrived from the Assembly to rescue the family and to offer asylum. Leading the way they forced a passage through the mob: a man carrying a long pole shouted, 'No, no, they must not enter.' Roederer seized the pole and tried to calm him. 'The King has a right to go to the Assembly.' The people redoubled their cries, 'Down with him, down with him.' A guardsman, a man from Provence, placed himself at the King's side, calling to him, 'Sire, don't be afraid. We are decent people but we don't want to be betrayed any longer. Be a good citizen, Sire, and don't forget to sack those sky-pilots you keep in the palace.'

At the doorway into the Assembly, the Royal Family were torn apart in the crush. The tall guardsman carrying the Dauphin thrust his way through and deposited the boy on the desk of the Speaker. The King squeezed through the doors; the rest followed, and the guards slammed the door in the faces of the milling mob. The band of courtiers was left outside.

After a final struggle in the packed lobby, the family and their attendants succeeded in making their way into the hall. In the stunned silence Louis walked up to the President Vergniand and said, 'I have come to prevent a great crime and I believe that I cannot be safer anywhere than in the midst of the representatives of the nation.' His voice trembling with emotion, Vergniand replied, 'Sire, you can count on the firmness of the National Assembly. It knows its duties and its members are sworn to uphold the rights of the people and of the constitutional authorities.'

From the direction of the Tuileries came the exultant cries of the people of Paris. A burst of musketry fire announced that the faithful Swiss were defending the palace.

3

THE MASSACRE
OF THE SWISS

John Moore awoke at 9 a.m. His slumbers had been disturbed by the rumbling of cannon and he heard cries of 'To arms, citizens, to arms'. Looking from the window of his hotel he watched men running half frantic through the streets. Moore dressed and went out; he saw bodies of men, some dragging cannon, rushing along the quays towards the Tuileries, and he noticed that cannon had been set up on the Pont Royal, on the river side of the palace. Another English visitor, Richard Twiss, watched immense hordes of men rushing along the streets like a torrent and some, he observed, were carrying pikes to which heads were affixed. Many of the men were accompanied by women who carried their muskets, some with large sausages, pieces of cold meat and loaves of bread stuck on the bayonets. All were laughing and singing the revolutionary songs, the *Ça Ira*. Philippe Morice, aged sixteen, a lawyer's clerk, was over-come by curiosity. On the pretext that he was visiting a café, he slipped from his office to ascertain what was happening. He got more than he bargained, for he was swept up by a crowd of ruffians and deposited on the Pont Royal where, fortunately for him, the company to which he had been 'assigned' was blocked from further progress by the huge crowd that filled the Carrousel.

The vanguard of the rioters were pounding on the gates of the Tuileries; the column from the Faubourg Saint-Antoine, the stalwarts of the Revolution, came up and broke them open. A huge crowd thrust through the gates into the courtyard and, immediately, the last remaining artilleryman of the National Guard turned their cannon on the palace. The rioters surged across the courtyard yelling, 'Down with the Swiss!'

The main body of the Swiss stood drawn up in battle array at the foot of the grand staircase; others guarded the stairs and the galleries at either side. 'Do not allow yourselves to be taken,' ordered Maréchal de Mailly who had assumed command of the palace. According to the eye-witness account published in 1819 by Colonel Pfyffer d'Altishoffer, the stairs and windows of the palace were lined by the red-coated Swiss. 'Down with the Swiss! Down!' yelled the rioters as they surged forward. The officers gestured to the people to retire. The assailants, states Madame Campan who was within the palace, did not know that the King and his family had betaken themselves to the Assembly, and those who defended the palace were equally ignorant. If both sides had been informed, she thinks, the siege of the Tuileries would not have taken place.

Frightened by the soldierly bearing of the Swiss, the mob halted. The situation was hair-triggered. The people were determined to reach the King and the Swiss guards were determined to prevent them from entering the palace. 'For a while,' states an anonymous observer whose diary of the day's events is preserved in the Ministry of Foreign Affairs, 'both parties inveighed against each other by cries and signs.' The pause lasted for about fifteen minutes. The rioters brandished their pikes and guns but they did not dare to advance across the courtyard; more and more people poured in through the gates. Some patriots, bolder than the rest, advanced to the foot of the staircase and began to parley with the soldiers, trying to turn them against their officers and induce them to lay down their arms. 'We are Swiss, and the Swiss only lay down their arms with their lives,' replied Sergeant Blazer.

The rioters became more audacious. They thrust forward their halberds, which terminated in hooks, trying to catch the men standing on the staircase. They dragged down five Swiss and disarmed them of their sabres, muskets and cartridge-boxes, to the joy of the crowd who greeted the discomfiture of the Swiss with shouts of laughter. Encouraged by the success of this manoeuvre, the rioters pressed forward and killed the five guards who had been disarmed. A pistol shot rang out, one of the mob fell dead. Two officers, Captains Zusler and Castleborg, gave the order to fire and a volley swept the crowd.

The undisciplined rabble fell back on the Carrousel, leaving the courtyard strewn with bodies, guns and pikes. The gunners abandoned their cannon and ran with the rest. Some of the rioters fell flat on their faces, feigning death and rising occasionally to glide to the walls to escape the withering fire. Within a few minutes the Swiss had cleared the courtyard. Two officers, de Durler and de Pfyffer, led a sortie at the head of 120 men. They rescued the cannon and re-took the gates. A detachment of sixty soldiers formed themselves into a hollow square and advanced into the Carrousel, sweeping it with fire. Another contingent, commanded by Count de Salis, turned the cannon on the columns that were trying to escape into the narrow streets leading from the square. Napoleon Bonaparte, who watched the incident from a distance, says 'The Swiss handled their artillery with vigour', and he states that the Marseillais were chased from the square and did not return until the Swiss had withdrawn.

A miracle happened. The undisciplined section guards halted and reformed. The men of Marseilles, led by their commander, Fournier, who was called 'the American' because he had fought in San Domingo with Touissant L'Overture, rallied the fleeing men. The Marseillais swirled their cannon and fired against the palace. John Moore, who was watching, says that at each discharge, a group of women fell a-clapping and crying 'Bravo, Bravo.'

The thunder of the cannon, and the crash of musketry that accompanied it, was carried into the Riding School.

On his arrival in the hall in which the Assembly was sitting, Louis, exhausted by the heat and by the turmoil of his passage from the Tuileries, sat himself down on a chair beside its President. Hardly had he taken his seat when a deputy, Chabot, an unfrocked priest, pointed out that the Constitution forbade the Assembly to debate in the presence of the Sovereign. To overcome this obstacle, the King and his family were transferred to the reporter's gallery, behind the President's chair, where they were shut up in the box of the reporter of the *Logographe*, a miserable hole measuring six feet high and twelve feet wide. It was intended for the use of one person and into it were crammed the whole family and some of their attendants. Louis sat in front and his family squeezed together on a bench in his rear. It was stiflingly hot.

At the sound of the cannon the deputies turned pale and leapt to their feet. A man burst into the hall to announce that the

Swiss were massacring the people and a deputy shouted that the killing was being done at the order of the King. Hostile glances were thrown towards the royal box. A second messenger, an officer of the National Guard, rushed in screaming 'We are pursued, we are overpowered', and he reported that the people were preparing to storm the palace. The boom of guns redoubled and several deputies who had ventured out of the Riding School returned to report that a murderous fire was being directed against the people. From the gardens of the Tuileries came terrible cries. Marie Antoinette leaned forward, her lips parted, her face kindling, her eyes blazing.

Before leaving the Tuileries Louis had given orders that the guards were not to resist the people. Now, believing he had been disobeyed, he said that the firing must be stopped. Who would be bold enough to carry his order? One of the King's elderly retainers, M. d'Hervilly, offered to go. At first, the King and Queen refused his offer, saying that the mission was too dangerous. 'I beg Their Majesties,' cried the old man, 'not to think of my danger, for my duty is to brave everything in their service; my place is in the midst of the firing and if I am afraid of it I would be unworthy of my uniform.'

Unarmed, and hatless, d'Hervilly made his way through the fusilade of grape and musketry fire. The rebel cannon thundered; the aim of the amateur artillerymen was bad and many of the balls flew above the palace roofs and others rebounded from the walls. The Swiss kept up their accurate fire, killing 400 of their opponents. D'Hervilly, when he reached the courtyard, could hardly make himself heard above the din. He passed on the King's order. Captain Durler refused to accept a verbal message and he ran to the Assembly. He begged the King to allow the Swiss to defend the palace. 'Lay down your arms, place them in the hands of the National Guard. I do not wish brave men to perish,' Louis told him and, taking a piece of paper, he wrote 'The King orders the Swiss to lay down their arms immediately and to retire to their barracks.' Louis had signed the death warrant of the Swiss.

The drums beat the retreat and the Swiss withdrew in two columns. As they retreated through the gardens, they were fired upon at point blank range by the National Guardsmen. They marched on as if on parade. One column proceeded to the barracks and the other turned towards the Assembly. On reaching its door the men stacked their arms. Count de Salis ran into the building waving his sword, expostulating at the order to abandon the defence. At both places, in their own barracks and outside the Assembly, the disarmed Swiss were set upon by the mob. Two hundred Swiss had been killed already; another 400 were massacred and the remainder were imprisoned. The bodies of the dead were torn to pieces by the enraged citizens of Paris, Next day, John Moore saw their naked bodies lying on the ground, some lying singly, some in heaps, objects of curiosity to crowds of spectators. 'Never have any of my battlefields given an idea of so many dead as did those Swiss,' Napoleon said in later life. Not more than 200 remained alive, and they died in the massacre of September 2nd.

When she was told of the fate of the Swiss, Marie Antoinette burst into tears. Louis hung his head. 'What, wretched man, have you no cannon to sweep out this rabble,' remarked Lieutenant Bonaparte as he watched the triumphant citizens invade the palace.

The Swiss people did not blame Louis XVI for the murder of their sons. In after years they raised at Lucerne a monument, a colossal stone lion, to their memory. The lion, struck by a lance and lying down, holds tightly within its claws the royal escutcheon engraved upon a shield adorned with the fleur-de-lis. Beneath the sculpture are inscribed the names of 800 Swiss soldiers who died in defence of the monarchy to which they had given loyalty beyond the price of their service.

The Parisians were masters of the Tuileries. A howling, screaming mob climbed the grand staircase and invaded the building. An anonymous eye-witness describes the scene:

'The mob, master of the grand staircase, proceeds to seize upon the interior of the palace. In a few minutes it floods all the apartments, and massacres all the Swiss whom it finds there. The corridors, the roofs, the offices, all the private outlets from the château, and even the cupboards and wardrobes, are visited, and all the hapless wretches who had concealed themselves in these corners and by-ways ruthlessly butchered. Others are thrown living from the windows, imploring in vain for their lives to be spared, and are pierced by pikes on the terrace and the pavement of the courts. A hundred of them effect their escape by the Cour de Marsan, but are stopped in the Rue de l'Echelle and slain by

35

blows and thrusts from sabres and pikes. Their bodies, despoiled, naked and mutilated, for the most part in a manner impossible to describe, are piled up on the pavement, and remain exposed to the eyes of all until the next day. More than a hundred of the servants of Louis and his family, even to the ushers, doorkeepers, grooms of the chamber and so forth, experience the same fate. Blood flowed in great streams, both in the state apartments and in the most private cabinets. A very small number of other servants and some soldiers escape the carnage disguised in the uniform of militiamen, or hide themselves in the chimney-flues, where they wait until the third day to avoid the fury of the victor.'

Morice, the notary's clerk, and Mercier, a liberal-Republican, also witnessed the scene of carnage and destruction. Mercier ran about and he boasted afterwards that he had written his book, *Le Nouveau Paris*, 'with his legs'. At the outset he witnessed a horrible scene. Many of the rioters made for the kitchens; they seized an under cook, pressed him into a boiler and exposed it to the blazing fire of the furnace. They then seized the food he had been preparing: one made off with a spit adorned with quails, another a turbot, still another a Rhine carp. In the wine cellars the rioters lay dead drunk on the floor beside the corpses of their victims. A musician played his violin over the body of the man whose throat he had cut. Men and women danced for joy in a welter of blood and wine, and a jumble of broken bottles. In the courtyard dishevelled hags roasted on braziers the limbs of the Swiss who had died in the fighting. Dense clouds of acrid smoke arose in the clear blue sky. A light snow of down floated over the Carrousel as the looters tore up eiderdown quilts and feather beds.

The staircases resounded with the tread of thieves and ruffians who ascended, descended, jostled and ran up and down the corridors searching for loot. What they could not carry they destroyed. They broke open desks, seizing money, watches, jewels, trinkets, diamonds, caskets, everything of value. They plundered wardrobes, stripped lace from coats and took plate, silverware and candlesticks. They shattered costly porcelain vases to obtain the far less valuable silver fastenings. They broke mirrors, and on the Queen's bed were enacted scenes of shameless and infamous obscenity. They wrecked the Chapel, tearing down pulpits, and throwing violins on the altar. A young man climbed up into the organ loft and played a ribald tune on the pipes.

Bleeding corpses lay everywhere, attracting hosts of flies, greedy for blood. Women chased the servants who had escaped the carnage: those who had hidden in cupboards were dragged out and murdered.

Two ushers of the King's Chamber, M. Pallas and M. de Marchais, guarded the door of the Council Chamber, sword in hand. Madame Campan heard them say, 'We don't want to live any longer; this is our post and here we will die'. They were hacked to death. M. Dieu died at the door to the Queen's apartment, where Madame Campan and several other women were sheltering. A man with a long beard burst into the room. When he saw them, he shouted 'Spare the women; don't dishonour the nation'. Madame Campan went to another room to seek her sister. She found a man, one of the Queen's footmen, sitting on a bed. 'Fly,' she told him. 'I cannot,' replied the man, 'I am dying of fear.' As he spoke a number of men broke into the room and threw themselves upon him. Madame Campan saw the footman murdered.

Several of the Queen's ladies had taken refuge in another room. They closed the shutters and lighted a candle. Pauline de Tourzel had an idea; 'Let us light all the candles, the sconces and the torches,' she cried. The brilliance of the lights would astonish the rioters, and give the ladies time to speak. When the invaders broke in, sabres in hand, they stood stupefied. 'Spare women; do not dishonour the nation,' chanted the ladies.

Madame Campan ran towards a staircase, followed by these women. The assassins tried to follow but they were impeded by the narrowness of the stairs. Madame Campan felt a terrible hand clutching at her back, seizing her clothes. She heard a man's voice call from below, 'What are you doing above there? We don't kill women.' She fell on her knees. 'Get up, you jade. The nation pardons you,' her would-be executioner told her. She and her companions were seized by several men who sat them on benches and forced them to recite 'The Nation Forever'. Returning to the royal apartments, Madame Campan stumbled over corpses; one she recognised as the body of the aged Viscount de Brèves whom, she recalled, had been told by the Queen the night before to go home.

Madame Campan escaped from the palace and she reached the house of her brother-in-law. The other women, including Pauline de Tourzel, were taken to the Abbaye prison, from where they were later released. Cléry, the King's valet, escaped the massacre; he fled to a neighbouring house whose master hid him from the armed troops that came to search. François Hue escaped by jumping into the Seine from which he was rescued by boatmen.

Satiated with slaughter and loaded with plunder, the majority of the rioters left the devastated palace, now on fire in several places. Two thousand people, at least, had lost their lives because Louis XVI could not bear the thought of violence.

A royalist sympathizer, a man named Dufour of whom nothing is known other than his name, came upon the scene later in the day. At the palace everything was quiet; the Grand Staircase was covered with corpses, piled one upon another. A thousand thoughts flashed through Dufour's mind. 'I pictured a murdered King, and with him all his family and many another victim, among whom, perhaps, there might be some still breathing, to whom I could bring help.'

Inspired by this idea Dufour went through the rooms amidst a silence that he found amazing. He met no one at first and, then, hearing a noise, he hid himself in the King's bedchamber; peering out he watched the last of the marauders making off and from these maniacs, as he calls them, he learned of the King's flight to the Assembly. He decided to follow. Entering the hall he saw the unhappy Royal Family 'delivered into the hands of their cruel enemies', as he puts it. The corridors of the Assembly were filled with terrorists who were loudly demanding the death of the King and a general massacre of their adherents. National Guardsmen, idlers, mob-orators, blood-soaked rioters, dishevelled women, and enthusiasts of every shade of opinion jostled each other in the doorway. From within the hall came the sound of a mighty uproar. The fate of the Revolution was being decided in strife and turmoil.

Events in the Assembly had moved quickly since 9.00 a.m. when the King and his family had been granted asylum. Louis XVI entered the Assembly as the reigning King of France, the constitutional monarch its deputies had sworn to defend; he left it a deposed King, a prisoner. 'He had thrown himself into the lion's den, to avoid fighting a flock of sheep,' says Frénilly.

While the battle for the Tuileries raged, the real leaders of the insurrection had remained in hiding; Robespierre stayed in his house; Marat had not quitted his cellar and even the 'audacious'

Danton did not show himself until the echoes of the last shot had died away. Those who now shouted the loudest had spent the night in fear and trembling; they left Hughenin, the president of the Commune, and his partisans at the Hôtel de Ville, to organize the assault on the Tuileries.

On the morning of August 10th, Hughenin came boldly to the Assembly and told the deputies, 'The people is your Sovereign.' He demanded the deposition of the King. Thoroughly frightened, the deputies agreed. Tamely, Vergniand signed the decree suspending the monarchy. The determined minority had triumphed over the moderates who marched with their eyes shut. The Assembly, the elected representatives of the people of France, was powerless against the armed citizens of Paris, and the deputies found themselves as much the victims of the insurrection as the King.

The final acts in the drama were lacking neither in spectacle nor in satiric, macabre humour. Members of the Commune stood at the bar of the Assembly, shouting down the moderates who dared to question their commands. Around the hall men stood on chairs, women leaned over balustrades and children climbed columns to gaze on the royal captives, howling insults and threats against them. Louis sat at the front of the box from which the protecting iron bars had been removed, an operation in which he had cheerfully assisted by demonstrating his skill as an amateur locksmith. Peering at the deputies through a large opera-glass, he listened imperturbably to the invectives poured upon him, and leaning over to speak to a deputy seated near the box, he remarked with the greatest tranquillity, 'What you are doing here is not very constitutional.' He believed that he would be back in the Tuileries by nightfall. He leant forward, his elbows on the front of the box, apparently a disinterested spectator to the fall of the monarchy. Someone gave him the leg of a chicken; he ate it with relish. Marie Antoinette shuddered; accustomed as she was to her husband's gluttony, she could not hide her chagrin at his behaviour.

The foetid odour of unwashed, perspiring bodies arose from the hall. As the day advanced the fierce August sun scorched the room; the temperature mounted; it was stiflingly hot. Grimy, red-faced rioters poured into the hall, brandishing blood-stained weapons and carrying the trophies wrested from the Tuileries.

From the Carrousel was wafted the acrid stench of burning flesh; the people were at work burning the corpses of their victims. Every hour brought news of some fresh horror. The standards of the murdered Swiss were borne triumphantly into the Assembly and deposited on the President's desk. Silver, rich brocades, caskets, spoons, forks, silver dishes, even homely utensils from the royal kitchens, were strewn on the floor.

Marie Antoinette sat white-faced, shuddering. As long as the combat had lasted she had been thrilled by a secret, vain hope. When the decree suspending the monarchy was voted, she closed her eyes in anguish; a second later, she haughtily raised her head. Madame Elizabeth wept unrestrainedly; Madame de Tourzel nursed the Dauphin in her arms. She and the boy shared a special fear; her daughter, Louis Charles's devoted friend, had remained in the palace. Madame de Tourzel saw Maréchal de Mailly brought as a prisoner into the Assembly; he was covered with blood and his clothes were torn. François de la Rochefoucald tried to staunch the old man's wounds.

The Royal Family were kept prisoner in their white-walled, suffocating dungeon for seventeen hours, subjected all day to the jibes and insults of the frenzied populace, gloating over their fall. Every minute the Revolution grew stronger; the elected deputies abdicated their authority. A new government was formed, headed by Danton, who was appointed Minister of Justice. Behind him massed the bayonets of the Commune.

The agony of the Royal Family was not over. At 10 p.m. they were released from their cramped positions and led to the Convent of the Feuillants, at the rear of the Riding School. With them went some of their attendants. The faithful d'Aubier describes the transfer: 'We crossed the yard through a mass of spears still dripping blood. The way was lighted by candles placed in the mouths of muskets. Ferocious cries demanding the heads of the King and Queen added to the horror. One madman, raising his voice above the others, cried that if the Assembly delayed delivering them to the people, he would set fire to their jail.'

The family were lodged in four tiny cells, uninhabited for years, their walls peeling and their floors cracking. These cells opened on to a corridor which was flanked by a grating through which the gloating crowds below could be heard clamouring for the death of the Queen, the chief object of the people's hatred.

'Throw down her head', shouted a number of men who had succeeded in climbing up to the grating. 'Why, what has she done to them?' asked the uncomprehending King. Dufour had been busy. Learning that the family were to be transferred to the Convent, he bethought himself of their comfort; he collected a number of mattresses and he persuaded a dozen porters to carry them to the building. Louis occupied one cell; D'Aubier and the Marquis de Tourzel watched by his side. The Queen and her daughter took another cell; Madame Campan, who had succeeded in joining the family, found her in 'indescribable affliction', waited upon by a stout woman, the keeper of the apartments, who appeared tolerably civil.

When the Dauphin was brought in by his governess, Marie Antoinette exclaimed, 'Poor children, how heartrending it is, instead of handing down to them a fine inheritance, to say it ends with us.' The Queen was eager for news of those she had left behind in the palace; Madame Campan gave her the names of the servants and courtiers who had been killed. The Queen then touched upon a delicate topic; her distaste for the behaviour of her husband who, since leaving the palace, had placed 'no restraint upon his great appetite'. She had warned him that his gluttony had produced a bad effect on the Assembly, 'but no change could be effected'.

The Dauphin shared a cell with Madame Elizabeth, the Princess de Lamballe and Madame de Tourzel. Worn out by fatigue, none of the women could sleep and they spent the night in prayer. Louis, on the contrary, fell asleep quickly; before he succumbed, he told the watchers at his side, 'People regret that I did not have the rebels attacked; but what would have been the result?' Their plans, he said, had been laid too well, and the result would have been the same. Having thus dismissed the matter, Louis wrapped his head in an old cloth and went to sleep. To D'Aubier, the King's sleep seemed truly wondrous. The windows were without bars and, during the night, two bloodstained revolutionaries climbed up to the window; even they were astonished at the King's innocence. Peering in, their blackened faces distorted villainously by the light of the flickering torches they held, they burst out laughing when they saw the King, and went away. Louis, disturbed by the unexpected intruders, awoke and he asked, 'Are the Queen and my children sleeping?' Marie Antoinette came into the cell; she believed that the family would be murdered during the night and she sought consolation from her husband, but he had fallen asleep again.

In the morning several of their attendants were allowed to join the Royal Family and among them François Hue, and to the joy of seven-year-old Louis Charles and the relief of her mother, Pauline de Tourzel. Hue found the King asleep; he awoke and, taking his officer's hand, he congratulated him on having the consolation of escaping the massacre. Dufour continued to perform his self-appointed duties; he went to a nearby eating-house and brought back breakfast for the family. But none of the ladies had any appetite, although Louis ate the food with relish. At 7 a.m. the family were taken back to the Assembly. As they walked through the gardens separating the two buildings, the Queen involuntarily inclined her head to the curious spectators who had gathered to watch the procession: a voice from the crowd called out, 'Don't put on so many airs with that graceful head; it is not worth while. You'll not have it much longer.'

The Royal Family were lodged again in the reporter's box, and all day they sat listening to the clamour of the members of the Commune who came to the bar of the Assembly demanding the passing of several decrees; one to encompass the death of the captive Swiss, another to pay thirty sous a day to the victorious Marseillais, and yet another ordering the overthrow of the statues of former Kings. John Moore, who had gained admittance to the Riding School, watched the Queen, whose beauty, he thought, had gone. But he did not observe the 'provoking arrogance' a person standing near him remarked. On the contrary, Marie Antoinette's behaviour in the trying circumstances seemed full of propriety and dignified composure. The height from which the unhappy princess had fallen, and her present deplorable situation, inclined Moore to view her with additional interest, and he was surprised to find 'that the edge of that rancour which has pervaded in this country against her, seems to be in no degree blunted by her misfortunes'.

At the close of the session, the family were returned to their cells, where they found that Dufour had provided dinner; a task that brought upon him the insults of the people through whom he was forced to make his way. He kept them quiet by saying that he was the proprietor of the eating-house and that he would suffer if they took the food, as they seemed inclined to do. Dufour laid a table in the corridor, to which he escorted the Royal Family who were exposed to the insults of the people who crowded it: one man in particular urged the people to massacre the whole family. Dufour took particular note of this monster's face and when he reappeared next day, he chased him away. On her return to her cell, the Queen found a parcel of clothes for the Dauphin, which had been left by Lady Gower. Several of their attendants offered the King and Queen money. When M. d'Aubier ventured to offer fifty livres for the royal expenses, the King told his friends, 'Keep your pocket books, Messieurs, you will need them more than we do for you will, I hope, have longer to live.'

The debate on the twelfth to which the Royal Family was forced to listen, concerned their own fate. It became a duel between the moderates in the Assembly and the Jacobin extremists, who employed the threats of the Commune to bully the deputies. Several deputies suggested that the Royal Family should be housed in the Luxembourg Palace, where they could be held as hostages against the counter-revolutionaries, the *émigrés* and their Prussian and Austrian supporters. When they heard this suggestion put forward, the faces of the King and Queen lighted up, for imprisonment in a palace implied no great fall from royal estate. But the members of the Insurrectionary Commune would not have it. The Luxembourg Palace contained subterranean passages which might facilitate escape. This was only a pretext; they were determined to get the King into their own hands. They demanded that he and his family should be imprisoned in the 'Temple'.

Marie Antoinette shuddered when she heard the word 'Temple' mentioned; she understood the full horror of their position. Their enemies intended to incarcerate them, not in the commodious palace of the Grand Prior of the former Knights Templar, but in the tower that adjoined it, a tall, grim, medieval dungeon with narrow windows and stone walls nine feet thick. 'You will see,' she told Madame de Tourzel in an undertone, 'they will put us in the tower and make it a regular prison for us.' She had always had a horror of the tower and a thousand times she had begged her brother-in-law, Comte d'Artois, who had occupied the Prior's palace, to have it pulled down. She had a presentiment of evil, she told her companion, and when Madame de Tourzel tried to dispel the Queen's fears, Marie Antoinette replied, 'You will see if I am wrong.'

'The Temple offers,' stated a member of the Commune, 'accommodation which Louis XVI, by his misfortune, has a right to expect from a people which wishes to be severe only to be just.' The Assembly bowed to the Commune's *coup d'état* and it decreed that the King and his family should be entrusted 'to the safekeeping and virtues of the citizens of Paris'.

The full implication of this illegal move was not lost upon the King and Queen. They were no longer royalty; they were criminals who might be brought to justice. That night they were told that they would only be allowed to take with them one person to wait upon the King and four women to serve the Queen, the Princesses and the Dauphin. 'Things may yet come right,' soothed M. d'Aubier. Louis shook his head. 'Charles I was more fortunate than I am; they left him his friends until the scaffold,' he groaned.

4

THE TEMPLE

At 5 p.m., two hours later than had been planned, on Monday, August 13th, two large coaches were brought to the door of the Feuillants. The King, the Queen, their two children, Madame Elizabeth, Princess de Lamballe, Madame de Tourzel, her daughter Pauline, Major Pétion, Manuel, the City Procurator, and a municipal officer named Cologne, eleven people in all besides the coachman and footman entered the first coach, a staggering weight to be drawn by two horses, which is vouched for by François Hue. In the second coach rode the four women servants, who were named Thiband, Angie, Basire and Navarre, and the two valets, Hue and de Chamilly. Madame Campan was not included in the party; we shall hear of her again before she disappears from the scene. The coaches, which had been brought from the royal stables, were driven by the usual coachmen who, however, no longer wore the royal livery: they were dressed in inconspicuous grey in order to accentuate the lofty heights from which the family had fallen. In his pocket Pétion carried the Commune's order committing the King and his family to the Temple; the word 'tower' had been scratched out and their true destination was kept secret.

The Commune took no chances, either that the royalists might attempt to stage a rescue, or that the people of Paris might lynch the prisoners they had so triumphantly seized from the Assembly. The city gates were closed and the entire route along the *grands boulevards* and through Montmartre and St Denis, to the gateway of the Temple, was lined by National Guardsmen, all of whom had been assembled for the occasion. Other guardsmen, with their arms reversed, marched on either side of the coaches which were preceded by an escort of cavalry, headed by Claude Santerre, the Commander of the National Guards. The procession moved at walking pace, due both to the weight of the coaches and the

45

vast hostile multitude who impeded the way. This pace, Madame de Tourzel thought, was intended to give an opportunity to the sightseers to press against the coaches 'with their eyes gleaming with rage'. Hue says that 'nothing was heard except threats and imprecations'. Pétion and Manuel became anxious, putting their heads out of the windows and entreating the mob in the name of the law to allow the coaches to proceed, and Pétion advised the Queen to lower her glances, in order not to infuriate the mob by her haughty stares. Several times the coaches were brought to a halt.

In the Place Vendôme, Pétion called a special halt to enable the King to contemplate at his leisure the equestrian statue of his ancestor Louis XIV, which had been thrown from its pedestal and trodden under foot. 'Look, Sire, this is how the people treat their Kings,' sneered Manuel. Louis was quick in repartee; 'Would that their fury confined itself to inanimate objects,' he retorted. The statues of Henry IV, Louis XIII and Louis XV had been similarly treated, he was informed.

The journey took more than two hours and it was dark when the procession reached the gateway of the Temple. Santerre, who led the way into the great courtyard which was filled by members of the Commune and other privileged spectators, made an interrogative sign to the municipal officers who stood massed upon the steps of the palace of the former Grand Prior, as if to say 'Is the tower ready?' 'No, not yet,' they signalled.

The cavalry escort drew to one side and the coaches lumbered into the courtyard and stopped in front of the palace which was brilliantly illuminated. When the order was given to open their doors, the escorting guardsmen tried to separate the King from his family and take him alone to the tower: when Louis refused to budge there was a great uproar until Pétion calmed the men down and, stepping from the coach, led the family into the vast and richly furnished palace.

The Temple, all the buildings of which were demolished in the nineteenth century, was far more than a palace; it was a miniature city, having its own gates and custodians, its own courthouse and magistrates, gardens, stables, market, cemetery, priory, church and medieval dungeon, the Great Tower, as it was known, which in August 1792 was in a dilapidated condition. The Great Tower was joined to the palace by a long, covered passage and it was abutted by a smaller building called the Little Tower, which had been inhabited since 1782 by M. Berthèlemy, the Keeper of the Archives of the Order of the Temple, an elderly and fussy bachelor who had turned it into a comfortable residence. Alas, the measured calm of M. Berthèlemy's well-ordered life was soon to be rudely interrupted.

On their arrival at the palace, the family were led into the brilliantly illuminated main salon, a vast room with ten windows, which was filled by municipal officers; small tradesmen and artisans who, in order, perhaps, to overcome their awe of the sumptuous surroundings in which they found themselves, puffed themselves up with importance and strutted about or lounged on settees, studiously keeping their hats on their heads. Madame de Tourzel thought they were dressed in 'the dirtiest and most disgusting clothes', whereby she probably meant that these common citizens were unaccustomed to dictates of good breeding. They behaved in the most revolting manner, treating the King and Queen with insolence and familiarity.

Louis refused to be offended and he displayed, says Hue, 'a tranquillity which evinced a conscience undisturbed.' The true explanation seems that the good-natured King understood that the boorish officials were overcome by their surroundings and he tried to put them at their ease. They, states Madame de Tourzel, asked the King a thousand ridiculous questions. One man who was lounging on a settee wanted to discuss the 'happiness of equality'. 'What is your profession?' enquired Louis. 'Cobbler,' replied the man, who is thus identified as the notorious Antoine Simon of whom we shall hear a great deal more later. Another official, Germain Truchon by name, who was known as 'the man with the long beard' because it reached his thighs, adopted a very free and easy manner, punctuating his remarks by the repetition of the bourgeois title *Monsieur* by which he addressed Louis. Madame de Tourzel says that Truchon was a man of bad character and a bigamist; a crime of which he had been accused but not convicted. Louis was in good spirits; believing that he was going to live in the palace, he invited the officials to show it to him; he admired the paintings and tapestries and as he progressed he allotted rooms for the use of the members of his family and the servants. No one dared to tell him that he would be imprisoned in the medieval dungeon, the roof of which could be discerned above the small buildings that surrounded it.

The Great Tower was uninhabitable, Pétion found when he went to inspect it. He took himself at once to the Hôtel de Ville, where he informed the Committee of the Commune that the ex-Royal Family had been lodged in the palace of the Temple and that 'he had not considered it his duty to comply with the decree' that had ordered their incarceration in the tower. The Commune refused to budge from the decision it had taken and it ordered Pétion to make the tower habitable and escape-proof and, meanwhile, to lodge the King and his family in the adjoining Little Tower, the residence of the Archivist.

Poor M. Berthèlemy had been disturbed by the tumult that accompanied the arrival of the procession at the Palace. Considering it no concern of his, he sat in his comfortable little residence occupied with his unending task of sorting the Archives of the Order. Shortly after 10 p.m. he was disturbed by a great noise and by the tramp of heavy feet on his own staircase. One instant later his pleasant little drawing room was invaded by a crowd of men who announced the startling news 'that he must move at once', for the King, the Queen, their children and their attendants, fourteen people in all, were to be lodged in his house. Everything, his furniture, his paintings, his books and even his personal belongings, must be removed at once. A gang of labourers rushed into the room, loaded his furniture on to their shoulders and hurried down the staircase. Bewildered and stricken by the sudden change in the circumstances of his well-ordered life, Berthèlemy ran about imploring help, but no one would pay any attention to him. Where would his possessions be put? Where would he find shelter at that late hour? The only answer he was given was that his furniture would be stored in a near-by church, of which one of the officials had the key. Satisfied at least on that score, the distracted archivist ran up and down stairs, hesitating whether to save first his rare old books or his equally rare old wine bottles. Scarcely had he decided which to take with him, as he himself states in his 'papers', which were collected and preserved by Madame Gustave Blavet, than the order to remove his furniture was countermanded. His furniture was brought back and additional beds and mattresses were brought in from the Tuileries whence they had been carried on handcarts. M. Berthèlemy was ejected from his house by the Commissioners of the Commune, who took possession of the building and forbade him to re-enter it. M. Berthèlemy plaintively laments that he was forced to wander the streets of Paris the whole night, seeking shelter, and dumbfounded at the sudden misfortune that had overwhelmed him.

In the palace itself, Gagnié, the head cook from the Tuileries, who brought with him a host of lesser cooks, had been preparing dinner for the Royal Family and for the municipal officials which was now served in 'the salon of the four mirrors' brilliantly lit by candles. It was served by a number of menials, among them a man named François Turgy who had filled the position of waiter in the *Bouche* at the Tuileries. He needs more than passing mention for he remained with the captive family for a year, wherein he rendered great services which were recognized in 1814 by his appointment to the houshold of the Duchesse d'Angoulême, as Madame Royale had by then become, whom he served as *valet de chambre*. Turgy, or Thurgé as Madame Royale calls him, had already proved his loyalty in October 1789, at the time when the royal apartments at Versailles had been invaded by a mob of women who had marched from Paris; in the nick of time Turgy had opened a door which enabled Marie Antoinette to escape by a private passage. Before he died in Paris in 1823, Turgy had been made an officer of the Legion of Honour and granted a patent of nobility. In her *Relation du Captivité* Madame Royale paid tribute to the 'unfailing courage, fidelity, zeal and intelligence' with which Turgy served her family.

On August 10th Turgy, who did not live in the Tuileries where accommodation was cramped, had failed to gain admittance and his attempts to get into the Feuillants were equally unavailing. Hearing that the King was to be removed to the Temple, Turgy hurried off to see M. Manard de Chousy, the Commissary-General of the King's household, to beg the favour of being employed there. He was given the promise that, if a single manservant of any kind were needed, no one but he would be nominated for the post. Foreseeing, however, that once the King was in the Temple it would be impossible to gain admittance without various formalities, and appreciating that he had nothing to recommend him to the enemies of the Royal Family, Turgy said to two of his fellow servants who were in like case, 'Let us simply go to the Temple; perhaps if we show a bold front they will let us in.'

The three waiters arrived at the main entrance at the very moment when one of the officers of the guard was allowing a man to pass in, supplying him with a ticket. Turgy, recognizing the man as being in the King's employ, said that he and his companions also belonged to the household. 'Take my arm, and make your companions take yours, and I will get you in,' the man told Turgy, and the three waiters were taken to the kitchens. Finding no supplies of any kind, whereby he probably meant table linen, crockery and utensils, Turgy made three separate journeys outside the Temple to procure them, leaving and gaining re-admittance by a side door, and taking the precaution of making the porter and the guards look at him well, so that he should be able to come and go at will.

The long delayed dinner, or more correctly 'supper', for in eighteenth century France dinner was eaten in mid-afternoon, was served at 10 p.m. It was a silent meal and Manuel, in Pétion's absence, stood by the side of the King's chair. Only an appearance of eating was gone through, states Madame de Tourzel on whose lap the Dauphin sat, dozing. He became so overcome with sleep and fatigue that he begged to be put to bed at about 11 p.m. An official came to say that the boy's room was ready and he took the sleeping child in his arms and hurried off with such rapidity that Madame de Tourzel had great difficulty in keeping up with him. He crossed three large rooms and entered a long corridor which to the anxious woman appeared to be a subterranean passage. At the end of this covered way, which connected the palace to the dungeon, the man turned into a large Gothic chamber and ascended two flights of stone stairs, and a third flight of wood, which brought them into M. Berthèlemy's billiard room in the Little Tower; the fear of being separated from her charge and the dread of irritating the municipal officer prevented Madame de Tourzel from asking any questions. Without saying a word she put the boy to bed in one of the two folding beds that had been brought from the Tuileries, and sat herself down by his side, a prey to gloomy forebodings. She shuddered at the thought of being separated from the King and Queen.

After supper the King and Queen were taken back into the salon where, at long last, Louis was informed that his lodging was not to be in the palace but in the dungeon, and that he and his family were to reside temporarily in the Little Tower. A municipal officer, carrying a lantern, led the way; Hue and de Chamilly were sent ahead to prepare the King's room. They were taken to the top floor of the Little Tower and shown a room containing only a dirty old bedstead, which had all the appearance of being infested with vermin, and three chairs. The two valets looked at each other without saying a word. A pair of sheets was given to them and they did all they could to make the bed comfortable and the room as clean as possible. The King when he came in showed neither surprise nor displeasure, until he noticed that the walls of the room were hung with engravings, most of which were of an indecent nature. 'I cannot,' said he, 'suffer such things to be seen by my daughter', and he took them down with his own hand. He then went to bed and slept tranquilly. De Chamilly and Hue sat up all night by his bedside, contemplating, relates Hue, the 'awful calmness of virtue, struggling with misfortune and subduing it', and wondering how it was 'that he who exerts such a command over himself, should not be formed to command others'.

Madame de Tourzel's anxieties were relieved by the arrival of the Queen, who took the governess's hand and said, 'Did I not tell you truly?' Only then did Madame de Tourzel understand that they were lodged in one of the two towers of the Temple. Marie Antoinette stood looking down at her sleeping son, holding back her tears. Then she retired to M. Berthèlemy's drawing room, into which his bed had been carried and which had been prepared for her by her two lady's-maids whom M. Pétion had thoughtfully provided. She sent them away, 'not able to support the presence of strangers', her daughter says, for she preferred to arrange everything herself. Madame Royale slept at her side on a camp bed. Princess de Lamballe occupied a small room on the same floor and Madame Elizabeth and Pauline de Tourzel were housed in 'a frightfully dirty kitchen' which opened onto the guardroom, whose occupants talked and laughed all night. The sentries who were posted on every landing and who, says Turgy, were all Marseillais, never ceased singing throughout the night, their chief refrain being:

> 'Madame monte à sa tour
> Ne sait quand descendra'.

Work started next day to render the Great Tower habitable and secure and M. Paloy, who had gained both fame and fortune as the demolisher of the Bastille, was again given the contract. The miscellaneous buildings surrounding the two abutting towers were pulled down, trees were uprooted, and a high wall was built around them, completely isolating the family's prison. Even the windows of the neighbouring houses were walled up. This work occupied several weeks, a delay in events within the Temple that provides an opportunity to follow Madame Campan who, it will be recalled, had not been permitted to accompany the family to the Temple. She was worried about a portfolio of papers with which the King had entrusted her and for which, she knew, the whole of the Tuileries had been ransacked by the revolutionaries whose appetites had been whetted by the discovery of a letter from the King's brother, the *émigré* leader, Comte d'Artois, the contents of which indicated a continued correspondence, possibly of a treasonable nature.

Madame Campan spent several restless nights at her house, wondering what to do for the best, and fearing to be denounced as a suspected person. Her fears were increased by the rumour, brought by her servants, that her house was about to be surrounded by fifty armed men. She had just received this intelligence when M. Gougenot, the King's *maître d'hotel* and Receiver-General of Taxes, entered her room. At first, he refused to help Madame Campan. The Queen had told her, she explained, 'This portfolio contains scarcely anything but documents of a most dangerous description in the event of a trial taking place, should it fall into the hands of revolutionary persons', and she had ordered her to destroy all the documents, save one. They included, said Madame Campan, letters from the Comte d'Artois and others relating to the early days of the Revolution, and all had been initialled by the King. One document, for example, invited the *émigrés* to return to France; an incriminating letter, for it implied that the King had encouraged the counter-revolutionaries.

At that moment Madame Campan heard a great noise in the street; M. Gougenot agreed to take the portfolio and, after extracting from his fellow conspirator an oath of silence by all she held sacred, he put it under his cloak and made off, a few minutes before the house was invaded by a number of armed men who, after placing sentinels at the outlets, broke open secretaires and closets, searched flower pots and boxes, and examined the cellars. Their Commander frequently ordered 'Look particularly for papers'. After the men had gone, M. Gougenot returned to report that all the documents had been burned except the one the King required, which he returned to Madame Campan; the *procès-verbal*, signed by all the Ministers, which authorized the King in April, 1792 to declare war against the invading powers. Next day, Madame Campan went to live at Versailles, tormented with the thought that she was unable to inform the King that his orders had been obeyed.

On the day following their arrival at the Temple, the family were permitted to inspect their new home; to people accustomed to life in a palace, even M. Berthèlemy's elegant little residence represented destitution, and in the light of morning it was still a gloomy building. By now, Louis knew it was only a temporary prison and after breakfast he was allowed to inspect the Great Tower, the floors and walls of which were piled high with the Archives of the Order of Malta, contained in thousands of boxes and bundles. In the afternoon the family were allowed to walk in the gardens of the Temple where they were accompanied by Manuel and Santerre.

The King and Queen (as we may continue to call them) had not even the consolation of being alone with their family for, apart from their attendants to whose presence they were accustomed, the small rooms, staircase and corridors of M. Berthèlemy's residence were crowded by guards and by the Commissioners of the Temple, the gaolers appointed by the Commune, who never let the family out of their sight. Several of these men wrote their recollections of their service in the Temple and one, Town Councillor Daujon, who should not be confused with Jean Pierre André Daujon, a member of the Insurrectionary Commune, and who will later on show himself to have been a man of courage as well as a convinced revolutionary, explains the rota system by which the commissioners were selected.

Eight commissioners, who composed the 'Council of the Temple', were sent from the Hôtel de Ville to undertake a forty-eight-hour spell of duty, and every evening the General Council of the Commune nominated four men to relieve the four who had been longest on duty; two spent the day with the prisoners and the rest remained in the guard room on the ground floor. The commissioners gave orders to the sentries and decided on any step that seemed good to them. They consulted with the Commune 'whenever they felt the matter so important that they ought to secure its approval before taking action'. At night the four fresh commissioners drew lots with those that remained to decide which four men should spend the night with 'Capet', as Daujon calls Louis, and the women and children. They followed them into their respective rooms and remained there all night. The commissioners they relieved retired downstairs, locking behind them not only the doors to the rooms, but also the seven doors on the staircase of the tower. Finally the great outer door was secured with an enormous padlock which had been brought specially from the Châtelet prison and all the keys were deposited in a cupboard in the guard room, the key of which was pocketed by the oldest commissioner. The commissioners who were not on duty slept on folding beds which were put up each night in their room. This was connected with the rooms above by bells which summoned them if they were required.

Duty at the Temple, due to the responsibility involved, became so unpopular that each evening when the time came for the selection of the commissioners many members fled from the Hôtel de Ville, and nomination was changed to selection by lot: even so the introduction of the urn from which the lots were drawn led to a hurried exodus and the difficulty was only overcome by the passing of an order by which the reluctant commissioners could be taken to the Temple by force. That such action was considered to be necessary refutes the calumny that service at the Temple was popular, due to the excellence of the cuisine. In the early days of the family's imprisonment, the food supplied to the commissioners was so unpalatable that, says Daujon, they often suffered from colic. Only later on were the commissioners fed the same food as their prisoners.

The King and his family were granted every possible indulgence except liberty. The Assembly had voted the sum of 500,000 livres for the upkeep of the deposed royals and this they proceeded to spend lavishly for, except for the clothes in which they were dressed, they were destitute of everything. Even so the deputies who had granted this sum were amazed by the extent and cost of the articles which constituted necessity to royalty.

The *Papiers du Temple* show that the family were supplied with a white wood bed with head board and hangings for the Dauphin, a bath for the little princess, a gold watch for the Queen which was supplied by her own jeweller at the cost of 900 livres, toys for the Dauphin, which included a large balloon', a whipping top and whip, a set of nine-pins, two pairs of rackets, twelve kites, a set of draughts and another of dominoes. A small knife with a tortoise-shell handle and a blade of gold was bought for him at the cost of 160 livres.

Louis ordered a dark-coloured dress coat made of fine cloth, kerseymere breeches in several colours, several dimity jackets, grey silk stockings, white dimity trousers, buckled shoes, some 'tafata for the feet', skins for the legs, a face sponge and another for the teeth, six razors, a pair of scissors, and an instrument for lacing and unlacing brodekins. These articles were supplied by his usual tailors and purveyors who, like the other shopkeepers who now rushed to re-equip the family, had to wait a long time for their money. The authorities were in fact so lax in the payment of these bills that Pétion and Hue had to sacrifice 2000 and 600 livres respectively from their own salaries in order to appease some of the importunate tradesmen.

To satisfy the requirements of the Queen and her ladies, thirty dressmakers worked feverishly, making, amongst other articles, *pierrots* of pink and white, blue and white cotton cambric; a *pierrot of toile de jouy*, a chemise frock, a frockcoat of Florence taffeta of a colour called *boue de Paris*, which fastened in front and was provided with a watch pocket, white silk stockings, a taffeta neckerchief 'which can be tied behind', lawn caps trimmed with narrow lace, lawn sleeves and collars for cotton dimity dresses, blue, grey and puce coloured shoes, one pair of Chinese sabots, 'a jockey shaped hat of black castor' and various 'head coverings', one of which was so admired by Madame Elizabeth that she ordered a similar one. The bill for scent alone came to 551 livres.

In addition to these personal items, the family was supplied with furniture which was obtained from a merchant named Masson at the cost of 63,000 livres. He delivered fifteen mattresses, fifteen coverlets, fifteen bolsters, fifteen folding beds, and sheets and pillows for each, as well as a dining-room suite, tables, corner buffets, dumb waiters and a water filter. In one week the King's personal laundry composed fifteen shirts, thirteen collars, sixteen handkerchiefs, four neck-ties, one vest, two pairs of silk hose, ten towels, four nightcaps, eight napkins, one cotton cap, three pairs of underwear and two sheets. He was supplied with a set of fourteen volumes of *Missel et Breviare de Paris*, and his sister, Madame Elizabeth, ordered a number of prayer books.

Food for the family and their attendants was supplied from the kitchen of the Grand Prior's palace, which was staffed by twelve domestics, who included a head cook, a plain cook, an assistant cook, a scullion, a turnspit, a steward, an assistant, a boy, a keeper-of-plate, and three waiters. The report, made to the Commune in early September, shows how the family fared.

'*Breakfast*. In the morning the steward provides for breakfast seven cups of coffee, six of chocolate, a coffee-pot of double-cream, a decanter of cold syrup, another of barley water, three pats of butter, a plate of fruit, six rolls, three loaves, a sugar basin of powdered sugar, another of loaf sugar, a salt cellar.

'Not all of this is consumed by the prisoners. The remains are devoted to the use of three persons who wait upon them in the tower, and of the twelve domestics mentioned above.

'*Dinner*. For dinner the head cook provides three soups and two courses, consisting, on days that are not fast days, of four *entrées*, two dishes of roast meat, each containing three joints, and four *entremets*; and on fast days of four *entrées*, at least three of them, and perhaps all, being of meat, two roasts, four or five *entremets*. *Dessert*. The steward generally adds by way of dessert a plate of pears, three compotes, three plates of fruit, three pats of butter, two kinds of sugar, a bottle of oil, a bottle of Champagne, a little decanter of Bordeaux, another of Malvoisie, another of Madeira, and seven rolls.

'For those who dine on what is left, a two-pound loaf and two bottles of *vin ordinaire* are added.

'*Supper* consists of three soups and three courses. On days that are not fast days they are composed of two *entrées*, two roasts, and four or five *entremets*; on fast days of four *entrées* not made of meat, two or three of meat, two roasts, and four *entremets*. *Dessert*. The same as for dinner except as regards coffee.

'Louis XVI's son generally has a little supper separately.

'The increase of the number of dishes at dinner and supper on fast days arises from the fact that Louis XVI fasts regularly on the days prescribed by the Church, while his companions do not. He alone drinks wine; the others only drink water.

'What is left over is given to the three servants in the tower, who hand on the remainder to the servants in the kitchen and pantry. One or two dishes are added with bread and wine.

'During the first twenty days the baker supplied bread to the value of 100 livres at four to five sous a pound. The butcher furnished about 100 lbs. of meat a day at thirteen sous a pound. The pork-butcher supplied about twenty-five pounds of bacon a day at sixteen sous a pound. Between August 16th and September 9th fowls to the value of 1544 livres fifteen sous were supplied, that is to say fifty-six pounds weight a day. The consumption of fish—including both sea and river fish—varied from nine to ten pounds a day. At the same period a fruiterer sent in a bill for vegetables which only amounted to four livres; but at that time and until the end of October a messenger from Versailles was bringing vegetables from the palace gardens to the amount of fifteen pounds a load. The same fruiterer supplied, between August 13th and 31st, fruit to the value of 1000 livres, including eighty-three baskets of peaches for 425 livres.

'Of butter, eggs and milk the quantity used was about forty pounds a day : and, during the first twenty-seven days, 428 lbs. of butter, 160 smalls pats of butter, 2152 eggs, some absolutely new-laid, and some laid any time within the week, 111 pints of cream, both double and single, forty-one pints of milk, 228 bottles of Champagne and *vin ordinaire*. Several bottles of it came from the cellars of the *ci-devant* King. A water-carrier supplied water to the value of four livres a day.

'During the same period 1516 livres' worth of wood, 245 livres' worth of coal, and 400 livres' worth of candles were supplied.'

This report to the Commune was printed in the form of a placard, and sold in Paris, with the following sensational heading:

'A very strange Report, laid before the Commune of Paris, on the enormous expenses of the prisoners in the Temple.

'Do not be surprised, Citizens, if food becomes dearer. The

cannibals of Temple Tower, whom you imagine are being treated like prisoners, only consume about 100 lbs. of beef and twenty-five pounds of bacon a day, and during twenty-five days have only eaten fowls to the value of 1544 livres, 15 sous. See the following Report to the Commune.'

The enemies of royalty still contrived to make the prisoners of the Temple responsible for the general famine!

No wonder that Town Councillor Charles Goret, one of the Commissioners of the Temple, of whom we shall hear more later, described the meals supplied to the family as 'sumptious'.

The routine for the serving of meals is described by Turgy in an account which differs little from that recorded by Daujon. Turgy relates:

'Before dinner or any other meal someone went to the Council Room to summon two of the municipal officers. They came to the serving room, where the dishes were prepared and tasted before them, so that they might see there was nothing concealed in them, nor anything suspicious about them. In their presence the decanters and coffee-pots were filled. The covers for the decanters of almond-milk were torn, according to their directions, by any person and from any piece of paper they chose. Then we all proceeded to the dining room, but we did not lay the table till we had shown it, above and below, to the officers; we unfolded the table-cloths and napkins before them: they tore the rolls in halves and probed the crumbs with forks, or even with their fingers.'

The same routine, states Daujon, was followed in the case of medicines, which, after being tasted by the apothecary, were sealed by him with his own seal and delivered thus to the prisoners. The prisoners were not allowed the indulgence of paper, ink, or pencils. Nevertheless, as we shall learn later, Turgy was often able to outwit the vigilance of the commissioners and transmit messages to the King.

Other than that they were well fed and clothed, the family led a monotonous life. The King, says Hue, on the day he came to the Temple, formed a plan of life to which ever after he constantly adhered. When he had dressed he shut himself in a small room adjoining his chamber where he said his prayers and read until breakfast time. He then joined his family and did not leave them again until after supper, when he retired to his bedchamber, reading until eleven o'clock. Every night and morning he read *The Imitation of Jesus Christ*, and he borrowed extensively from M. Berthèlemy's small but well-chosen library, selecting many books on history, his favourite subject.

During the day, says his daughter, Louis instructed his son in his studies, particularly in geography; the Queen coached him in history. The study of arithmetic, however, was forbidden later, lest the Dauphin might use figures for secret correspondence. The Queen worked on her embroidery. About five o'clock in the evening the King and Queen took a walk in the gardens, not so much at their own inclination but for the benefit of their son whom they dared not let go out alone, states Madame de Tourzel, 'for the fear of giving the commissioners the idea of taking possession of him'. On this subject, she says, they had several times heard very sinister remarks.

No one from outside was allowed to visit the prisoners without producing a decree issued by the Commune, and every kind of article, whatever its nature, books, soiled linen, other garments and plate and crockery carried in and out of the Little Tower, was examined very carefully by the commissioners on duty.

A watch was kept upon the royal servants. On the day following the family's arrival at the Temple, three officials of the Commune—Chabot, who is described as a 'deputy', Santerre, the Commissary-General of the National Guard, and Billand-Varennes, the acting procurator-general—came to identify all the people who had remained with the Royal Family, and to make a list of their names. Turgy was asked if he had been formerly in the King's employ, to which he answered entirely correctly that he had. 'But who let you in here?' asked the perplexed Chabot, consulting the list of the people who had been allowed to accompany the King from the Feuillants. Quite untruthfully, Turgy replied that he and his two comrades, Chretien and Marchand, had been allowed to come in by Pétion. This lie satisfied Chabot who told Turgy, 'In that case it must be because you are good citizens. Remain at your posts and the nation will take better care of you than the tyrant ever did.' When they were alone again, the two other waiters, who were much alarmed, said to Turgy; 'Do you want to be the death of us all? You tell the town councillors that we were sent here by the Assembly, and you tell the deputies that we were sent here by the Commune.

We wish we were well out of it.' Nevertheless they remained and were faithful to their duty, relates Turgy.

For six days the family's attendants kept up the pretence of a phantom court. Then, on the night of August 18th–19th, at one o'clock in the morning, Madame de Tourzel was awakened by a disturbance on the staircase and she overheard a conversation between the commissioners, or the 'municipals' as she calls them, that caused her considerable uneasiness.

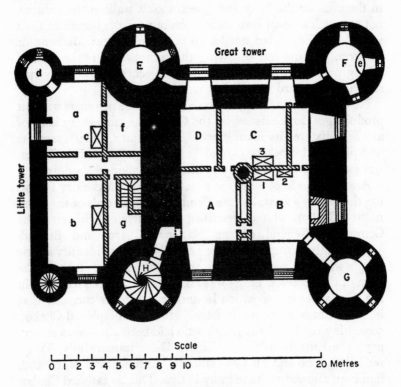

Small Tower, occupied by Louis from August 13 to September 29, 1792: *a*, king's room; *b*, kitchen; *c*, Hue and Chamilly's room; *d*, king's reading-room; *e*, king's bed; *f*, washroom; *g*, staircase.

Large Tower, occupied by Louis from September 29, 1792, to January 21, 1793: *A*, antechamber; *B*, king's room; *C*, Cléry's room; *D*, dining-room; *E*, food-house; *F*, wardrobe; *G*, king's oratory; *H*, staircase.

5

THE PRISONERS

The apartments in the Little Tower were suddenly invaded by commissioners and guards. Two commissioners entered the room where Hue and de Chamilly were lying on a mattress at the sleeping King's side. 'Are you the *valets-de-chambre*?' they demanded. Hue and de Chamilly answered in the affirmative. They were ordered by the two commissioners to rise and follow them. Hue's and de Chamilly's hands met and they pressed them together warmly, recalling that only that morning one of the commissioners had said in their hearing, 'the guillotine is permanent and is cutting off the pretended servants of Louis'. Their last hour had come. Going down to the Queen's ante-chamber, they found Princess de Lamballe and Madame de Tourzel under arrest. The Queen was holding them in her arms; in order not to leave the sleeping Dauphin alone, she had dragged his bed into her room. Madame Elizabeth arrived from the second storey bringing Pauline de Tourzel with her, and the three lady's-maids came from the floor below. Little Madame Royal watched dumbfounded. The King, though awakened, did not leave his room. 'Being assembled in the same place,' says Hue, 'we awaited our fate in silence.'

The Commune had decided to separate the Royal Family from their attendants, possibly because its members disapproved of the deference that was paid to the deposed King and Queen but, more probably, because they lived in daily dread of a royalist plot to abduct them. Despite their triumph on August 10th, the revolutionaries felt insecure; they had reason to, for the invading Prussian and Austrian armies had crossed the French frontier on July 18th and there was a strong royalist 'fifth column' in France.

The royal attendants were taken to the courtyard of the Palace, put into carriages and conveyed under guard to the Hôtel de Ville into which they were ushered, says Madame de Tourzel, 'through that horrible little door used in the case of criminals going to execution'. They were shown into a large hall which was occupied by women, and even children, and by members of the Commune, some of whom were asleep on the benches. They were examined separately. Hue was ordered to return to the Temple, to his great joy. The other servants were released (de Chamilly was guillotined later), and Princess de Lamballe and the de Tourzel mother and daughter removed to the prison of La Force where only the Princess was detained. Madame and Pauline de Tourzel did not return to the Temple and both women survived the Revolution.

On his return to the Temple, Hue flew to the King's room where he found Louis up and dressed. Hue showed by his looks that it would be prudent to say nothing at the moment and the King resumed his reading. About six in the afternoon Manuel came to say that the other servants would not return and that the Commune would send others to replace them. 'I will have no others,' replied Louis and he said that he and his family would look after themselves. Next day, Pétion sent a man and a woman to do the rough work, a former clerk of the toll-gates, fifty-seven-year-old Pierre Joseph Tison and his wife, who was later joined by their daughter, Pierrette. The menial servants, and the large staff employed at the Palace, many of whom had enjoyed their sinecures for many years, were not disturbed and they remained at their coveted posts. Within three days, the King's personal staff was increased by the arrival of Hanet Cléry, who had acted as the Dauphin's valet since his infancy. When he heard of the removal of the royal servants from the Temple, Cléry, who after his escape from the Tuileries had gone into the country, applied to Pétion for permission to rejoin the Royal Family, a duty which forced him to abandon his wife and children and which led him, eventually, to a series of adventures. Cléry, like Hue and Turgy, wrote his memoirs of the captivity he shared.

Madame Royale, before her release, wrote a diary of her captivity, and in reference to this early period she says that her father was insulted by the workmen in the garden and tormented by the turnkey, Rocher, who sang revolutionary songs and, knowing that the King did not like the smell of tobacco, puffed smoke into his face at every opportunity. Madame Royale, who was only thirteen at the time, wrote very briefly and the best account of the family's imprisonment in the Little Tower comes from the pen of François Hue who, in his recital of 'the barbarities to which His Majesty was exposed', claims that 'the picture must be given in all its details for from a sketch no true idea could be formed'.

On his return to the Temple, Hue resumed his duties, helping the King to dress and afterwards, while he said his prayers, the Queen. It was the only part of the day when she was alone for, after Hue had arranged her hair, the commissioners entered the chamber and stayed with her all day. During the day the King read or taught his son and the Queen and Madame Elizabeth sewed, being forced to mend their own and the King's clothes, or worked on their tapestries. The family at this stage, before their new clothes were delivered, were deprived of everything, and for some nights Hue was forced to make the Dauphin's bed with sheets that had holes in many places.

Hue goes on to say: 'After dinner (which was served at two in the afternoon and was followed by supper at nine), the King generally went into the library of the Keeper of the Archives of the Order of Malta, who had previous occupied the apartment of the tower. The library remaining there, His Majesty went to it to take books. One day, being in that room with him, he pointed to the works of Rousseau and Voltaire, and said to me, in a low voice: "Those two men have ruined France." With the view of recovering the habit of the Latin language, and of teaching, during his confinement, the Dauphin the first lessons of it, the King translated the Odes of Horace, and, sometimes, Cicero. As a relaxation from his reading and study, to which he was always eager to return, the Queen and Madame Elizabeth played with him after dinner, sometimes a game of piquet, sometimes of backgammon: in the evening, one of the Princesses read a play aloud.

'At eight o'clock I laid the Dauphin's supper in Madame Elizabeth's room; where the Queen stayed with him while he ate. Then, when the municipals were out of hearing, Her Majesty made her son say the following prayer: "Almighty God! who made and redeemed me, I adore thee. O preserve my father's life, and the lives of my family! Defend us against our enemies! Grant to Madame de Tourzel the strength she stands in need of to support the ills she suffers on our account!"

'After this prayer, I put the Dauphin to bed. The Queen and Madame Elizabeth stayed with him by turns. When the family went to supper, I carried something to eat to whichever of the Princesses was sitting by the Prince. When the King rose from the table, he went immediately to see his son. After staying a few minutes, he took the Queen and Madame Elizabeth by the hand, kissed Madame Royale, and returned upstairs to his own chamber. Then going into his little room, His Majesty remained there till eleven o'clock, his bed-time.

'This interval,' continues Hue, 'was the time in which I had to endure the most. Alone with the municipal on guard, I was obliged to hear all the horrors that the man pleased to utter against the King. The usual charge turned on His Majesty's hating and betraying the people. "Is not that true?" said one of them. "You certainly think as we do? If not, you must be the accomplice of this enemy to the Nation." A frozen air and dead silence were my only notice of these speeches. "You do not answer; then you are not a patriot." I continued dumb, resigned to whatever might happen.

'It was only at the moment of his going to bed, and of his rising, that the King ventured to talk to me. Sitting within his curtains, what he said was not heard by the commissioner. One day His Majesty, having heard the abuse heaped on me by the municipal on guard, said to me: "You have had a great deal to bear today. For my sake, continue to bear all; make no reply." I had no difficulty in obeying this order. The heavier misfortune weighed upon my master, the more sacred was his person in my eyes. Another time, when I was placing a black pin at the head of his bed to hang his watch on, he slipped into my hand a piece of paper rolled up. "Here is some of my hair," said he; "it is the only present I can make you at this time."

'The King, I am certain, foresaw that I should soon be taken from the tower. The thought tormented him. One of the doors of the room in which I slept opened into His Majesty's chamber, the other on the staircase. By the latter, the municipals often broke in suddenly, in the middle of the night, to see if I was not employed in secret correspondences. Once particularly, the King being wakened by the noise made by a municipal in his nocturnal visit, was uneasy on my account. As soon as it was light, His

Majesty, without shoes or stockings, and in his shirt, softly opened a little door between his chamber and mine. I woke. The sight of the King, and the situation in which he was, alarmed me. "Sire," said I, agitated, "does Your Majesty want anything?" "No," replied the King, "but hearing a noise in your room to-night, I was afraid that they had taken you away from me." How was my heart affected! The King went to bed again and slept tranquilly.'

Each time the family visited the garden, says Hue, they were insulted by the guards, who joked about the King's inevitable fate. However much he tried, Hue found it difficult to learn what was in store for the prisoners, until he realized that the voices of the news-criers could be heard within the prison.

Hue goes on to say: 'I went up to the Little Tower at the time the criers were passing. There, hoisting myself up to the height of a window, two-thirds stopped up, I remained till I could catch the most interesting intelligence. I then returned to the room before the Queen's chamber. Madame Elizabeth crossed at the same time into her own chamber, whither I followed her on some pretext, and communicated to her what I had been able to collect. Going back to the Queen's room, she went into a balcony at the only window that had not undergone the fate of the others, the apertures of which were nearly all blocked up. The King, without giving the municipals the least ground of suspicion, went to the same window, as if to take the fresh air, and his sister repeated to him what I had reported to her.'

By this means the King learned of the death of two friends, M. de la Porte, the Intendant of the Civil List, and Durosoy, the Editor of the *Gazette de Paris*, who were guillotined on August 24th and 25th.

The Commissioners of the Temple came to suspect, Hue believed, that the prisoners were obtaining information from the news-criers, and they ordered the hawkers to cry the most disastrous intelligence, that the Royal Family were to be separated, which caused the Queen such terror that she was in danger of fainting. And, asserts Hue, they tortured the King with petty slights, forcing him to turn out his pockets in a search for imaginary weapons, and they withheld from him the funds that had been voted for his upkeep, so that he was forced to borrow money from Hue to pay the most pressing tradesmen. Several of the commissioners, he says, persisted in remaining in the Queen's chamber until she was in bed. A further tyranny was exacted on August 24th:

'Between twelve and one in the morning, several municipals went into the King's chamber. Wakened by the noise, I got up as fast as I could; I saw them approach His Majesty's bed. "In execution of a decree of the Commune," said one of them, "we are come to search your chamber, and to take away whatever arms may be found in it." "I have none," replied the King. They searched, notwithstanding, but found nothing. "This will not do," said they; "you had a sword when you came to the Temple; give up that." Obliged to bear all, His Majesty ordered me to bring his sword. To assist, however involuntarily, in disarming my King was a shocking thought to me. I gave the sword into the King's hand. "Gentlemen," said he, "I deposit it with you. The more this sacrifice costs me, the more it proves my love of the public peace."'

Such was the constant restraint in which the prisoners were kept that Hue had few opportunities to speak to the King and Queen in private. Occasionally he was able to follow one or the other from one room to another on the pretence of performing some duty. On one of these occasions the Queen whispered to him, 'Everything tells me that I must be separated from the King; I hope you will remain with him.' Hue promised to stay as long as he was able to do so. In his will, Louis XVI paid tribute to the devoted service given to him by François Hue, and by his other officer of the bed-chamber, de Chamilly.

Meanwhile events had been stirring. The combined Prussian and Austrian armies, 75,000 strong, having taken Longwy, had marched on Verdun, which they now besieged. From Paris, 20,000 National Guardsmen, raw recruits, were sent to join the French armies in the east to stem the Duke of Brunswick's apparently inexorable advance on Paris. On August 24th it was learned that 7,000 royalists in the Vendée had revolted and royalist conspiracies were reported in Dauphiné and Brittany. In Paris there were daily riots and murders. The fate of the Revolution hung in the balance. An extraordinary tribunal was set up to detect, arrest and bring to justice suspected counter-revolutionaries, and on August 21st the guillotine, which had been set up in the Place du Carrousel, claimed its first political victim, Louis Conolot d'Angremont, who had been condemned to death that morning for the crime of raising irregular forces for the royal service.

The Parisians went mad with fear: the foreign invasion was expected to be the signal for royalist risings. Arms were requisitioned, homes were searched, railings were turned into pikes, church bells welded into cannon; soldiers guarded the streets and bridges. Hundreds of priests and suspected royalists were rounded up and thrown into the understaffed and overcrowded prisons, it being openly said that when the Duke of Brunswick reached Paris they would break out to lead the counter-revolution. It would be safer to massacre these suspects, suggested Marat.

The morning of Sunday, September 2nd, in the Temple began like any other day. The family were walking in the gardens. Suddenly Cléry, who was with them, noticed uneasiness amongst the commissioners, and the King and Queen and their children were taken hurriedly into their tower. Hue heard a confused noise coming from the streets adjacent to the Temple.

The best description of the dramatic moment comes from the pen of Daujon, one of the commissioners of whom we have heard already. The King, or 'Capet' as Daujon continues to call him, on his return from the gardens stood with Daujon at a window from where they watched the workmen demolishing a house near the tower. Louis called Daujon's attention to pieces of stone that were on the point of falling and as each piece fell he laughed heartily, showing his good humoured enjoyment. His pleasure was brief. The loud report of a gun checked it, a second report quenched it, a third replaced it with terror.

Daujon recognized the sound of the alarm guns: it was followed by a clamour of the tocsins and by the beat of drums. The red flag of emergency had been hoisted at the Hôtel de Ville, he was told. The workmen below downed their tools and left their work. A moment later, Manuel, the Procurator of the Commune, came into the room. 'Verdun is about to fall,' he announced.

6

THE PRINCESS
DE LAMBALLE'S HEAD

'To arms, to arms, citizens, the enemy is at the gates,' called the horsemen who had been sent galloping through the streets of Paris. Volunteers flocked to assemble in the Champs de Mars. In each section the minute-men paraded. The clamour of the tocsins and the roll of drums beat the air. Danton mounted the Tribune of the Assembly, electrifying the people by his cry, '*de l'audace, encore de l'audace, toujours de l'audace et la France est sauvée,*' (to dare, to dare, and still to dare and France is saved). The Parisians were convinced that the Prussians and Austrians were only a few leagues from the city. The terror, the fear that the Duke of Brunswick would live up to his promise and extract a terrible vengeance for their crime in deposing the King, gripped the revolutionaries; the rumour that the royalist sympathizers, the despised priests and hated aristocrats, were plotting to overthrow the Revolution, spread like wildfire. The mad panic released one of the most horrible and one of the most callous massacres in history. It was carried out by a few cut-throats, by no more than 150, probably. The ministers and the municipal officials made no attempt to stop it. 'I don't care a damn for the prisoners; let them shift for themselves,' announced Danton.

The bands of ruffians invaded the prisons to which the counter-revolutionary suspects had been taken, and butchered over 1,000 priests, aristocrats and the remnant of the Swiss guards, along with several hundred ordinary criminals, thieves, pick-pockets, prostitutes and even the children who were held in the House of Correction. Their bodies were dragged into the streets and fearfully mutilated. Princess de Lamballe was taken from her cell at La Force to a room in which she was interrogated by the executioners who brandished bloody weapons. Sickened by the odour of blood, she fainted. When she recovered consciousness, she was asked her name and rank. She said that she was Superintendent of the Queen's Household. Invited to swear 'Liberty, Equality and hatred to the King and Queen', she agreed to swear the first two. 'I cannot swear the last for it is not in my heart,' she told her interrogators. A man whispered in her ear, 'Swear it; if you do not swear you are a dead woman.' The Princess put her hands over her eyes. 'Let someone release Madame,' said one of her judges. This phrase was the death signal. Two men took her by the arms and forced her to walk over corpses to the threshold. A sabre slashed into the back of her head. She was despatched with pikes, and her body was thrown on to a pile of corpses. The mob fell upon it. They tore out the heart and sex organs and cut off her head, affixing these trophies to pikes which they lifted high into the air.

The bearers of the pikes marched at the head of the procession. An old friend of the Princess, Madame de Lebel, the wife of a painter who was trying to get near the prison in the hope of getting news of her friend, seeing the great commotion in the crowd, inquired the cause. 'It is Lamballe's head that they are carrying through Paris,' she was told. Seized with horror, Madame de Lebel took refuge in a hairdresser's shop on the Place de la Bastille. Hardly had she done so when the murderers entered the shop, demanding that the hairdressers arrange the head of the Princess. They were forced to wash off the blood and comb and powder the hair. 'Now, at any rate, Marie Antoinette can recognize her,' one of the assassins gleefully cried. The procession resumed its march, other individuals dragging along the headless corpse. The Princess's murderers were obsessed by the idea of making the dead woman gaze upon the scenes in which her life had moved, for in their delirium they thought their victim's remains were still conscious, despite their outrages.

An English spy named Burger considered the incident worthy of a despatch which he sent to the Foreign Secretary, Lord Grenville, on September 8th; he described the murder of Princess de Lamballe and he added:

'When this murder took place on Monday, Lindsay [William Lindsay, the British Chargé d'Affaires] and some other Englishmen were at the Palais Royal with the Duc d'Orléans. While they were waiting for dinner they heard a large crowd making a great noise, and going to the window they saw Madame de Lamballe's head. Overcome with horror at the sight, they drew back into the further end of the room, where the Duc d'Orléans was sitting. He asked what was going on. They answered that the mob was carrying a head on the end of a pike. 'Oh,' he said, 'is that all? Well, let us go to dinner!"

'While they were at dinner he asked if the women in the prisons had been massacred, and having received the answer that several of them had suffered this sad fate, he said, "Tell me, pray, what has become of Madame de Lamballe." M. Walkiers, who was seated beside him, intimated by a movement of his hand round his neck, that she had been killed. "I understand you," said the Duke, and immediately began to speak of something else.'

This story had a sinister implication, for the Princess de Lamballe was reputed to have been the mistress of the Duke of Orléans, who had sided with the revolutionaries from the early days of the Revolution.

The crowd swept on through the Rue des Franc-Bourgeois and the Rue de la Corderie. It was about three o'clock in the afternoon of September 3rd.

The King and Queen in the Temple knew nothing about the massacres. Following the excitement of the news from Verdun, which encouraged the hope that their rescuers were approaching, the Royal Family had been confined to their quarters; when the King and Queen appeared at the windows, people in the street threw stones, and a woman in the house opposite wrote on a square of cardboard 'Verdun is taken', and held the card in her window for a moment. Madame Elizabeth was able to read it without the guards noticing. Hardly had the news of the fall of the fortress been confirmed than a new Commissioner, a former Capuchin friar named Mathieu, entered the room in which the family were assembled. 'He was inflamed with rage,' states Madame Royale, and he vented it on the King whom he warned, 'If they (meaning the Prussians and Austrians) come here, we shall all die, but you will be the first.' Louis listened calmly to Mathieu's insults; Louis Charles burst into tears and ran from the room, and Madame Royale had the greatest difficulty in consoling her brother. Some of the guardsmen told Louis that the invaders were marching against France and killing French soldiers at his order. 'I have done everything for the happiness of the people, and there is nothing more for me to do,' he replied resignedly for, states Madame Royale, he was dreadfully upset by this slander.

Scarcely had Louis finished speaking when Mathieu called out, 'I arrest you.' 'Whom? I?' asked the King. 'No, your *valet-de-chambre*,' said Mathieu, indicating François Hue. 'What has he done?' Louis asked and before Mathieu could answer he went on; 'He is attached to me; that is his crime.' Hue was taken to the Hôtel de Ville, the approaches to which were filled by immense crowds, most of whom brandished swords, pikes and guns. 'Good, good, here's guillotine's game. He is the tyrant's valet,' screamed the sightseers. Hue was examined by a deputy-procurator who accused him of smuggling disguises into the Temple for the purpose of the Royal Family escaping, and of having obtained a waistcoat and breeches of Savoyard colour, proof positive of an intelligence with the King of Sardinia. Other charges included that of using hieroglyphic characters to carry on a secret correspondence ('These hieroglyphics,' says Hue, 'were nothing more than a book of arithmetic I used every night, before the Dauphin went to bed, to put on his bolster that he might in the morning learn the lesson which the King had set him') and the unpardonable crime of having sung a song in the Temple which implied that the King had been deserted by his people. The further charge that marked kindness was shown to him by the Royal Family, in marked contrast to their behaviour towards the Commissioners of the Commune to whom they hardly spoke, struck Hue dumb.

Hue was finally accused of holding the clue to the plot, laid within the Tower, to betray the sovereign people, and he was confined in a dungeon at the Hôtel de Ville, fortunately for him, for if he had been sent to one of the prisons he must surely have been massacred. Eventually he was released. He wrote his story in 1806, and he lived to see the restoration of the Bourbons in 1814.

The King, states Daujon, complained bitterly at the arrest of his confidential servant but 'the women far surpassed him in acrimony; especially Elizabeth who strode up and down the room, giving vent to her anger in a loud voice and darting menacing glances at us all'. In an aside, Daujon adds this statement, one which gives us a further insight into the characters of the captive family:

'I have always observed in her (Madame Elizabeth) a great deal of deliberate and consistent kind of pride that seemed to have neither end nor object, that was roused without cause and that nothing could conciliate. A good many people, and perhaps she herself, took it for dignity. Marie Antoinette seemed deeply affected by this separation. "It was plain," she said, "that the object was to part them from all the people who were most attached to them, and in whom they had placed their confidence." I do not know to what degree the prisoners confided in this *valet-de-chambre*, but I was extremely surprised at the civility and kindness—at the little attentions even—shown him by Marie Antoinette. They never had anything especially nice to eat without sharing it with M. Hue. "You like this: I have kept some for you," they would say. Absent or present, he was in their thoughts. "He takes so much trouble. He is so obliging." I think the Queen would have waited on him if she had dared.'

That night Cléry (whom Mathieu had warned 'Take care how you behave or the same thing may happen to you') took over Hue's job and he slept at the King's side. Unable to sleep, the Queen lay awake listening to drums beating the call to arms, but she did not know what was happening. Next morning, September 3rd, she heard that some people connected with the court had been massacred in the prisons, but her fears for her friend were relieved at 10 a.m. when procurator Manuel called to say that Princess de Lamballe and the other women who had been removed from the Temple were quite safe. Hue would also be safe, Manuel assured the King who was anxious about his valet. As he left the royal apartments Manuel whispered to Cléry, 'You are charged with a difficult duty; I exhort you to courage,' a remark that made Cléry fear that the people might attack the Temple.

That morning the family were refused permission to take their usual walk. About three o'clock, shortly after they had finished dinner, and were occupied in playing backgammon, they heard fearful cries and the noise of guns. An immense crowd was approaching the Temple, Daujon was informed by a mounted orderly who had been sent out to reconnoitre. Cléry had gone downstairs to dine with Tison and his wife. He and the Tisons had hardly seated themselves before they saw through the window a head affixed to a pike. Madame Tison screamed loudly and the murderers, thinking they heard the Queen's voice, raised their victim's head, so that it could not escape her sight. Cléry recognized Princess de Lamballe; though bloody the head was not disfigured and her blonde hair, which was still curly, floated around the pike. The cries from the street grew louder and the crowd began to chant the Marseillaise and the *Ca ira*.

Cléry ran upstairs, his face blanched with terror, hoping to hide the news from the Queen, until he had warned the King privately, but two commissioners were present in the room. 'Why do you not go to your dinner?' the Queen asked. 'I do not feel well,' was all that Cléry could say. Another commissioner entered the room and spoke mysteriously with his colleague. 'Are we safe here?' the King asked. 'The people want you to appear at the window, but we shall not allow it,' one commissioner replied. The cries and insults increased. A National Guards officer, wearing two epaulettes and carrying a large sabre, entered the room.

Addressing himself to this new arrival, the King asked what was happening. The young officer told him, 'Very well, Monsieur, as you wish to know I will tell you,' and indicating the commissioners, he said 'they want to prevent you seeing the head of Madame de Lamballe which the people have brought here, to show you how they avenge themselves on tyrants.' They were dragging her body with them and were demanding the person of the ex-Queen.

The Queen was frozen with horror. One of the commissioners scolded the young officer for his disclosure, but Louis ('with his usual good nature' remarks his daughter) excused him by saying that it was his fault for having asked the officer, who had merely answered his question.

Cléry ran to support the Queen who had fainted and Madame Elizabeth helped him place her in an arm-chair. The children burst into tears and tried to revive their mother by their caresses. Rocher, the turnkey, uttered cries of joy on seeing the head of Princess de Lamballe and, says Madame Royale, he scolded a young soldier who was sick with horror at the spectacle. Louis, his good humour gone, turned on the officer and said firmly, 'But you might have refrained from telling the Queen of that dreadful thing.'

One of the commissioners shut the window and drew the blinds, but Cléry, looking through a chink, saw the head again. The man who carried it mounted a pile of rubbish, debris from the demolished house; another man, he who dragged de Lamballe's body, tried to force the gates of the tower. In less than five minutes, realized Daujon, the mob would reach the door. To Daujon belongs the glory of preventing the massacre of the royal family. He tells the story in his own words:

'Two commissioners were instantly despatched to meet them, to find out their intentions, and to fraternize with them ostensibly if circumstances demanded it. Above all they were to secure the man who was carrying the head, for it was certain that he would lead the mob, and if he could be guided according to our wishes the crowd would be more easily restrained.

'Two other commissioners were despatched into the neighbouring districts, to impress upon those who seemed most excited that if they were to commit so abominable and useless a crime, Paris could never be cleansed from the stain of it. These commissioners were reinforced by several good citizens, who promised us to employ every effort to bring the most obstinate to reason.

'The clamour increased and our difficulties with it. The officer on duty asked us for orders, adding that he had four hundred well-armed men for whom he could answer, but that he would take no responsibility. We told him that our intention was to employ force only as a last resource for the protection of life; that it was our duty first to make use of persuasion; and that his business, therefore, was to see to the security of his arms. He made his arrangements accordingly.

'In the streets the throng was already prodigious. We had both sides of the great gate opened, in order that those outside might be pacified by seeing our peaceable intentions, of which further evidence was supplied by a portion of the National Guard, who stood unarmed in a double line from the outside entrance to the inner door. Nonetheless, all the arms, doors, and passages were well guarded in case of a surprise.

'We heard prolonged and violent shouting, and then at last they came! A tricoloured sash, hastily hung in front of the main entrance, was the only rampart that the magistrate consented to raise in opposition to the torrent, which seemed really uncontrollable. A chair was placed behind the tricolour; I climbed upon it and waited. Soon the bloodthirsty horde appeared.

'At the sight of the honoured symbol the murderous frenzy in the heart of these men, drunk with blood and wine, seemed to yield to a feeling of respect for the national badge. Everyone tried with all his strength to prevent the violation of the sacred barrier; to touch it would have seemed to them a crime. They were anxious to appear right-minded, and actually believed themselves to be so; for public opinion, which constitutes the moral law of the people, has an unbounded influence over such men as these, who bow down before it even while they are outraging it.

'Two men were dragging along a naked, headless corpse by the legs. The back was on the ground; in front the body was ripped open from end to end. They came to a standstill before my tottering rostrum, at the foot of which they laid out this corpse in state, arranging the limbs with great particularity, and with a degree of cold-blooded callousness that might give a thoughtful man food for much meditation.

'On my right, at the end of a pike, was a head that frequently touched my face, owing to the gesticulations of the man that carried it. On my left a still more horrible wretch was with one hand holding the entrails of the victim against my breast, while he grasped a great knife with the other. Behind them a huge coal-heaver held suspended at the end of a pike, just above my forehead, a fragment of linen drenched with blood and mire.

'As they appeared on the scene I extended my right arm, and there I stood, absolutely motionless, waiting for silence. I obtained it.

'I told them that the municipal body chosen by themselves had been entrusted by the National Assembly with a charge for which they, the Commune, were responsible not only to the Assembly but also to the whole of France, having sworn to deliver it up in the state in which they had received it. I told them that when we heard the people had designs on the life of the prisoners we refused to oppose them by force of arms; we had rejected the idea with horror, being persuaded that if just arguments were once laid before a Frenchman he would not fail to listen to them. I made them see how impolitic it would be to deprive ourselves of such valuable hostages at the very moment when the enemy was in possession of our frontiers. And on the other hand, would it not be a proof of the prisoners' innocence if we did not dare to bring them to trial? How much more worthy it is of a great people, I added, to condemn a King guilty of treason, to death upon the scaffold! This salutary example, while it strikes well-justified terror into the hearts of tyrants, will inspire the peoples of the world with a devout respect for our nation. I ended by entreating them to resist the counsels of a few ill-disposed persons who wished to drive the men of Paris into behaving with violence in order afterwards to poison the minds of their provincial brethren against them; and then, to shew them the confidence of the Council in their good intentions, I told them it had been decreed that six of them should be admitted to march round the garden, with the commissioners at their head.

'Instantly the barrier was removed and about a dozen men entered, bearing their spoils. These we led towards the tower, and were able to keep them fairly in check till they were joined by the workmen, after which it was more difficult to restrain them. Some voices demanded that Marie Antoinette should come to the window, whereupon others declared that if she did not show herself we must go upstairs and make her kiss the head. We flung ourselves upon these maniacs, swearing they should only carry out their horrible design after passing over the bodies of their municipal officers. One of the wretches declared I was taking the part of the tyrant, and turned upon me with his pike so furiously that I should certainly have fallen under his blows, if I had shown any weakness, or if another man had not opposed him, pointing out that in my place he would be obliged to act as I did. My air of unconcern impressed him, and when we went out he was the first to embrace me and call me a fine fellow.

'In the meantime, two commissioners had thrown themselves in front of the first inner door of the tower, and prepared to defend the approaches with devoted courage; whereupon the others, seeing that they could not win us over, broke into horrible imprecations, pouring out the most disgusting obscenities, mingled with fearful yells. This was the final gust of the storm, and we waited for it to blow over. Fearing, however, lest the scene should lead to some climax worthy of the actors, I decided to make them another speech. (This seemed to me the last gentle means that remained to us; and I am convinced, by the effect I saw produced upon my barbarous audience as I went on, that I only gained my end by the big words I used—words that in such a context were an insult to reason and humanity. If I had failed I should have seized the sabre of a National Guard and killed the first man who had dared to come forward. When a man loves everything connected with the glory of his country, and is deeply sensible of the duty it entails, there is nothing he will not attempt, and I would almost say, attempt successfully.) But what could I say? How could I find the way to such degraded hearts? I attracted their attention by gestures; they looked at me, and listened. I praised their courage and their exploits, and made heroes of them; then, seeing they were calming down, I gradually mingled reproach with praise. I told them the trophies they were carrying were common property. "By what right," I added "do you alone enjoy the fruits of your victory? Do they not belong to the whole of Paris? Night is coming on. Do not delay, then, to leave these precincts, which are so much too narrow for your glory. It is in the Palais Royal, or in the garden of the Tuileries, where the sovereignty of the people has so often been trodden under foot, that you should plant this trophy as an everlasting memorial of the victory you have just won."

' "To the Palais Royal!" they cried; and I knew my ridiculous harangue had won their approval. They left the place; but first nauseated us with their horrible embraces, redolent of blood and wine.'

Next day, a friend, Bazire, a member of the Committee of Surveillance, in whom Daujon had every confidence, told him that several of the ruffians had come to the Committee to hand over the contents of de Lamballe's pockets, and one man had stated that he had torn out her heart and had eaten it on the spot; he had never tasted anything so delicious. As proof of his story, he drew attention to the blood with which his lips were stained. He pulled from his pockets various parts of a woman's body, which he said he had cut off the de Lamballe. Daujon found it difficult to believe the truth of this story, and we may remark that a man named Jacques-Charles Hervelin was charged before the Committee with having 'eaten the heart of the former Princess de Lamballe after having it grilled'. Another version states that he cooked it in wine. Hervelin denied the charge.

The murder of the Queen's friend, and the revolting circumstances of her death, greatly increased the Royal Family's anxieties, which were little relieved by the appearance of Mayor Pétion who, according to Daujon, arrived in a desperate state, for he believed that the mob had forced the Queen to kiss de Lamballe's head. 'How could they have permitted anything so horrible?' he asked the Commissioners of the Temple. He was delighted to hear that the people had not been allowed to enter the tower, and he at once announced the purpose of his visit; the payment to the King of some of the money owed to him for his expenses by the Commune, and which he badly needed, a task that little Madame Royale thought callous under the circumstances. While the money was being counted, the municipal officer who had sacrificed his tricolour sash to prevent the mob from entering the Temple came to demand the cost of it. Louis paid him, and he congratulated Daujon on his great firmness and resource in preventing the people from gaining access to the Tower. 'You have saved our lives; thank you,' Louis told him.

All was quiet that night by eight o'clock, says Cléry. The riot on September 3rd was followed by a period of brooding silence in the Little Tower. Unknown to, or not fully understood by the captive Bourbons, great events were stirring on the eastern frontiers of France.

7

THE LITTLE TOWER

Madame Royale and Cléry both employ the word 'tranquil' to describe the days that followed the murder of Princess de Lamballe, in contrast no doubt to the horror of that day, and both supply information which depicts the daily life of the family. Discipline, says Madame Royale, became stricter; nevertheless, two of the commissioners, whom she does not name, alleviated her father's misery by showing him kindness and encouraging him to hope. She mentions, also, the case of a sentinel who 'never ceased weeping all the time he was at the Temple', and who had a conversation with her aunt through the keyhole. She asked Heaven to reward this man for 'his loyalty to the King'. She occupied her time studying the rules of arithmetic and copying out extracts from books, 'with a municipal always looking over my shoulder, thinking I was planning some sort of conspiracy'.

Cléry, who had taken over Hue's duties, describes the daily routine in the Little Tower, in which the King occupied a large room, with a smaller room leading off it, which Cléry calls 'the cabinet', on the third floor; the second floor had been converted into two bedrooms for the Queen, the Dauphin, Madame Elizabeth and Madame Royale.

'The King arose usually at six in the morning; he shaved himself, and I arranged his hair and dressed him. He went at once into his reading room. That room being very small, the municipal guarding the King sat in the bedroom, the door being half-open in order that he might not lose sight of the person of the King. His Majesty prayed on his knees for five or six minutes, and then read till nine o'clock. During that time, and after having done his room and prepared the table for breakfast, I went down to the Queen. She never opened her door until I came, so as to prevent the municipal from entering her bedroom. I then dressed the young Prince and arranged the Queen's hair; after which I went to perform the same service for Madame Elizabeth and Madame Royale. This moment of their toilet was one of those in which I could tell the Queen and the Princess what I heard and what I knew. A sign told them I had something to say, and one of them would then talk to the municipal officer to distract his attention.

'At nine o'clock the Queen, her children and Madame Elizabeth went up to the King's room to breakfast; after having served them I did the bedrooms of the Queen and the Princesses; Tison and his wife helped me only in that sort of work.'

Tison, states Cléry, had been sent to the Temple by the Commune to spy upon the commissioners and to denounce them, and he says that Tison was 'an old man, hard and malignant by nature, incapable of an emotion of pity and destitute of all feelings of humanity.' One at least of the commissioners, as we shall learn, was fully aware of Tison's role.

Cléry continues his account of the daily routine:

'At ten o'clock the King came down with his family into the Queen's room and passed the day there. He occupied himself with the education of his son, made him recite passages from Corneille and Racine, gave him lessons in geography, and taught him to colour maps. The precocious intelligence of the young Prince responded perfectly to the tender care of the King. His memory was so good that on a map covered with a sheet of paper he could point out the departments, districts, towns, and the course of the rivers; it was the new geography of France that the King was teaching him. The Queen, on her side, was occupied with the education of her daughter, and these different lessons lasted till eleven o'clock. The rest of the morning she spent in sewing, knitting, and doing tapestry. At midday the three Princesses went into Madame Elizabeth's room to change their morning gowns; no municipal went with them.

'At one o'clock, if the weather was fine, the Royal Family were taken down into the garden; four municipal officers and a captain of the National Guard accompanied them. As there were numbers of workmen about the Temple, employed in pulling down houses and building new walls, the Royal Family were allowed to walk only in the horse-chestnut alley. I was permitted to share these walks, during which I made the young Prince play either at quoits, or football, or running, or other games of exercise.

'At two o'clock they returned to the tower, where I served the dinner; and every day at the same hour Santerre, the general commanding the National Guard of Paris, came to the Temple, accompanied by two aides-de-camp. He searched the different rooms. Sometimes the King spoke to him; the Queen never. After the meal, the Royal Family returned to the Queen's room where Their Majesties usually played games at piquet or backgammon. It was during that time that I dined.

'At four o'clock the King took a short rest; the Princesses sat by him, each with a book in her hand; the deepest silence reigned during that nap. What a spectacle! a King pursued by hatred and calumny, fallen from a throne to a prison, yet sustained by his conscience and sleeping peacefully the sleep of the just! his wife, his sister, his children contemplating with respect those august features, the serenity of which seemed increased by troubles, so that even then there could be read upon them the peace he enjoys today! No, that sight will never be effaced from my memory.

'When the King awoke, conversation was resumed. He made me sit beside him. I gave, under his eyes, writing-lessons to the young Prince; and I copied out, under his selection, passages from the works of Montesquieu and other celebrated authors. After this lesson, I took the little Prince into Madame Elizabeth's chamber, where I made him play ball or battledore and shuttle-cock.

'At the close of the day the Royal Family sat round a table; the Queen read aloud books of history or other well-chosen works suitable to instruct and amuse her children; sometimes un-expected scenes corresponding to her own situation occurred and gave rise to painful thoughts. Madame Elizabeth read also in turn, and the reading lasted till eight o'clock. I then served the supper of the young Prince in Madame Elizabeth's bed room; the Royal Family were present; the King took pleasure in amusing his children by making them guess the answers to conundrums taken from a file of the *Mercure de France* which he had found in the library.

'After the Dauphin's supper, I undressed him; it was the Queen who heard him say his prayers; he said one especially for the Princesse de Lamballe; and by another he asked God to protect the life of Madame de Tourzel, his governess. If the municipals were very near, the little Prince himself took the precaution to say these last two prayers in a low voice. I then made him go into the cabinet, and if I had anything to tell the Queen, I seized that moment. I told her what the newspapers contained, for none were allowed to enter the tower; but a street-crier, sent expressly, came every evening at seven o'clock and stood near the wall on the rotunda side within the Temple enclosure, where he cried, with several pauses, a summary of what was taking place in the National Assembly, the Commune, and the armies. I stationed myself in the King's cabinet to listen; and there, in the silence, it was easy to remember what I heard.

'At nine o'clock the King supped. The Queen and Madame Elizabeth took turns to remain with the Dauphin during this meal; I carried them what they desired for supper; that was another opportunity to speak to them without witnesses.

'After supper the King went up for a moment into the Queen's room, gave her his hand in sign of adieu, also to his sister, and kissed his children; then he went to his own room, retired into his cabinet and read there till midnight. The Queen and the princesses closed the doors of their rooms; one of the municipals remained all night in the little room between their two chambers; the other followed the King.

'I then placed my bed beside that of the King; but His Majesty waited, before going to bed, till the municipals were changed and the new one came up, in order to know which one it was, and if he was one the King did not know, he always told me to ask his name. The municipals were relieved at eleven in the morning, at five in the afternoon, and at midnight. The above manner of life lasted the whole time that the King was in the Little Tower.'

Cléry refers to Antoine Simon, the shoemaker who had been given the duty of supervising the finances of the Temple prison and who, he says, never quitted the building.

'This man affected the lowest insolence whenever he was in the presence of the Royal Family; often he would say to me, close to the King, so that His Majesty might hear him: "Cléry, ask Capet if he wants anything, for I can't take the trouble to come up a second time." I was forced to answer, "He wants nothing." '

It was this Simon, says Cléry, who was later put in charge of the young Dauphin and 'who, by well-calculated barbarity, made that interesting child so wretched', and he adds, 'There is reason to think that he was the tool of those who shortened the Prince's life'; two assessments we shall need to consider later in respect to the controversial problem of the fate of Louis Charles.

Cléry recalls several anecdotes relating to the period when the family were confined in the Little Tower. One day, at the Queen's order, he made a multiplication table to teach the Dauphin how to reckon, but 'a municipal declared that she was showing her son how to talk in cipher and they made her renounce the lesson in arithmetic'. The same thing happened over the Queen's tapestry which she asked permission to send to a friend, but the municipals thought its designs represented hieroglyphics and they obtained a decree forbidding the work to be sent out of the Temple.

Cléry refers also to some of the insults to which the family were subjected. A municipal named Turlot said one day in Cléry's hearing, 'If the executioner doesn't guillotine that s . . . . family, I'll do it myself.' One of the sentinels, Cléry found, had scribbled on the wall the words 'The guillotine is awaiting the tyrant'. He made a motion to efface them but the King stopped him.

Rocher, the turnkey of whom Madame Royale speaks, was, says Cléry, 'a horrible object':

'He dressed as a *sapeur*, with long moustaches, a black fur cap on his head, a large sabre and a belt from which hung a bunch of big keys, presented himself at the door whenever the King wished to go out; he would never open it till the King was close beside it, and then, under pretence of choosing the right key from his enormous bunch, which he rattled with a frightful noise, he kept the Royal Family waiting, and drew back the bolt with a crash. Then he would hurry down the stairs, and stand by the last door, a long pipe in his mouth, and as each member of the Royal Family passed him he would puff the smoke in their faces, especially those of the Princesses. Some of the National Guards, who were amused by such insolence, would gather near him, and laugh loudly at each puff of smoke, permitting themselves to say the coarsest things; some, to enjoy the spectacle more at their ease, would even bring chairs from the guard room, and, sitting down, obstructed the passage, already very narrow.'

On their return to the tower the family were forced to endure the same insults and often, records Cléry, the walls were covered with most indecent apostrophes, written in such large letters that they could not escape their eyes, such as: 'Madame Veto shall dance'; 'We will put the fat pig on diet'; 'Down with the *Cordon rouge*'; 'Strangle the cubs'. Once the guards drew a gibbet on which dangled a figure, and beneath it was written: 'Louis taking an air bath'. At another time it was a guillotine with these words: 'Louis spitting into the basket'. The King and Queen were forced to endure this torture for the sake of their children who would not otherwise have had any fresh air or exercise.

But not all the guardsmen were so vile, as Cléry remarks:

'A sentinel mounted guard one day at the Queen's door; he belonged to the *faubourgs*, and was clean in his dress, which was that of a peasant. I was alone in the first room reading. He looked at me attentively and seemed much moved. I rose and passed before him. He presented arms and said in a trembling voice, "You cannot go out." "Why not?" "My orders are to keep you within sight." "You mistake me," I said. "What! Monsieur, are you not the King?" "Then you do not know him?" "I have never seen him, and I would like to see him away from here." "Speak low," I said, "I shall enter that room and leave the door half open; look in and you will see the King; he is sitting by the window with a book in his hand." I told the Queen of the sentry's desire, and the King, whom she informed, had the kindness to go from one room to the other and walk before him. I then went back to the sentry. "Ah! Monsieur," he said, "how good the King is! how he loves his children!" He was so moved that he could hardly speak. "No," he continued, striking his chest, "I cannot believe he has done us all that harm." I feared that his extreme agitation would compromise him, and I left him.'

Another sentry, who was posted in the garden, who may have been the tearful man to whom Madame Royale refers, seemed anxious to communicate something to Cléry, but he was too timid and the valet failed to receive his message. Despite Cléry's attempts to gain information from the cries of the news vendors, the family can have had only the haziest of notions about what was going on outside their prison, though Turgy's ingenious attempts to pass notes and signal by code may have told them more. At first, Turgy wrote little notes which he rolled into pellets and dropped into dishes. Later, for greater caution, he and Madame Elizabeth devised a code by which Turgy informed them of the progress of the foreign armies which he was in an advantageous position to secure by his duties which took him outside the Temple in search of provisions two or three times a week. Sometimes he met François Hue, at lonely places inside the city and even outside Paris. Only rarely was Turgy searched on entering or leaving the Temple because, as he recounts, 'I was very careful to supply the warders with everything they asked for when they visited the kitchens'. This made them more amenable and he says that, in spite of the vigilance of the commissioners, 'hardly a day passed during the fourteen months I was at the Temple, that I did not deliver notes or communicate by signs'. The signal code that Turgy describes only came into operation after the family had been transferred to the Great Tower, and it will be quoted in due course.

The family learned that the course of events was apparently swinging in their favour, for their predicament, which posed a dangerous threat to royalty everywhere, had aroused the indignation of the Great Powers. Lord Gower,[1] the British Ambassador, had quitted Paris on August 23rd after delivering a sharp note in which King George III expressed 'his solicitude for the position of Their Most Christian Majesties and the Royal Family', which was a diplomatic way of conveying a veiled threat to the revolutionaries. The British Chargé d'Affairs, William Lindsay, asked for his passports on September 2nd, and Chauvelin, the French Ambassador in London, was politely told that he would no longer be received at court. Catherine, Empress of Russia, expelled the French Chargé d'Affaires, and the Bourbon King of Spain instructed his Ambassador in Paris to ask for his passports. Thus revolutionary France fell under the ban of monarchial Europe. As September advanced the net tightened.

The threat from the east became even more pressing as the Duke of Brunswick, following his capture of Verdun, moved farther into France. There seemed nothing to prevent him from

1 Who became Duke of Sutherland.

reaching Paris, where panic reigned; several of the more timorous revolutionaries advocated the establishment of a 'redoubt' in the plateau of central France, a pusillanimous retreat which was jeered to scorn by Danton. In a spirited counter-attack the revolutionaries sought to woo to their cause the downtrodden subjects of the tyrant kings who threatened the establishment of liberty, and they conferred the rights of French citizenship on such illustrious foreigners as, for example, Jeremy Bentham, the English philosopher, Clarkson and Wilberforce, the Negro slavery abolitionists, George Washington and Thomas Paine, and several distinguished Germans, Italians and Poles.

Above all, the revolutionaries pinned their faith on the French armies standing on the eastern frontier. Though numerically stronger than the combined Prussians and Austrians, the French regular troops were believed to have been paralysed by the emigration *en masse* of most of their officers, and the reinforcements who had been rushed from Paris were raw recruits, undisciplined *sans-culottes*. But this 'blue uniformed' rabble, as opposed to the 'white breeches' worn by the regulars, formed only a small part of the forces that General Dumouriez now massed around Sedan. Combining his own army of 20,000 men with Biron, who commanded a further 25,000, Dumouriez linked forces with Kellermann, who led 28,000 men, in the Argonne, the traditional route of foreign invasion. Brunswick advanced ponderously with his well-disciplined monarchial armies, forcing Dumouriez to the south. The road to Paris lay open.

With great boldness, Dumouriez thrust his armies behind Brunswick, occupying a ridge in the rear. Brunswick, fearing to progress further without dislodging the French, turned to attack, bringing up 34,000 Prussians, with 15,000 Austrians on either flank, and 5,000 French *émigrés*, commanded by the Comte de Provence, in the rear. The battle of Valmy was fought on September 20th: it decided the fate of the Revolution, yet it was no more than a long-distance cannonade. The Prussians advanced in massed parade-ground formation, expecting the despised *sans-culottes* to fly in terror. The French regulars stood their ground and Brunswick was forced to retire. Ten days later he led his soldiers back across the frontier. Wolfgang Goethe, who witnessed the battle, summed up its result: 'From this place and this day dates a new era in human history.'

The eye-witnesses within the Little Tower do not mention the family's reaction to the news of the French victory which they must have heard within a few days. It spelled death to their hopes of an early rescue; another piece of news seems to have pleased Louis.

On September 21st the newly elected National Convention, which replaced the Assembly, formally abolished the monarchy and declared a Republic in its stead. That afternoon a municipal officer named Lubin marched to the Temple, accompanied by *gendarmes* on horseback and followed by an enormous crowd. The delegates halted outside the tower; the trumpets sounded and a great silence fell. In stentorian voice, intended for the hearing of the people within, Lubin announced the new decrees. Cléry is again our source of information:

'Hébert, so well-known under the name of Père Duchesne, and Destournells, afterwards Minister of Public Taxation, happened to be on guard that day over the Royal Family; they were seated at the moment near the door, and they stared at the King, smiling treacherously. The King noticed them; he had a book in his hand and continued to read; no change appeared upon his face. The Queen showed equal firmness; not a word, not a motion that could add to the enjoyment of those two men. The proclamation ended, the trumpets sounded again. I went to the window; instantly all eyes turned to me; they took me for Louis XVI; I was loaded with insults. The *gendarmes* made threatening motions towards me with their sabres; and I was obliged to retire in order to stop the tumult.'

Louis, says his biographer,[1] was not displeased at the news of the abolition of the monarchy:

'Often in the past he had wished he could resign with a clear conscience, and now that responsibility was taken off his shoulders, he felt, perhaps for the first time in his adult life, really serene. He had, moreover, cause to hope that he would no longer be molested, now that France was a republic and the ex-King safely in prison. Thus consoling himself, Louis settled down happily to a long period of reading.'

Yet, remarks Padover, Louis XVI was a 'magic talisman' who

[1] S. H. Padover, *Louis XVI*, 1928.

had to be destroyed before the new order could feel itself secure. The Jacobins and the Paris mob were convinced that as long as the King was alive the republic was in danger, and they began a ruthless propaganda campaign against 'Louis the Last,' as they named the deposed King.

On September 29th Louis was informed that the apartment prepared for him in the Great Tower was ready for occupation.

8

THE COMMISSIONERS

At ten o'clock in the morning six commissioners entered the Queen's room where the family was assembled. One of them, a man named Charbonnier, read to the King the decree of the Commune which ordered 'the removal of paper, pens, ink, pencils and written papers, whether on the persons of the prisoners or in their rooms, and also from the *valets-de-chambre* and all other persons on service in the tower'. Charbonnier added, 'If you have need of anything, Cléry will come down and write your requests on a register which will be kept in the Council Chamber.' The King and his family, without making any protest, searched their persons and handed over their writing materials, and the Commissioners searched the room, carrying off all means of written communication.

Suspecting that something out of the ordinary was afoot, Cléry learned from a member of the delegation that the King was to be transferred that evening to the Great Tower, and he whispered the information to Madame Elizabeth, who told her brother. Louis was not therefore taken completely by surprise when, after supper, the commissioners reappeared and read to him the official order transferring his prison; nonetheless he was visibly affected and his distressed family tried, in Cléry's words, 'to read in the eyes of the commissioners to what length their project went'. They learnt nothing and the King was forced to leave them in the utmost alarm and uncertainty. 'It was one of the cruellest moments Their Majesties passed in the Temple,' says Cléry, who followed the King to his new prison. His room on the second floor of the Great Tower contained only a bed, and the painters and paperers were still at work, which caused so intolerable a smell that Cléry feared that the King would become ill from it. He passed the night sitting on a chair at the King's side, and next day Louis, with great difficulty, obtained an adjoining room for his valet.

Convinced that the Commune intended to separate the family permanently, Cléry sat disconsolate on the morning following the transfer, until he was aroused by the King standing at his side. 'They seem to have forgotten your breakfast, take this, the rest is enough for me,' Louis said, giving his valet a piece of bread and a bottle of lemonade, all that the servitors had brought that morning. Touched by his master's concern, Cléry could not restrain his tears; the King saw them and his own flowed.

The Great Tower, the fortress built by the Knight Templars on the model they had established in the East, had remained unchanged since it was constructed in the thirteenth century, and it had been so solidly built that no repairs had been required for five hundred years. In 1792 the square donjon was dark, sombre and forbidding. 150 feet high, it was capped by a spire, surrounded by battlements, and flanked by four turrets which rose from the ground at the angles of the Tower. The Great Tower abutted on the Little Tower, between which there was no internal means of communication. Both buildings were demolished in the nineteenth century, and their location is marked by the Place du Temple.

The Council of the Temple took over the ground floor which comprised a single chamber, thirty-five feet wide, the roof of which was supported by a central column rising into Gothic arches, and there the commissioners on duty, other than the two who were upstairs, dined, slept and kept their registers. The massive outer door, which was six to eight inches in thickness, had been strengthened with strong iron bands, iron locks and four enormous bolts on the inside. A narrow, dark staircase within one turret led to the first floor which was occupied by forty citizen-soldiers who were on duty continually, in addition to their comrades and the gunners, about 250 men in all, who guarded the Temple precincts, under the command of an officer and an adjutant-major.

The fourth floor was uninhabited, and the second and third floors had been converted for the use of the King and the Dauphin, when his son joined him, and the three women, by partitioning each floor into four rooms of roughly equal proportions, and some attempt had been made to render them habitable by stretching canvas across the ceilings, to disguise the Gothic arches, and by covering the walls of the partitions with paper. Large porcelain stoves had been installed on both floors, the smoke from which, because there were no chimneys, was conveyed outside the building by sheet-iron pipes, the construction of which necessitated the blocking up of a window on each floor. The remaining windows brought in little light, for their embrasures were nine feet thick, and they were closed by thick bars and iron shutters.

The King's apartments on the second floor were entered from the staircase through two doors, one of wood and the other of iron, both secured by locks and bolts and penetrated by a sliding 'judas' for inspection. These doors opened into the ante-room in which stood the stove, and from it led two doors, both of clear glass, one into the narrow dining room and the other into the King's bedroom, behind which there was another room where Cléry slept. It was connected to the King's room by a passage which gave entry to the water closet *à l'anglaise* in the turret. Another turret had been converted into a wood store.

The ante-room was furnished with eight chairs, upholstered in pink velvet, a desk and a table, and one wall bore 'The Declaration of the Rights of Man', depicted in three colours. Louis' bedroom contained a four-poster bed, which had been brought from the palace of the Temple, which had curtains and covers of green velvet, a spring mattress, four coverlets and a bolster enclosed in white taffeta. The Dauphin's folding bed stood at the foot of the King's bed. The furniture included a wash-stand, an arm-chair and four upright chairs, which were covered in damask to match the bed materials, a chest of drawers with a marble top, a desk with a green morocco top and a large mirror over the fireplace. There was also a mahogany pot-cupboard, and a mahogany *bidet* with a china receptacle. On the mantelpiece stood a clock which bore the legend 'by Lepanti, Clockmaker to the King', but the word 'King' had been blotted out. Adjoining the bedroom, a small study had been constructed in the turret, containing a small stove, two cane chairs and a table. The dining room was furnished with a folding table, five cane chairs, a dumb-waiter and two corner cupboards.

The third floor had been partitioned on the same plan as the second floor. The Queen and her daughter shared the room above the King's, Madame Elizabeth occupied the room above Cléry's and the Tisons slept above the dining room. There was no corridor on this floor and the only access to the water closets was through Madame Elizabeth's room. The Queen's room was furnished with a four-poster bed, wash-stand, a couch and rush-seated chairs, a clock representing, of all ironical things, Fortune and Her Wheel, and a clavichord which, like the rest of the furniture, had been brought from the palace, and on which Mozart was reputed to have played. The three waiters, Turgy, Chretien and Marchand, lived in the outbuildings of the Palace and each day they carried the food that had been prepared for the prisoners the 200 yards that separated the kitchens from the tower, which by October had been completely isolated by the thirty-two foot high wall built by M. Paloy.

No ray of sunlight entered either floor and their occupants were subdued. Uncertainty and a sense of disquiet weighed them down and even the children had lost their gaiety. Marie Antoinette bent over her sewing and Louis and his sister paced aimlessly to and fro, bowed by indefinable anguish. The description of the topography of the new prison, which is essential to the story, has carried us ahead of events for the record of which, at this time, we rely on Cléry.

On the morning following the King's transfer to the Great Tower, Cléry found a pretext to revisit the Little Tower; the commissioner on duty sanctioned the King's request to obtain books from M. Berthèlemy's library but, as he could not read, he could not select them. The man's ignorance gave Cléry his opportunity: he found the Queen and her children in her room with Madame Elizabeth. They were weeping and they asked Cléry a thousand questions about the King, to which he could only answer with reserve. Addressing the commissioner who had accompanied Cléry, the Queen asked, with sobs of grief, that the family should at least be allowed to dine together, a request to which he agreed for that day, pending the decision of the Commune for the future. The Queen and her children were overjoyed and their gratitude brought tears to the eyes of the commissioner, the only tears, says Cléry, he ever saw shed by any of them in that dreadful place. The incident would not be worth recalling except that it re-introduces the enigmatic figure of Antoine Simon, who had been one of the representatives of the Commune deputed to organize the transfer of the Royal Family from the Feuillants to the Temple and who, in October, was appointed to supervise the finances of the Temple prison. Noticing the tears of the Queen, Simon remarked, 'I believe those bloody women will make me cry,' and turning to the Queen he accused, 'When you murdered the people on August 10th *you* did not cry.' Later on, when Simon is appointed to be the Dauphin's special gaoler, we shall need to consider whether or not he was the unmitigated scoundrel that tradition makes him out to be, the man whose callous brutality reduced the bright and gay little boy into a deaf and dumb beast.

Dinner that day was served in the King's new room; nothing more was said about the decree of the Commune, and the King and his family met every day for dinner, which was followed usually by a walk in the garden. After dinner the Queen was allowed to inspect her future apartments which she begged the workmen to finish quickly, but it was three weeks before she was allowed to rejoin her husband. The temporary separation, says Cléry, increased the watchfulness of the commissioners and made them uneasy; their distrust made it even harder for him to gain information from outside the Temple, a task in which, however, he was aided by visits from his wife, which were sanctioned by the Council. Though closely watched he learned what was going on. Turgy also picked up news on his visits outside and, though forbidden to speak to Cléry, he was often able to pass on scraps of gossip. Cléry whispered the news to the King when he dressed him in the morning. At first, he says, the commissioners were rude to him, but by showing gentleness in return he was able to gain their goodwill and inspire their confidence, which made the passing of messages easier.

On October 7th Cléry was ordered to go down to the Council Chamber where he found twenty of the commissioners assembled and presided over by Manuel, the procurator of the Commune. His presence made Cléry anxious. He had come, Manuel explained, to strip the King of his orders and decorations and he accompanied the valet upstairs, where they found the King seated and reading. Cléry thought the conversation that ensued as remarkable for the indecent familiarity of Manuel as for the calmness and moderation of the King. 'How are you? Have you all that is necessary?' asked Manuel. 'I am content,' replied Louis.

When Manuel pressed the point, Louis added, 'I thank you, I have need of nothing,' and he resumed his reading, a picture, thought Cléry, of great resignation and unalterable serenity. 'You did right,' Louis remarked when Cléry told him later that he had handed over the decorations.

The family were reunited on October 28th when the Queen, her sister-in-law and the two children were transferred to the third floor of the Great Tower, where night and day, along with the King, they were subjected to the surveillance of the commissioners, two of whom were always on duty which consisted 'in never losing sight of the prisoners for a single instant, in speaking to them only when answering their questions, and in never telling them anything of what was happening, in giving them only the title of *Monsieur* or *Madame*, but in saying nothing which might offend or disturb them, and in always keeping their hats on'.

It was a difficult situation for both the commissioners and the prisoners. Whatever were their true sentiments, the commissioners needed to show their revolutionary fervour, for they knew that any deviation from republican principles would be denounced to the Commune, and several of them were embarrassed at finding themselves in the presence of the august persons of which they had once stood in awe. The King and Queen tried to put them at their ease and they ignored the boorishness of the fanatics who tried to humiliate them. The records give no hint of the regal hauteur with which revolutionary tradition sought to discredit the ex-Royal Family. Louis, Marie Antoinette and Madame Elizabeth behaved with dignity in the most trying circumstances, as the stories of their captivity show, even when we allow for the natural bias of their authors.

The ex-Commissioners of the Temple who wrote after the Bourbon restoration in 1814 desired to show themselves in a favourable light, and their recollections are coloured by that event. The royal servants, on the other hand, needed no exoneration, for they had proved their loyalty in royalty's darkest hour: the martyrdom of their master and mistress turned them into worshippers who could find no fault. One only of the prisoners survived to tell her story; Madame Royale's diary reflects the views of a child who had seen her father and mother taken to the guillotine, and her brother, as far as she knew, murdered by neglect.

No one wrote objectively about the imprisonment of the ex-Royal Family.

Publicly, Hébert, following his tour of duty 'over the Temple menagerie', denounced the Royal Family in terms familiar to the readers of his satirical sketches; Louis became a 'rhinoceros foaming with rage and panting with thirst for blood', and the Queen, 'the tigress who swam in the torrents of blood she had spilled', had assumed 'the treacherous face of a cat', and she behaved weakly and had drawn in her claws 'the better to choose her time and still to give a few scratches'. Madame Elizabeth came in for his special fury and he describes her 'as a strapping woman who appears to have a good appetite' and who 'had the air of a miller's wife rather than a princess'. He had been re-volted, Hébert told the readers of his scurrilous publication *Père Duchesne*, by 'this wretched race leading as merry a life as in the past'. But privately he told a friend that the little Dauphin ' is as beautiful as the day and as interesting as can be'.

Charles Goret, who served several tours of duty at the Temple, and who had seen the Royal Family at Versailles at the zenith of their splendour, provides a very different picture. 'We are glad to see you,' the Queen told him, recognizing him as a previous visitor, and she tried to put him at his ease by inviting him to read his book by the window rather than in the dark corner in which he had secluded himself. When the King suggested it was time for the afternoon walk in the garden, Madame Elizabeth told Goret, 'Perhaps you do not know the correct rules of proce-dure. I will teach them to you,' and she invited him to lead the way. In the garden Goret sat talking with the King and Queen while Cléry played ball with the children. Back again in the salon, Madame Elizabeth leant over Goret's chair and began to sing a little song in which she invited her niece to join. The child proved obstinate, which nettled her aunt, who gave up her song and retired to her room. Goret was left alone with the Queen, who took from a little cabinet a handful of twists of paper which she unfolded before him, saying, 'This is my children's hair at such and such an age.' She put them away and returned, rubbing her hands with scent and waving them near his face so that he might smell the scent which was very sweet.

Goret was clearly captivated by the consideration he was shown which did not, however, make him lax in his duty. When the family retired for the night, 'after first showing their affection for each other with every mark of tenderness and respect', he followed Louis into his bedroom, and he attempted to join him in the little turret room while he said his prayers. 'I shall not run away; do not be afraid,' remarked the King, indicating that the room was too small to hold two people without inconvenience. After Cléry had helped the King to bed, Goret threw himself down on his sofa in the ante-room fully dressed, in the hope of obtaining a little rest, 'but this I found impossble, for no sooner did the King lie down than he fell into a sleep that not only appeared to be profound, but was accompanied by continuous and truly remarkable snoring'.

On his second visit to the Temple, early in November, Goret found the previously happy atmosphere had gone:

'The Queen sat in her room quietly, but Madame Elizabeth walked to and fro like the King, and often had a book in her hand. The children came and went in the same way; and the appearance and behaviour of the whole family was very different from what I had observed before they were moved to their present quarters. Everything seemed to foretell the still greater misfortunes that we witnessed later on. The father, wife, and sister were much seldomer together, and conversed much less frequently. It seemed as though they feared to aggravate their ills by speaking of them; and this is the saddest of all states to be beyond the reach of consolation. The children had lost the playfulness they had hitherto preserved. In a word, everything reflected the gloom that had been cast over this place by preventing the light from entering except through the top of the windows.'

But the Queen's politeness was not diminished. When the young prince failed to greet Goret, the Queen spoke to him severely, 'My boy, come back, and say "Good Morning" to the gentleman as you pass him,' which he did. This incident, Goret thought, showed that the teachings of the child's mother were very different from those that slander imputed to her later.

Other commissioners were not so considerate as Goret and the family regulated their behaviour accordingly. One, a stone-cutter named Mercerane, came dressed in filthy clothes, stretched himself on the Queen's damask couch and put his feet on the firedogs, making it impossible for the prisoners to warm themselves at the fire. Another, a tailor named Lechenard, swallowed a pint of spirits before ascending to take guard in the Queen's ante-room. In the morning 'the bed and floor bore witness to his intemperance,' and the Queen, when she opened her door, recoiled in horror, crying to her sister-in-law, 'Sister, don't leave your room.'

Another commissioner, who was named Moelle and who was fearful of being denounced by Tison if he showed leniency towards the prisoners, spent his first night of duty in a state of the liveliest agitation, 'due to mingled sensations of alarm, sympathy and respect' for the august family, and for the 'best of kings'. Moelle, who had drawn the surveillance of the King, was awakened at half-past six in the morning by Cléry, who took him into the King's bedroom:

'Beside the King's bed was the uncurtained one of M. le Dauphin, whom our entrance did not awake. The King drew his curtain, and his first glance rested on me. As this was the first time he had seen me it was natural that I should be of some interest to His Majesty. While this silent by-play was going on Cléry lit the fire. When the King rose he threw a dressing-gown round him; he sat on the edge of the bed while his shoes and stockings were put on; and he shaved himself. Cléry completed his toilet for him, and then dressed M. le Dauphin, who from the moment he awoke and throughout the process of dressing was full of the gaiety and playfulness that is so charming in children, which he possessed to a special degree. [Louis XVI's wardrobe in the Temple was composed of two coats that were exactly alike, which he wore alternately. They were of a pale reddish mixture, lined with fine unbleached linen; the buttons were of filigree work in gilt metal. Some waistcoats of white piqué, some breeches of black silky material, and a greatcoat of the colour known as *cheveux de la Rein*, constituted the rest of his wardrobe.] The King smiled sadly, and looked at his son with all the tenderness of a loving father. Then, when M. le Dauphin was dressed, he said his prayers in the presence of his august father, who immediately afterwards retired, according to his custom, to meditate in the little turret room that served him as an oratory.'

The scene made a vivid impression on Moelle who thought, 'how simple is the King in his private life, how susceptible he is to natural affection and how carefully he fulfills his personal duties'. It was impossible that so pure a life could be the outcome of any but the most virtuous character.

The heart of Jacques François Lepitre, who was a Professor of Literature, stood still and he could hardly breathe when, at the drawing of lots, he found it was his fate to guard the Queen and the princesses, the relatives of 'the best of Kings'.

Lepitre, who was accompanied by a colleague, spent an uneasy night in the Queen's ante-room with only a thin coverlet to protect him from the cold; he complained bitterly next day and obtained the addition of sheets. He was awakened by Tison, whom he describes as 'this crafty, cruel man', a person of insinuating ways, and against whom he had been warned. Nonetheless, says Lepitre, 'I fell a victim to him'. Continuing with his narrative Lepitre who, as we shall learn, showed his loyalty to the royal prisoners when it was highly dangerous to do so, describes the Queen's levée:

'At eight o'clock the Queen opened her door and went into Madame Elizabeth's room. Her keen glance dwelt upon us for a moment, and it was easy to see she was trying to discover the nature of our feelings with regard to her. We were decently dressed; indeed, our appearance was a contrast to that of the commissioners. The respect that misfortune claims from us all was plainly written upon our faces. Madame stood at the door of her room and scrutinized us for some time, and then both she and Madame Elizabeth came out to us and asked the names of our *section*, observing that this was the first time we had visited the Temple. During breakfast, at which another commissioner appeared (for no meal was served except in the presence of a member of the Council), we remained in the outer room, for we dared not place any confidence in our colleague.'

For breakfast Louis and his son joined the women who wore ordinary gowns of white dimity which they changed later in the day for garments of dark brown cloth with a pattern of little flowers. After breakfast the King returned to his apartment, where he gave his son lessons and read. On the day when Lepitre was first on duty his colleague tried to play a few notes on the clavichord, or harpsichord as he calls it, but it was in such a bad condition that he was forced to give it up. Lepitre had it tuned and, when friendly commissioners were on duty, the instrument was used for impromptu little concerts. Lepitre and Moelle both found a bond with the King in their knowledge of Latin, and were able to discuss the merits of Tacitus and Vergil. Lepitre on his second visit was accompanied by a colleague whom the Queen, to his amusement, nick-named 'the Pagoda', because he never gave answer but a movement of his head. Dinner, says Moelle, was served in the King's room: 'The royal prisoners were most abstemious, the Princesses and M. le Dauphin drinking nothing but water, of which the King mixed a great deal with his wine. At dessert he indulged in a single glass of sweet wine. His skill in carving meat was remarkable; and he showed this skill in various kinds of manual work, with which he had been in the habit of amusing himself in happier times. The Royal Family spoke little, for reserve was forced upon them by the presence of the commissioners.'

We shall hear more again of Lepitre, in connection with another commissioner named Toulan. Both men risked their lives in the Queen's cause. Yet, when he came first to the tower, Cléry thought Toulan to be one of the worst enemies of the Royal Family.

For three months, states Cléry, the family had only been visited by members of the Commune. On November 1st a deputation came from the National Convention. They asked the King how he was treated and whether he was given all necessary things. Louis replied, 'I complain of nothing.' Shortly after this visit, he suffered from toothache and his request for his dentist was refused. The infection turned septic and the King's Chief Physician, M. le Monnier, had to be sent for. When he came to the Tower he was searched and ordered only to speak in a loud voice, so that the Commissioners could watch his words. Louis's illness lasted ten days; the Queen attended him by day and Cléry by night. Then the young Prince fell ill with fever: the Queen was allowed to visit him by day but, despite her urgent request, permission to stay with him at night, or to carry him to her bedroom, was refused. Both the Queen and Cléry contracted the fever.

The Princesses nursed Cléry and the Dauphin, who had recovered, hardly left him for the six days he was in bed. One night, after he was up again, about eleven o'clock when he was preparing the King's bed, Cléry heard the little Prince calling him in a low voice. Fearing he was ill, Cléry went to him. 'My aunt gave me this little box for you,' he said, and I would not go to sleep without giving it to you; it was high time you came, for my eyes have shut up several times.' Opening the box Cléry found that it contained tablets for his throat. His eyes filled with tears; the boy saw them and kissed him, and two minutes later he was sound asleep.

The Dauphin, by his gaiety, vivacity and charm, and by his little rogueries, made his parents forget for a moment their cruel situation. Although he was only seven years old, Louis Charles knew he was in prison and watched by enemies, and his behaviour and his talk, says Cléry, had acquired that reserve which is inspired by danger. He never mentioned subjects that could remind his father and mother of painful memories. When he saw some Commissioner on guard who had shown himself to be kinder than his colleagues, he would run to his mother and say with an expression of great satisfaction, 'Mamma, it is Monsieur such-a-one today.'

One day, shortly after his arrival in the Great Tower, Louis Charles stood watching the mason who was cutting holes in the wall of the ante-chamber to carry the enormous bolts designed to hold the door. While the man ate his breakfast, the boy amused himself with the tools and his father showed him how to use them. Impressed by the King's skill, the mason said, 'When you get out of here you can say you worked at your own prison.' 'Ah,' answered the King, 'when and how I get out.' Louis Charles burst into tears and the agitated father strode up and down with hasty strides.

Another story about the Dauphin was passed to a newspaper by one of the commissioners who, like most of his colleagues, fell under the spell of the seven-year-old boy with his beautiful flaxen hair, laughing eyes and clear voice, who ran about the apartments, disarming even the most severe of critics and touching their hearts with his innocence. At dinner one afternoon, he eyed an apple longingly, which led his aunt to remark, 'You appear to desire that apple, yet you do not ask for it.' 'Aunt,' he replied, adopting a serious tone, 'my character is frank and firm. Had I desired that apple I should have asked for it at once.' Like his father Louis Charles was very fond of *brioche*. One day when the remains of a cake was being removed from the table, he exclaimed, 'If you like, Mamma, I will show you a cupboard where you can lock up the remains of the *brioche*.' 'And where is the cupboard?' asked the Queen. 'Here,' replied her son, pointing to his mouth.

So the time went by. The King read, borrowing 157 books from M. Berthèlemy's library. The Queen sewed. The children learned their lessons and romped in play. Beneath the gallant exterior lay gnawing anxiety, the fear what fate might bring. Turgy and Cléry tried to keep the King informed of outside events; on November 6th the French army defeated the Austrians at Jemappes and a week later General Dumouriez entered Brussels as a conqueror. The Revolution was secure, for the time being at least.

Below stairs in the Council Chamber, the six commissioners who were not on duty on the second and third floors, slept and ate, and according to Parisian gossip, drank to excess. Whether or not this rumour was true, it gave rise to the story of 'the Orgy of the Temple', that went the round that fall. After supper, the lights were extinguished, the punch was lit and the brandy flowed. The geometrician James, it was said, became so overjoyed that he played leap-frog with his colleague Nicolas Jerome. At the next session of the Commune, members grumbled about the commissioners' over-indulgence which 'sullied the Revolution'.

Within the Temple security was tightened. No one was allowed to enter or leave the Great Tower unless he carried a card on which was printed the word '*Sûrété*', and the commissioners were required to carry a card bearing the words '*Officier Municipal*', and even then they were not allowed to enter the Tower unless the card bore the special visée '*Pour le tour*'.

The members of the Temple Council, the commissioners, states Moelle, were honest but weak men, controlled by fear and events'. Other than the occasional fanatic, such as the unfrocked priest Jacques Roux, who during his tour of duty in the Queen's ante-room sang all night at the top of his voice, they interpreted their duty without meanness. Only at the Hôtel de Ville did they need to make their revolutionary fervour apparent; there they were often malicious, uttering depraved epithets against the imprisoned family. One commissioner, a hosier, accused the Queen of teaching her children 'the most bloody tragedies', and he remarked that the royal women were more voluptuous than any *fille* in the Rue Saint-Jean–St. Denis district, a notorious area for prostitutes. The members of the Commune, to their credit, hooted with laughter at the hosier's extravagance and the *Journal of the Debates* records that 'the General Council disapproved of those words which offended humanity and decency'. Another member criticized the King's appetite for books and he remarked 'he is assured of hardly a fortnight's existence and the books he demands would suffice to last the longest life'. He suggested that 'Capet' should be given the *Life of Cromwell*, the English regicide, to read.

The Commune was anxious to bring Louis to trial to answer for the crime of treason to the sovereign people but, so far, it had not been able to unearth any evidence upon which to base the charge. This was provided when, on November 20th, the King's secret safe, which had been concealed in the wall of a passage at the Tuileries, was discovered.

Early in December, records Cléry, the number of the commissioners at the Temple was increased, and the new men were coarser than their predecessors. Two commissioners at a time kept surveillance over the King and Queen, day and night, and the prisoners were forced to give up their knives, razors, scissors and other sharp instruments. The commissioners made a thorough search, taking away even a ruler for rolling hair, and little instruments for cleaning teeth. The Queen was reduced to breaking her sewing thread with her teeth, and Louis offered the fire-tongs, asking 'Are not these sharp instruments?' Each day brought harsher decrees. The Queen and Madame Elizabeth were struck with the presentiment of some fresh catastrophe. Cléry learnt the truth from his wife; on her visit on December 7th Madame Cléry, between her remarks which were made in the loud voice demanded by the watchful commissioners, whispered,'Next Tuesday, the King's trial will begin.' That was in four days' time.

9

THE FIRST VICTIM

The discovery of the iron safe in the wall of the Tuileries and the 627 documents it contained made certain the trial of the King, although these papers, bills, receipts, petitions, and the letters Louis had *received*, were largely innocuous. This safe had been constructed for the King by François Gamain, a locksmith, who, believing that he had been poisoned by the royalists, disclosed the secret to the Minister of the Interior, Roland. He hurried to the palace, where he opened the safe and removed the documents without witnesses, thus creating the suspicion that he may have tampered with its contents by extracting papers that might have incriminated his own faction. Roland carried the documents to the National Convention, which appointed a Commission of Twelve to examine them.

The discovery of the papers created excitement out of all proportion to their value, and it was employed by the Jacobin extremists to whip up enthusiasm for the trial and execution they were determined to achieve. The question of putting Louis on trial on the charge of treason to the sovereign people had been mooted from the time of his dethronement when he became an ordinary citizen, amenable like others, it was claimed, to the penal code. But the alleged acts had been committed while he was the Constitutional King, when he was inviolate. Thus, whether or not Louis had committed treason by conspiring with foreign rulers to crush the Revolution, and however great was suspicion that he kept up a treasonable correspondence, his trial would be an illegality. And by whom could he be tried? Only by the National Convention, as the emblem of the people's sovereignty, claimed the extremists. The majority of the deputies feared the responsibility of condemning the King and they hesitated to commit themselves; they argued that the Convention was a legislative body and not a Court of Law.

Two men stampeded the Convention. Striding to the Tribune, Antoine Saint-Just, aged twenty-five, in his maiden speech cut through the obstruction with ruthless logic: 'We are not here to judge him, but to resist him: Louis has fought the people and has been defeated. He is a barbarian, a foreign prisoner of war.' Robespierre carried the argument a stage further: 'If Louis is innocent all the patriots of France are guilty.'

Louis was the defeated enemy; to prove their innocence, the people of France needed to try and execute him. The trial of the ex-King was a political act. It had no legality. It was expedient that Louis should die, for it was necessary to destroy for ever the halo of sanctity that surrounded monarchy and to demonstrate, to the foreign rulers who threatened France, that the people were sovereign. As long as he remained alive Louis would be a source of counter-revolutionary infection. The Convention voted itself as a Special Tribunal.

Louis had been warned of what was afoot by Cléry and the rumour brought by Madame Cléry was confirmed by Turgy, who smuggled into the tower a newspaper which stated that 'Louis Capet is to be brought before the bar of the National Convention'. 'I shall not seem to be informed in order not to compromise you,' Louis told Cléry. The prisoners were forewarned when, at five o'clock in the morning on December 11th, they were awakened by the sounds of trumpets and drums and by the rumble of cannon and the tramp of feet in the Temple courtyard. Feigning ignorance they followed their usual routine. After breakfast the King with his son withdrew to the second floor in order to proceed with the day's lessons: the little boy wanted to play a card game and Louis hadn't the heart to say 'No'. The Dauphin lost all the games and Cléry noticed when he cried 'Every time I get to *sixteen*, I lose the game', that the King winced at the mention of the number.

The boy had settled to his reading by eleven o'clock when two commissioners entered the room. They had orders to remove his son, they told Louis, and they refused to give any explanation for the separation. The King kissed his son tenderly. Cléry followed the boy upstairs and on his return he was able to tell the King that he had left the child in his mother's arms, which seemed to calm him although he continued to pace up and down rubbing his hands on his thighs. Chambon, the Mayor of Paris (who had succeeded Pétion who had been elected President of the Convention), would be coming up to see him, one of the commissioners informed Louis.

Chambon, who was accompanied by Pierre Gaspard Chaumette, the Procurator of the Commune, Santerre and by several officials, entered the apartment at 1 p.m. 'I am charged,' he told the King, 'to inform you that the Convention awaits you,' and he nodded to Coulombeau, the Secretary of the Commune, who began to read the decree; 'Louis Capet is to be arraigned. . . .' Impatiently, Louis interrupted, 'My name is not Louis Capet; my ancestors once bore that name but I have never used it.' He became quite angry; he complained that his son had been taken from him, 'treatment which is but the sequel to all I have borne here for the past four months.' He would go to the Convention, he said, not to obey its order but because 'my enemies have the power to force me'.

Cléry gave him his overcoat and hat and Louis was taken to the courtyard which was filled with guards. He entered the awaiting coach and was driven through the strangely silent streets which were lined with soldiers. On the third floor of the Great Tower Marie Antoinette held her son in her arms. For the first time during her captivity she broke down and wept. When she was told that the King would be separated from his family, she exclaimed in bitter grief, 'From my son, my son who is only seven years old.'

Advised that the ex-King had arrived, the acting President of the Convention, Pétion's deputy, warned the 749 deputies, 'All Europe is watching you.' 'Louis Capet awaits your orders,' cried the guard at the door. Amidst death-like silence Louis walked to the bar. Wearing his overcoat, carrying his hat in his hand and unshaven for several days, he looked, thought one eye-witness, like an ordinary citizen coming to petition a court of law; yet there was an indefinable stamp of authority about the stoutish man of middle-class looks.

The President's voice broke the stillness: 'Louis, the French nation accuses you. Listen while the *"Act of Crimes"* is read. You may sit down.' Seating himself on a chair, Louis looked round the hall. For a moment his eyes met those of his cousin, Philip Égalite, one of the Parisian deputies. The *ci-devant* Duc of Orléans raised his lorgnette and stared at the prisoner. Louis looked away. Whether or not he recognized them in the sea of faces, his bitter enemies Marat and Robespierre were there.

Louis listened carefully while the list of his alleged crimes, which numbered thirty-three, were read. He was accused, amongst other things, of permitting the national cockade to be trampled before his eyes, of corrupting the people by bribes, of having done nothing to suppress the counter-revolution in the provinces, of giving money to the *émigrés*, of disorganizing the army and of assembling troops in the Tuileries on August 10th. Louis answered that he had done no more than fulfil his constitutional duties. He was good-humoured and self-possessed. He spoke clearly and confidently. 'He answers well,' thought the United States Ambassador Gouverneur Morris, who sat in the gallery. John Moore, who was there, wrote in his journal:

'The King's appearance in the Convention, the dignified resignation of his manner, the admirable promptitude and candour of his answers, made such an evident impression on some of the audience in the galleries, that a determined enemy of royalty, who had his eye upon them, declared that he was afraid of hearing the cry of *Vive le Roi!* issue from the tribunes; and added that if the King had remained ten minutes longer in their sight, he was convinced it would have happened.'

The deputies shifted uneasily in their seats. A wave of sympathy ran through their ranks: few of his audience could accept that this patient and rather sad-looking man, with his good-natured expression, was the arrogant tyrant and barefaced plotter they had been led to believe. And his crisp, always courteous answers, suggested that the accusations were weak indeed. The case against the ex-King was breaking down.

The Secretary of the Convention gathered up the papers that had been taken from the iron safe and thrust them under Louis's nose. Did he identify them? Louis said he did not recognize them and he denied that he had caused the safe to be constructed. He did not recognize the key that opened the safe. Yet it was proved to have been obtained from one of the King's ex-valets, Thierry. This lack of good faith on Louis's part destroyed the favourable impression he had created. His prevarication made the papers sound more incriminating than they really were. 'Do you identify these documents?' insisted the Secretary. 'I demand Counsel,' answered the King.

The King was sent into the waiting room while the Convention deliberated. After acrimonious debate, the Jacobins were forced to give way and on Pétion's motion that Counsel could not be refused 'without attacking all the principles of humanity', it was agreed that the King would be allowed to choose his defenders. Louis, who had been kept standing in the waiting room, was not informed and he was taken back to the Temple. 'Do you think they will allow me Counsel?' he asked the commissioner on duty, Arbeltier. The Constitution allowed it, he remarked, but the man did not know.

Louis was not permitted to rejoin his family. 'That is pretty harsh,' he exclaimed and he asked to be allowed to see his son. 'Your son is considered a member of your family,' was the reply. Louis ate his supper and retired to bed. On the floor above the Queen put her son in her own bed and sat by his side all night in silent agony of sorrow; her daughter and sister-in-law were so worried that they dared not leave her and they too spent a sleepless night. Next day Cléry fixed a string between the privies in the turrets on both floors by which the prisoners were able to exchange little notes, pricked out on paper by a pin, for their pens had been taken away. Cléry was ordered to serve the King only and before he went downstairs for the last time Madame Elizabeth whispered to him, 'The Queen and I expect the worst; we have no illusions of the fate they are preparing for the King.'

The decree authorizing Counsel was brought to Louis on the day following his examination and he asked for the services of two lawyers, Target and Tronchet. Target refused the dangerous duty, pleading illness, and the venerable Lamoignon de Malesherbes, an ex-Minister and an old friend of the King's, volunteered to undertake the duty which, the correspondence shows, many Frenchmen were anxious to undertake. Tronchet lived to become a Supreme Court Judge under Napoleon and de Malesherbes was guillotined in 1794.

Tronchet and de Malesherbes came to the Temple. Cléry watched Louis greet his old friend, whom he embraced tenderly. The task of reading and sorting the 107 documents selected by the Convention from those that had been taken from the iron safe so appalled the lawyers that they informed the Convention, 'It is physically impossible for two men, one of whom is a sexagenarian and the other more than a septuagenarian, to prepare a defence in such a short time'; the Convention agreed to their request for help and the young lawyer, de Sèze, was appointed to join the defence team. Nonetheless, it took several days to examine the documents, seventy-five of which Louis rejected; he initialled thirty-seven as genuine. To de Malesherbes Louis said, 'I am sure they will make me perish, for they have the power and the will; but in truth I shall win, for the memory I shall leave will be stainless.'

The work of reading and initialling the documents was finished by December 19th, an important date for Louis because it was both his daughter's fourteenth birthday and a Holy Day. His petition to see his child was refused. 'Well, I can still fast,' he told the astonished commissioner. His request for a razor was also refused and he remained unshaven. Cléry took the liberty to remark that if the King appeared before the Convention with several days' growth of beard 'the people would see with what barbarity the Council of the Commune had acted'. Louis shook his head: 'I ought not to try to influence people in that way in my fate,' he replied. Next day, the Commune relented and Louis was allowed to shave himself in the presence of two commissioners. De Malesherbes came in the evening to inform the King that his trial had been fixed for December 26th. Louis told him that if his life was spared, he did not wish to rule again. Death, he said, did not frighten him; he worried about his wife, for there would be no one to guide her. She was an unfortunate Princess; 'Our marriage promised her a throne; now what a prospect!'

Louis spent the day before the trial making his will or his 'testament', as he described it. It is a remarkable document, unpretentious and breathing the sincerity of a man who had no doubt of his innocence, and no hatred of his enemies. He did not love them, he confessed, and he did not pretend to judge them. He commended his family to the care of God and he begged his wife to forgive him 'for all the ills she has suffered for me and the griefs I have caused her in the course of our union'. She had nothing with which to blame herself. His son, 'if he has the misfortune to become King', he begged to reflect 'that he owes himself solely to the welfare of his co-citizens', and he urged him 'to forget all hatred and resentment, especially that which relates to the misfortune and griefs I have borne'. He must reign according to the laws but, he stressed, 'a king cannot make the laws respected unless he has the necessary authority'. Expressing his gratitude to his friends, Louis expressly mentioned Hue and Cléry, 'whose true attachment to me led them to shut themselves up in this sad place' and 'who came so near to being also the unfortunate victims of it'. He ended by declaring 'before God, and about to appear before Him, that I do not reproach myself with any of the crimes laid to my charge'.

Louis XVI was a willing martyr. He had no doubt of his fate and his only concern was for those he left behind and for his own reputation. He had done his best; it was his misfortune to have ruled when he did. He had the responsibility to his people to try to guide the Revolution; events had taken him unawares and he had not been able to entirely forget the past: behind Louis XVI lay a thousand years of absolute monarchy and ahead lay the sovereignty of the people. The wind of change blew too suddenly and too fast for him to bend to the gale. Kind and good natured, he resisted when he should have bowed and he bowed when he should have stood firm. Louis died because he had been weak, and the men who rode the whirlwind were unable to direct the storm. The Revolution they had expected to last for ever was short-lived.

On the morning of December 26th the sound of drums announced the arrival of the escort and Mayor Chambon came to the tower at 9 a.m. Louis was dressed and ready to go. The ten-minute journey was made by coach through streets lined with soldiers behind whom stood the people of Paris, silent and hostile. Louis was unperturbed and he chatted with his companions, the officials of the Commune, discoursing on the merits of the Roman authors and standing up for Seneca whom the Secretary of the Commune thought had been hypocritical in defending the tyrannical Nero before the Senate. About his own situation Louis said nothing. In the waiting room of the Convention de Sèze showed his client the lengthy speech he had prepared. Louis rejected it; 'Cut out the pathos, I don't want to arouse pity.'

In his address to the Convention de Sèze confined himself to the illegality of the trial and he claimed that the accusations

against the ex-King were invalid because his acts had been constitutional and there was no proof of treason. It was a complete
defence. Suspicion that Louis had conspired with the *émigrés*
and foreign powers to crush the Revolution was not proof. But
de Sèze failed to rouse the deputies; the moderates were prepared
to consider the accusations earnestly but they needed passion to
sway them from the vehemence of the articulate minority. 'The
King,' said de Sèze 'had shown himself always the consistent
friend of the people. They wanted liberty and he gave them
liberty.' The counter-accusations that might have won votes
could not be made by a counsel who hoped to keep his head.
Louis himself said nothing until he was accused of shedding
French blood. Raising his voice with all the consciousness of
innocence, he indignantly declared, 'No, Sir, I have never shed
the blood of Frenchmen'. The Englishman, Henry Redhead
Yorke, who sat in the gallery, saw a tear trickle down the King's
cheek. He instantly wiped it away with his hand. 'You may withdraw', Louis was told. On the return journey to the Temple, he
chatted as merrily as before.

The 721 deputies (twenty-eight were absent) of the Convention debated the verdict and the sentence from December 26th
to January 14th. Louis and Cléry remained on the second floor
of the tower; the Queen above heard his restless pacing to and
fro, which told her that her husband was still there. Cléry's wife
informed him that public opinion was swinging in favour of the
King; at the Théâtre Français he had been loudly applauded and
at the Vaudeville the audience insisted on the repetition of the
speech in which an actor was required to say to two old men,
'How can you be accusers and judges both?' Many of the deputies, Cléry heard, wished to pronounce for the penalty of imprisonment or banishment rather than death. 'May they have
that moderation for my family; it is only for them I fear,' Louis
exclaimed.

The voting was complicated. The deputies were asked to
decide three questions: 'Is Louis Capet guilty?' 'Should the sentence be submitted to the people for ratification?' and, if the
answer to that was 'No', 'What should be the sentence—death,
detention or deportation?' First, the deputies debated. Many
admitted that Louis had made mistakes, that he had been weak,
that events had caught up with him. Some thought that he was

more a victim than a conniver. Others clamoured for the death of 'the assassin'. The petition for delay presented by the English liberals, Lansdowne, Fox and Sheridan, was read and ignored. Each deputy claimed the right to justify his decision. The debate was interminable. The moderates who were in the majority were not strong enough to stand up to the Jacobins and they were unsure whether Louis was entirely guilty or entirely innocent; he seemed to have been guilty of something. Many deputies read aloud the letters they had received from their constituents; the Parisians demanded 'Death for the Tyrant'; the provincials were less certain. The alternative many sought was offered by the radical Thomas Paine, who was an honorary member of the Convention. He advised banishment to the country France had helped to become free. 'Let the United States of America become the asylum of Louis Capet', he wrote, for his French was not good enough for him to speak, for there he could contemplate 'that the true system of government is not that of kings but of representation'.

The voting took three days. Each deputy was required to walk to the Tribune and state his answers and give his reasons. On the question 'Is Louis Capet guilty of conspiring against public liberty and an attack on the general security of the State?', the vote was unanimous. Of the 721 deputies present, thirty-seven abstained from giving a definite answer, and 638 voted 'Guilty'. The referendum, the appeal to the people on sentence, was rejected by 425 votes to 286. It remained to decide the penalty. The voting began on January 16th at eight o'clock in the evening and it lasted for thirty-four hours. Once again each deputy mounted the Tribune and expounded his reasons. The galleries were packed; the condemnation of a king was a greater drama than any theatre could provide. Women wearing the briefest of *negligés* squeezed between workers and peasants. Hawkers sold oranges and bottles of wine. Many spectators had brought cards on which they noted the votes. The Jacobin supporters formed a noisy claque, which applauded and hissed the 'good' and 'bad' patriots.

Deputy followed deputy; many were tedious, few were brief. Slowly the roll call mounted. The votes for *'La Mort'* piled high, but the decision could still be close and every neck was craned when it became the turn of Philip Égalite to ascend the Tribune.

He had promised his friends that he would abstain from voting 'so as not to dishonour the family'. The spectators were struck by his startling resemblance to the King, and complete silence fell as he spoke. 'I vote for death', he announced. A cry of indignation swept the hall. 'Oh, the monster,' shouted a woman in the gallery. 'Fortunately, Louis is leaving us the one relative who can most disgust us with royalty', a deputy remarked to his neighbour.

Finally the votes were counted:

For detention or banishment	288
Suspended sentence of death	46
Death, but reprieve	26
Unconditional and immediate death	361

'The penalty is death', announced the President. De Malesherbes was instructed to inform the ex-King of the verdict and sentence.

The apparent closeness of the vote, 361 to 360, is misleading and it does not follow, as has been remarked, that the Duke of Orléans cast the deciding vote, for the twenty-six votes for 'death' were not necessarily conditional upon 'reprieve'.

The aged magistrate who had accepted the King's defence as an honour, came to the Great Tower at nine o'clock in the morning. 'All is lost', he told Cléry who met him at the door. Louis rose to meet his old friend. De Malesherbes threw himself at the King's feet, choking with sobs and it was some time before he could speak. When he began to say 'You are condemned . . .', Louis interrupted, 'I am not afraid of death'. De Malesherbes gave him the list of votes. 'I am much grieved that M. d'Orléans, my relative, should have voted for my death', exclaimed Louis, scanning the list. 'There is a plot to rescue you,' de Malesherbes assured the King. 'Do you know these men?' inquired Louis. 'No, Your Majesty, but I can find them,' answered de Malesherbes. 'Then,' commanded Louis, 'seek them out and tell them that I thank them for their zeal, but such an attempt would only endanger their lives and will not save mine. I will not have French blood spilled for my sake. I prefer to die, and I beg you to order these men, in my name, to make no movement to save me,' and, pausing for a moment, he added, 'In France the King does not die.' That night, after de Malesherbes had gone,

Louis sent Cléry to search M. Berthèlemy's library for a history of England which described the execution of Chares I. Marie Antoinette was not informed of the sentence. She did not believe, she told the commissioner who was on duty, that the people of France would kill their King, and the foreign powers would not permit it.

On Saturday, January 19th, the Convention rejected an appeal for reprieve by 380 votes to 310, and it decreed that the King's execution should take place on January 21st. The death warrant was sent to Charles Henry Sanson, the public executioner, who found it on his desk when he returned home on Sunday, together with several letters threatening him with death if he carried out the execution. His wife, an ardent royalist, was prostrate in her chair and a young man was in the room. He proposed, he told Sanson, to dress himself like the King and hide under the scaffold; Sanson's assistants could smuggle the King out of sight and he would take Louis's place. Recognizing him as a madman, Sanson showed him the door, and he ordered his assistants to meet him at six o'clock in the morning at the Place de la Révolution, now the Place de la Concorde, where the guillotine was installed.

Louis spent the Sunday morning alone with Cléry and the commissioners on duty. At 2 p.m. the door from the stair was suddenly thrown open to admit the twelve members of the Executive Council, the government of France. Their leader, Garat, his hat on his head, stepped forward and he ordered the Secretary to read the decree of the Convention. Louis listened impassively while the four articles were read. He showed indignation only when the word 'conspiracy' was mentioned, and he asked for three days' delay in order to prepare himself, for the attendance of a confessor, naming the Abbé Edgeworth de Firmont, an Irish priest, and for permission to see his family in private. Stay of execution was refused and his other requests were granted. Hébert, who was present, says that Louis listened to the sentence of death with rare coolness and he showed such dignity, nobleness and greatness that tears of rage rose to his eyes and he was forced to leave the room.

After the Ministers had gone, Louis sat down to dinner. 'I have no knife,' he remarked to the commissioner who stood at his elbow. 'They are no longer allowed', the man told him. 'Do they think me so cowardly as to take my own life?' Louis exclaimed and he cut up the beef with his spoon. Overcome with grief and indignation Cléry retired to his own room, bitterly angry that the Commune had chosen vile and ferocious men to guard the King in his last moments. Mercerant, the arrogant stone-mason, to Cléry, 'Everyone refuses to come, but I wouldn't give up this day for a great deal of money,' and the other commissioner, a young man, said he had offered to undertake duty at the Temple 'that I might see the grimaces he (the King) will make tomorrow.' Just after he had said this, Louis remarked on his youthfulness, and thanked him for volunteering for the distasteful duty. The young man did not know what to say.

The Abbé Edgeworth was brought to the tower. Louis took him into his little turret room and closed the door. At 8 p.m. he reappeared and asked the commissioners to bring his family, reminding them of the order that he could talk with them without witnesses. 'You will be in private, the door will be shut, but we shall have our eyes upon you through the glass partition,' Mercerant replied. While they waited, Cléry rearranged the room on the King's instructions, drawing the table to one side to give more space. 'Bring a glass and water that is not iced,' requested the King. His wife might need it and iced water made her ill. He sent Cléry to tell the Abbé to stay in the turret, for the sight of him might make his family unhappy.

Cléry, who remained in the ante-room with the commissioners, describes the last meeting between Louis and his family:

'At half past eight the door opening; the Queen appeared first, holding her son by the hand; then Madame Royale and Madame Elizabeth; they ran to the arms of the king. A gloomy silence reigned for several minutes, interrupted only by sobs. The Queen made a movement to draw the King into his room. "No," he said, "let us go into the dining-room, I can see you only there." They went there, and I closed the door, which was of glass, behind them. The King sat down, the Queen on his left, Madame Elizabeth on his right, Madame Royale nearly opposite to him, and the little Prince between his knees. All were bending towards him and held him half embraced. This scene of sorrow lasted seven quarters of an hour, during which it was impossible to hear anything, we could see only that after each sentence of the King the sobs of the Princesses redoubled, lasting some minutes; then the King would resume what he was saying. It was easy to judge from their motion that the King himself was the first to tell them of his condemnation.

'At a quarter past ten the King rose first; they all followed him; I opened the door; the Queen held the King by the right arm; Their Majesties each gave a hand to the Dauphin; Madame Royale on the left clasped the King's body; Madame Elizabeth, on the same side but a little behind the rest, had caught the left arm of her brother. They made a few steps towards the entrance, uttering the most sorrowful moans. "I assure you," said the King, "that I will see you to-morrow at eight o'clock." "You promise us?" they all cried. "Yes, I promise it." "Why not at seven o'clock?" said the Queen. "Well, then, yes, at seven o'clock," replied the King. "Adieu . . ." He uttered that "adieu" in so expressive a manner that the sobs redoubled. Madame Royale fell fainting at the King's feet, which she clasped; I raised her and helped Madame Elizabeth to hold her. The King, wishing to put an end to this heart-rending scene, gave them all a most tender embrace, and then had the strength to tear himself from their arms. "Adieu . . . adieu" he said, and re-entered his chamber.'

Cléry wished to support Madame Royale on the stairs but the commissioners turned him back, and closed the doors. Louis shut himself up again with his confessor until supper time, when he reappeared, eating little, but with relish. Abbé Edgeworth asked the commissioners to obtain the sacramental robes and furnishings required for him to say Mass in the morning, and these were secured. Cléry undressed the King; as he was about to roll his hair, Louis remarked 'It is not worth-while.' 'Wake me at five o'clock,' he asked as Cléry closed the curtains of the bed. Louis fell into a deep sleep at once and Cléry spent the night in a chair. Hearing the city clocks strike five he rose and lit the fire. The noise awakened Louis. 'Is it five o'clock?' he asked. He had slept well and he asked, 'Where did you sleep?' 'In the chair,' replied Cléry. 'I am sorry,' Louis said, and he pressed his valet's hand.

Cléry dressed the King and did his hair. Louis took his personal possessions from his pockets and laid them on the mantelpiece, his eye-glasses, his snuff-box and his wallet. All this was done in silence as the commissioners were watching. His toilet completed, the King told Cléry to call the Abbé. All the necessary articles had been assembled, and Cléry had arranged the room for Mass; the bureau served as the altar. When the Abbé Edgeworth had robed himself, the commissioners withdrew. The service began at six o'clock. The kneeling King listened with deep absorption while Cléry said the responses, and he took Communion. After Mass Louis returned to the turret and the Abbé went to Cléry's room to remove his robes. Cléry seized the opportunity to be alone with his master and entered the King's cabinet. Louis thanked him for his service and he asked him to care for his son. He pressed the valet to his bosom and gave him his blessing. Ever thoughtful for others, Louis told Cléry to return to the bedroom in order 'to give no cause for complaint against you'.

Marie Antoinette did not sleep all night, and she was denied her last meeting with her husband. The Abbé Edgeworth advised against it, and Louis accepted his judgement. 'Tell the Queen,' Louis instructed Cléry, 'that I beg her pardon for not having her come up. I wanted to spare her the pain of so cruel a separation.' A quarter of an hour later, Louis reappeared from his cabinet with a request for scissors. 'We must know what you wish to do with them before we can submit your request to the Commune,' the commissioners told him. 'I wish Cléry to cut my hair,' Louis replied. The Commune refused permission, despite Louis's assurance that he would not himself touch the scissors.

Paris had been under arms since dawn. All shops were ordered to remain closed and the citizens were forbidden the streets. There were whispers of a plot to abduct the King and on Sunday night one of the deputies who had voted for sentence of death, Le Peletier, had been assassinated by a royalist. The Jacobins took no chances. 100,000 soldiers and National Guardsmen lined the streets. Sanson reached the Place de la Révolution at 8.30 a.m. The morning was dank and bitterly cold.

Two members of the Convention came to the tower to escort the King. All the others had rejected the job with distaste; Jacques Roux and Pierre Bernard, two unfrocked priests, gloated at the opportunity to see their enemy humiliated. General Santerre accompanied them. Louis came out of his cabinet followed by the Abbé Edgeworth. Selecting the man nearest to him, Louis offered him his will and asked him to give the papers to his wife. He had chosen Roux, who spurned the papers and said, 'It is not my job. I am here to conduct you to the scaffold, not to run your errands.' 'Quite right,' answered the King, giving the papers to another man. Cléry offered Louis his overcoat. 'I have no need of it, but I will take my hat,' he said, and turning to Santerre, he exclaimed 'I am ready. Let us go.'

Louis was relieved to see the Mayor's coach in the courtyard. 'I expected an open tumbrel,' he told Santerre. He mounted the coach and Edgeworth sat by his side, facing the two armed *gendarmes*. The coach rolled into the Place du Temple where it was surrounded by 1200 soldiers who marched ahead and behind. Every foot of the route was guarded. Doors were closed and windows were shuttered. The unearthly silence was broken by the clatter of the horses' hooves and by the rumble of wheels. The King, says Edgeworth, maintained a profound silence; he read the breviary the Abbé had given him. An attempt was made, says Sanson, to save the King; as the coach and its escort were passing the Porte St Denis, four men with raised swords burst through the cordon crying, 'Come on, Gentlemen, save our King'. Two were cut down, and their leader, Baron de Batz, and his secretary escaped.

The coach reached the Place de la Révolution, the former Place Louis XV, at 10.15 a.m. and it halted in the open space that had been left around the raised scaffold. The square, says Edgeworth, was filled with an armed multitude as far as the eye could reach. There were also some privileged spectators. On the outskirts of the troops stood a carriage with its blinds drawn and within sat Philip Égalite, drawn by the torture of remorse to witness the finale of the tragedy in which he had played such an ignoble part. Within nine months he would die on the same scaffold as his cousin.

'We are arrived, if I mistake not,' Louis whispered to his companion, and he resumed reading his last prayer. Then he gave back the breviary and stepped from the coach. Dr Philip Pinel who was present noticed that he gazed aloft at the guillotine without flinching, as he mounted the platform which was raised a foot above his head. Edgeworth followed. Louis removed his hat and coat, spurning the aid of Sanson's assistants. The drums beat incessantly The assistants seized the King and attempted to pinion his arms. He shook them off. 'What, are you trying to bind me? I shall not consent to that. You shall never bind me.' Then, seeing the futility of resistance, he held out his hands. The executioners bound his hands behind his back and cut off his hair; one pocketed the locks. Louis tried to mount the steps that led to the guillotine, not an easy task for a clumsy man whose hands were tied. Edgeworth helped him. The drum beats rose to a crescendo of sound. 'Shut up,' called Louis and Edge-worth heard him shout, 'I am innocent of all the crimes laid to my charge.' Santerre called to the drummers to drown the King's words, and he shouted to Sanson, 'Do your duty.'

Sanson's two assistants dragged the prisoner to the platform, fastened him to the plank and forced his head into the groove. Sanson jerked the lever and the shining blade crashed down. The head was cut off so quickly that Dr Pinel thought that the King could hardly have suffered. At 10.22 a.m. Le Gros, Santerre's principal assistant, held up the dripping head. For a moment there was an awful silence, followed by a mass intake of breath which sounded like 'Ah!' It was broken by cries of *'Vive la République'*, a thousand times repeated. The drums beat louder and a salvo of cannon fired.

The King's body was taken at once by Sanson to the cemetery of the Madeleine, where it was buried in quick-lime. When, twenty-two years later, an attempt was made to give it a decent burial, only a handful of clay and some doubtful fragments of bone remained.

Marie Antionette shuddered when she heard the salvos of cannon. For the first time in a thousand years there was no one to cry, 'The King is dead! Long live the King!' The commissioners did not bother to tell the Queen that her husband was dead. She learnt it next day when the man on duty called her 'the Widow Capet'.

10

THE PLOTS

There is a hint in Turgy's *Recollections*, which he published in 1818, that, at the sombre moment of realization that her husband was dead, the white-faced Queen raised her sobbing son to her knee and she and the Princesses saluted him as the King of France. Turgy was in the room about that time, for at ten o'clock Marie Antoinette asked for food for her son, and in 1817 Turgy, when he was ordered to interview the pretender Mathurin Bruneau, who claimed to be the Dauphin, framed the questions: 'What occurred on January 21st when they heard the guns being fired? What did your aunt say and what did they do for you out of the ordinary?' Turgy states that, after January 21st, at table the boy was placed on a chair the seat of which was raised higher than the others, though, of course, this procedure may have been due to the boy's size. Goret, who was on duty in January, says that the Queen and Madame Elizabeth 'accorded the young Prince the rank and precedence to which his accession gave him a right'. Madame Royale passes over her father's death in understandable silence and of the details of that dreadful day we know only, from a report made to the Commune, that the young Dauphin implored the Commissioners of the Temple to allow him to go and ask pardon 'so that my father shall not die'.

Outside France the reaction to the execution of Louis XVI was swift and condemnatory. The Comte de Provence declared himself Regent for the boy King. In Britain public mourning was ordered and the French Ambassador was told to leave London immediately. The Empress of Russia accredited a minister to the court of the Comte de Provence and within a few weeks every European power, except Switzerland and Scandinavia, had joined the coalition against France.

In France jubilation at the death of the tyrant was mixed with shame. Parisians were stunned at the enormity of their crime and shops and businesses remained closed for three days. The moderates trembled; the triumph of the Jacobins frightened them. The people believed, stated the outspoken *Le Veridique*, 'that the death of Louis XVI has made one more saint, and a new king'.

Life in the tower was no longer the same. The Queen and the Princesses were allowed to order mourning dresses of the simplest kind and the Queen's former dressmaker, Mademoiselle Pion, came to the prison on two successive days. 'I cannot express,' she related to Madame de Tourzel with whom she had taken service, 'all I felt on seeing what a ray of consolation was brought into the faces of this august family by my puny person. Monseigneur the Dauphin, whose age excused his thoughtlessness, ran sometimes to me, then to the Queen, to the Princesses and even to the municipal officers. He took advantage of this to put to me, under the appearance of a game, all the questions the Royal Family might desire, and he played his part so well that no one would have imagined he had spoken to me.'

Cléry, who Goret says was 'in a terrible state', was not allowed to visit the Queen again and he was taken down to the Council room, where he found General Santerre, who took a delight in relating to him the gory details of the execution. Cléry was so upset that Goret took him to his bedroom and he passed the night there. Next day Cléry was removed to the Little Tower, where he was held prisoner until March 1st. He was released eventually and he visited several European countries, including Britain, where he was introduced to Sir Walter Scott, who remarked upon his fine manners and interesting conversation.

Of the servants who had chosen to share the privations of the Royal Family, only Turgy and his two colleagues of the pantry remained, and he stayed in the Temple until October 13, 1793. In spite of the vigilance of the commissioners, Turgy kept the prisoners informed of the progress of the foreign armies which they believed were coming to rescue them. The nature of some of his signals suggests that he was as ignorant of the true state of affairs as they. Turgy smuggled the code he had used out of France in 1796, when he went to Vienna.

'For the English: place the right thumb upon the right eye; if they are landing near Nantes, place it on the right ear; if near Calais, on the left ear.

'If the Austrians are successful on the Belgian frontier, place the second finger of the right hand on the right eye. If they are entering the country by way of Lille or from the Mayence direction, use the third finger as above.

'For the troops of the King of Sardinia, use the fourth finger in the same way.

'N.B.—Be careful to keep the finger stationary for a longer or shorter time according to the importance of the battle.

'When they are within fifteen leagues of Paris follow the same order for the fingers but be careful to place them on the mouth.

'If the Powers should be concerning themselves with the Royal Family, touch the hair with the fingers of the right hand.

'If the Convention should pay any attention to them, use the left hand: but should that body go on to the order of the day, use the right.

'If the Convention should withdraw, pass the whole hand over the head.

'Should the troops advance and be successful, touch the nose with one finger of the right hand, and use the whole hand if they are within fifteen leagues of Paris.

'The left side is only to be used to indicate the success of the Convention.

'In answering any question the right hand is to be used and not the left.'

The hopes that may have been raised by these signals were largely false. The Great Powers were concerned only in protecting their own interests in Europe and they made no attempt, other than by trying to defeat the French armies, to rescue the imprisoned family. The British campaign in the Low Countries was designed to prevent the French from opening the river Scheldt to commerce that could damage British trade, and the Austrians and Prussians had their eyes on Poland, the partition of which interested them far more than the safety of three women and a boy who were only minor pawns in the great game of territorial aggrandisement.

The family had firmer friends nearer at hand. Two commissioners plotted to aid their escape, as did other friends both within and outside France, though some of the plots that were hatched were no more than dreams such as the plan devised by the *émigré* Count Louis de Noailles, who schemed to snatch the boy King by means of a forged passport, to get himself from London to Paris, and two air pistols by which to intimidate the gaolers. The bold enterprise suggested by Count Alex de Fersen, who is reputed to have been Marie Antoinette's lover, for a body of 300 cavalry to thrust from the Belgian frontier to Paris, break into the Temple and carry off the prisoners, had the merit of surprise and it might have succeeded, but the Marshal Prince de Saxe-Coburg lacked enthusiasm for a scheme which seemed likely to lose him 300 of his best men.

François Toulan, 'the laughing cavalier of Gascony' as he has been called, did not survive to describe his part in the escape plot which he originated and which is known from the stories told by Turgy and François Lepitre. Toulan, who was guillotined on June 30, 1794, was an ardent revolutionary who had proved his loyalty on August 10th. He became an equally devoted partisan of royalty, though the reason for his change of heart is unknown. He came on duty as a Commissioner at the Temple first in December, 1792, and it seems that he was touched by the misfortunes of the Queen to whom he offered a plan of escape.

Toulan, says Lepitre, was 'clever enough to assume the mask of republicanism, and was able to serve the Royal Family all the better for this, since he was not suspected of being attached to them', and at the meetings of the Commune he was zealous in 'indulging in remarks about the prisoners that were, to say the least, inconsiderate, if not actually disrespectful'. At first he fooled Lepitre so completely that he ventured to ask the Queen if she were really sure of the man with whom she had been conversing. 'You need not be anxious,' Marie Antoinette told Lepitre, 'I know why he behaves like that. He is an excellent man.' Turgy, too, was surprised by Toulan's sudden conversion, until Madame Elizabeth reassured him and instructed the waiter to give Toulan the name 'Fidèle' in their secret correspondence.

Toulan brought Lepitre into the plot and the two commissioners devised a simple ruse whereby they were frequently on duty together in the Queen's apartments. Following the execution of the King the number of commissioners had been reduced to six, and the surveillance of the prisoners became lax. Lots were drawn every evening to decide which commissioners should go upstairs and the words '*jour*' and '*nuit*' were written on the papers. Toulan wrote '*jour*' on all the papers and when their colleagues had drawn their lots, he threw the rest into the fire and he and Lepitre went off together to their post. They met again during the day at Lepitre's house, where also came the Chevalier de Jarjaves, a devoted royalist, whose wife had been one of the Queen's ladies. The Queen insisted he must be brought into the plot, and she gave Toulan a letter to the Chevalier guaranteeing his sincerity. Toulan even succeeded in smuggling de Jarjaves into the tower, an audacious enterprise about which the Queen wrote, 'Take great care not to be recognised by the woman (Madame Tison) who is shut in with us here', and which is vouched for by the Queen's later words, 'I fully recognise your attachment in all you said to me here.'

Toulan's ready wit devised the strategem whereby to introduce de Jarjaves into the Tower. Each evening a lamplighter came to adjust the lamps in the building and to this man Toulan confided his desire to bring in a friend who was anxious to gaze on the royal prisoners. Would he allow the friend to take his place one evening? Flattered probably by the attention of a member of the Commune, whose loyalty could not be suspect, the lamplighter agreed and de Jarjaves donned his clothing, and aided by the man's pass, spent a few minutes with the Queen.

Though equally anxious to aid the Princesses, Lepitre had more to lose by his complicity than his comrades. He owned a prosperous school in the Faubourg Saint Jacques and he required financial compensation for its possible loss. On the Queen's instructions the banker, the Marquis Joseph de Laborde, although he thought the chances of escape for the whole family were 'chimerical', paid him 100,000 francs. The reluctant and possibly timid Lepitre was an essential ingredient to the plot for, apart from his membership of the Commune, he held the position of the President of the Committee of Passports, and could thereby supply the papers with which to facilitate flight once the escape from the Temple had been achieved.

Lepitre thought the escape plan dangerous but none the less possible and he brought in one of his clerks, his own cousin, Guy Richard. Turgy, who had already shown his brazen effrontery in getting him appointed to serve the Royal Family, thought the escape plan 'rash', though that did not deter him from agreeing to play a conspicuous part in its execution.

Lepitre describes the plan devised by Toulan:

'We had procured some men's clothes for the Queen and Madame Elizabeth, and we brought them in one by one, either in our pockets or on our persons, concealed under our pelisses. We also obtained two wadded cloaks, to hide their figures from too close scrutiny, and to make their gait less noticeable. Moreover, we provided them with two hats made on purpose for them, and added to them the scarves and tickets of admission that were used by the Commissioners of the Commune.

'The difficulties in the way of removing Madame Royale and her brother from the tower seemed to be greater. But we thought of a way of doing so. Every evening the man whose office it was to clean the lamps within the building, as well as those outside, came to light up the tower, accompanied by two children, who helped him in his work. He came in at half past five, and long before seven o'clock he had left the Temple.

'We examined the clothes of the two children with great care, and saw that similar ones were prepared for the young King and his sister. Above a light undergarment were the dirty trousers and the coarse jacket called a carmagnole; thick shoes were added, with an old peruke and a shabby hat to hide the hair; while the hands and face were to be in a proper state to complete the illusion. This disguise was to be donned in the turret next to the Queen's room, which Tison and his wife never entered, and we meant to leave the tower in the following way.

'It was arranged that Toulan was to take advantage of the Tisons' weakness for Spanish snuff, which he had lavished upon them while he was in the Temple, and was to give them some of it at a quarter to seven, mixed with so strong a narcotic that they would instantly fall into a profound sleep, from which they would not be awakened till seven or eight hours later, though they would not be in the least injured by it. This plan, innocent though it was, did not please any of us, but we had no choice; we should have been obliged to adopt it.

'The Queen was to leave a note behind her exonerating these two people; and then, dressed like a man, with the municipal scarf round her, was to pass out of the building escorted by myself. We had nothing to fear from the Temple guard; for if we had shown our cards of admission, even from a distance, the sentries would have been quite satisfied, and the sight of our scarves would obviate any suspicion. When we were out of the Temple we should have gone to the Rue de la Corderie, where M. de Jarjaves was to wait for us. A few minutes after seven, when the sentries at the Tower had been relieved, Guy, my clerk, armed with a card of admission such as was used by the workmen employed in the Tower, was to knock at the Queen's door with his tin box under his arm, and Toulan, scolding him for not seeing to the lamps himself, was to hand the children over to him. He would have taken them out with him and on the way to the trysting-place would have rid them of their clumsy garments. Soon Madame Elizabeth, in a similar disguise to the Queen's, would have joined us with Toulan, and we should instantly have started away.

'Our arrangements were such that no one could have started to pursue us until five hours after our departure. We had made most careful calculations. In the first place, no one in the Tower ever went upstairs till nine o'clock in the evening, when the table was laid and supper served. The Queen would have asked that supper might be at half past nine that evening.

'To knock repeatedly, feeling more and more surprised that the door was not opened, to question the sentinel, who, having been relieved at nine o'clock, would know nothing of what had occurred; to go down to the Council Room and inform the other members of the strange circumstances; to go upstairs with them and knock anew, and summon the sentries who had gone off guard and obtain vague information from them; to send for a locksmith to open the doors, the keys of which we should have left inside; to get them opened at last with the greatest difficulty, for one of these doors was of oak and was covered with large nails, and the other was of iron, and both of them had locks that entailed considerable excavations in the solid wall if they were not turned in the usual way; to look into all the rooms and turrets; to shake Tison and his wife violently without succeeding in waking them; to go down again to the Council Room; to draw up a Report and take it to the Council of the Commune, which, even if it had not broken up, would have lost time in fruitless discussions; to send messengers to the police and the Mayor, and to the committees of the Convention, asking what measures should be taken: all these things would have caused so much delay as to give us a chance of escaping successfully. Our passports would have been perfectly correct, for I was then President of the Committee and should have drawn them up myself. We should therefore have had no anxiety on the journey as long as the distance between us and our pursuers remained undiminished.

'We had discussed this project on several occasions. On one essential point opinions were divided. The Queen wished us to travel separately, but at a short distance from each other. She wished us to have three cabriolets, in one of which she would have been with her son and M. de Jarjaves while Toulan was with Madame Elizabeth, and I with Madame Royale. I combated this idea for a long time, pointing out that three carriages would be more noticeable than one in the little towns or villages through which we passed, and that if an accident should happen to one of them the two others would be obliged to wait and would rouse suspicion. If on the other hand they continued their journey there might be some fear of their losing their way, or the delay might lead one party into danger and expose the others to regrets that would be more terrible even than the danger. But the Queen met this by saying that a berline laden with six people (for Toulan would have hurried forward on horseback), and drawn by six horses, would be no less noticeable; and that, since we should be obliged to change horses at every posting-house, we should be exposed to the curiosity of the inhabitants, and still more to the indiscretion of the postillions. She pointed to the unlucky expedition to Varennes undertaken in very different circumstances.[1] Three light carriages would only require one horse apiece, and we should surely be able to find suitable relays at various points of our journey without having recourse to posting houses. In this way we should secure better horses, and should have to change them less often. Everything—economy of time, greater security, and the possibility of our all travelling in two carriages in case of an accident—seemed to point to the adoption of the plan proposed by the Queen. Being alone in my opinion, I yielded to the majority; but I confess it was with much trepidation that I thought of the moment when the sacred charge for

[1] The Royal Family's attempted escape in June 1791 failed because they were recognized.

which I was to be responsible should be confined to my care.

'It was not till the end of February that the goal of our journey was determined upon. La Vendée was now in revolt, and we might have found a refuge there. This was thought of first, but the distance seemed too great and the difficulties too numerous. It seemed easier to reach the coast of Normandy, and to secure some means of crossing to England. M. Jarjaves undertook to provide for everything. We could count entirely upon his ability and his unwearied zeal: he had money enough for the journey; and in whatever direction the Royal Family had chosen to travel they would have found the love and courage of more than one faithful subject ready to facilitate their escape by every necessary means.

'It may easily be imagined that this scheme demanded various modifications. But nevertheless it was sufficiently well thought out to give rise to hopes of success.'

All was ready by early March, when several circumstances combined to cause the plan's abandonment. De Jarjaves, who held an appointment in the Ministry of War, was ordered to join the Army of the Alps, a command he could not refuse, and a series of riots in Paris led to the suspension of the issue of new passports. A modified plan for the Queen to escape alone was rejected by Marie Antoinette, who refused to leave her children. She preferred 'death rather than remorse', she told Toulan. At the crucial moment Lepitre hesitated to compromise himself because 'we (he and Toulan) noticed in the Council that we were regarded with ill-concealed distrust and it was made plain to us by half-uttered rumours and vague suggestions that we had better be on our guard'.

The escape plot had not been revealed, but Toulan's 'imprudence' had aroused suspicion, for he had boasted that the Queen had given him a gold box, and 'I too,' says Lepitre, 'had drawn suspicion by making disparaging remarks about "Sans Culottes".' On March 26th he was denounced by the drunken tailor Lechenard as 'a false brother on whom the prisoners lavish politeness and amiability'. Toulan's facetious defence allayed suspicion, but neither he nor Lepitre were again chosen to represent the Commune as commissioners of the Temple. When Marie Antoinette learned of the failure of the plot she told

Toulan in a note smuggled out by Turgy, 'We have dreamed a beautiful dream, that is all.'

Only the prisoners suffered. A minute search of their apartments led to the discovery of a man's hat, which Madame Elizabeth said was a souvenir of her brother. It had been brought into the Temple as part of a disguise to facilitate escape, declared a suspicious member of the Commune; he brought the King's hatter before the Commune, and executioner Sanson who said that Louis's hat had been torn to pieces by spectators and taken as souvenirs. The true identity of the hat was not solved.

Of yet another plan for their escape the family may have been unaware, for Turgy, their only means of outside communication, does not mention it. Baron de Batz, the ardent and hot-headed royalist who had attempted to snatch Louis from his executioners, recruited a captain of the National Guards, the prosperous grocer Joseph Victor Cortey, who commanded a company of thirty men, all royalists, and a Police Commissioner named Michonis, who agreed to smuggle out the prisoners all of whom would be disguised in military cloaks and hats. The scheme was hazardous and it stood little chance of success, for no great thought had been given to the essential part of the plan, the escape from Paris, and it appears to have been betrayed.

The bold baron came in person to supervise the gaol break and he was taken into the Tower by Captain Cortey who, with his royalist guardsmen, were on duty that night. Michonis took his post in the Queen's ante-room. At that moment Antoine Simon turned up. 'Ah, there you are,' he greeted Cortey, 'if I had not seen you here I should have felt uneasy', and he ordered Michonis to report to the Commune, replacing him in the Queen's apartments. While Simon was upstairs Cortey allowed Batz to escape. Next day Simon informed the Commune that he had received an anonymous letter which warned him, 'Michonis will betray tonight. Be vigilant', but his colleagues refused to believe Simon. They said he was a simpleton who had been hoaxed and Michonis dispelled any doubts by treating the whole affair with good-humoured contempt. Either the members of the Commune were very naïve or there was more behind the 'hoax' than it appears, a matter in which we shall need to delve more especially when we come to consider the vexed questions, who was Simon's powerful protector and what did he hope to gain from possession of the boy King?

Whatever store the Queen and Madame Elizabeth may have placed in this maze of plots, and their desperate situation may have clouded their sense of realism, they still needed to live and to keep the children happy, a task in which they were helped by the kindness shown to them by several of the commissioners, such as Goret who, when the Queen refused to walk in the gardens because descent of the stairs required her to pass the door through which her husband had been taken to his death, obtained permission for the family to take the air on the gallery above the fourth floor, which was reached by a circular stairway within one turret, and he had seats taken up for them. During the period of his duties which ended in March, Goret says that the meals supplied to the prisoners were less sumptuous than before, but 'there was nothing lacking', and he describes Simon as being established more or less permanently in the Temple as a 'general factotum'.

Goret's words about Simon will need to be weighed carefully later. Of Simon he says, 'He was a wretched shoemaker, uneducated and ignorant, but apparently not so ill-disposed as other historians have made him appear. The Princesses summoned him fairly often to bring them anything they might require. His manner in their presence was rather free and easy. "What do you wish for, ladies?" he would say, and he would then try to do as they desired. If they asked him for something that was not in the stores of the Temple, he would run out to the shops. I have heard the Queen say, "We are very fortunate in having that good M. Simon, who gets everything we ask for." '

Lepitre, who does not mention Simon, supplies some details about the prisoners in whose welfare he became so concerned. After the death of the King, he says, Madame Cléry, who was a skilful performer on the harpsichord and harp (before her marriage she had played in the royal orchestra), wrote the music for a Commendatory song, which Lepitre took into the Temple, and which the young King sang to his sister's accompaniment; 'our eyes filled with tears, and for a long time we stood there sadly without speaking'.

'The daughter of Louis XVI sat at the harpsichord, and beside her was her mother with her son in her arms, trying, in spite of the tears that streamed from her eyes, to direct her children's playing and singing. Madame Elizabeth stood beside her sister and mingled her sighs with the sad tones of her royal nephew's voice. Never will this picture be effaced from my memory.'

Madame Elizabeth gave Lepitre locks from the hair of the whole family which he placed within a ring which he wore constantly. He was also the recipient of another present, the gift which caused no little fun. Lepitre had promised to obtain wool and knitting needles for Madame Elizabeth, but he forgot. On his next visit he found himself greeted with a formality he had not previously experienced, and the Princesses thanked him ironically for having been so energetic in keeping his word to them. While Lepitre was racking his brains to understand, 'they held out their hands, which they had been hiding behind their backs, and showed the knitting upon which they had been employed'. Another commissioner had been more obliging, they said. Lepitre was profuse in his excuses and was forgiven, and he was shown the knitting upon which Madame Elizabeth was engaged, which she called a stocking. Lepitre could not suppress a smile 'in view of the size of this so-called stocking'. He thought it would make a better cap. 'Very well, then, a cap it is,' answered Madame Elizabeth, 'and it shall be for you.' When she had finished it she presented it to Lepitre, after first extracting his promise that he would give to the poor the sum such a cap would be likely to cost. He obeyed scrupulously and it cost him ten francs. Even in her jokes, he says, Madame Elizabeth found means of influencing others to do good.

The dead King's sister, otherwise a rather shadowy figure, takes better shape from Lepitre's characterization:

'I have never seen a character in which the highest degree of genuine piety was combined with so much gentleness. Her tenderness for the children of her august brother was the tenderness of a mother. What efforts she made to help the Queen in educating the young Prince and Madame! For in spite of the lack of necessary aids, their education was not neglected and the resources of the two Princesses were such that they were able to a great extent to supply the lack of external means. Not a moment was ever wasted: even games were turned to good account. It was impossible not to be touched by the sight of the young King—barely eight years old—bending over his little table, reading the history of France with the greatest attention, then repeating what he had read, and listening eagerly to the observations of his mother and aunt. The most savage among the commissioners could not altogether restrain their emotion, though it is true they reproached themselves for it later on.'

Slowly the paralysing effect of the King's death wore off; it was succeeded by the calm of desolation, in which little occurred to alleviate the boredom of daily existence. Mostly Marie Antoinette sat silent, absorbed in contemplation of her last mementos of her husband, his seal and ring and a lock of his hair, which Cléry had smuggled to Turgy before he left the Temple. One day, the chimney in the Queen's room caught fire; on another came the Polish painter, Kocharsky, who drew a pastel portrait of Marie Antoinette with her head covered with a widow's veil. Madame Royale contracted a sore on her leg which required the attendance of Dr Brunyer, formerly physician to the royal children, who treated her for a month and who was able to talk with the Queen about the past and the present. The prisoners, we learn, had devised still another means of outside communication; for an old friend, Madame Launoy, had secured an apartment in a house in the Rue de la Corderie, which overlooked the tower, and from the third floor of which it was possible to see into her room. At night she set up a magic lantern with which she projected letters of the alphabet on to a sheet which the prisoners were able to read. Madame Launoy was very proud of her exploit and she told it in her old age to her grandchildren, who passed the story on within the family.

Below stairs the commissioners became bored with their duty as gaolers and one complained to the Commune that it was ridiculous for them to act 'as valets to Madame Capet and emptying her chamber pots', a piece of extravagance which failed to amuse his colleagues, most of whom, states Commissioner Moelle, 'enjoyed the good cheer', the food which was now supplied to them from the palace kitchen, to the quality of which they were unaccustomed. To the outraged commissioner's remarks about chamber pots, another member of the Commune, a man named Réal who is reputed to have been a toady of

Chaumette's, the Procurator General, retorted, 'It is not on account of Capet's wife that you go to the Temple, but because of her son.' The boy, he remarked, was a hostage who must be carefully retained, an early hint of concern for the fate of the boy King who would soon become a pawn in the web of individual jealousies and rivalries.

II

THE SEPARATIONS

Events in the war zone appeared to be moving in favour of the prisoners. The French army was defeated at Neerwinden in Holland on March 18th and eighteen days later Dumouriez, the hero of the Revolutionary War, deserted to the Austrians, declaring that he would restore Louis XVII and march on Paris at the head of 50,000 men. The royalist revolt in the Vendée flared and the Austrians captured Valenciennes and Mayence. Again the road to Paris lay open. The revolutionaries struck back by creating the Committee of Public Safety which was dominated by the Jacobins: the reign of Robespierre began. The exciting news of the apparent royalist triumph was conveyed to Madame Elizabeth by Turgy both by code and in little notes which he concealed in dishes, and the signals he describes indicate that the prisoners lived in daily expectation of the news that their advancing rescuers were 'within fifteen leagues' of Paris. Once again they were doomed to disappointment. Dumouriez's flagrant treason roused the French and only a 1000 men followed him; the moderates, the Girondins, fell from power and that boded ill for the prisoners, for their fate would now depend upon internal divisions within the ranks of the new rulers of France, the men who were interested in them, and in one of them particularly, as the means to enhance their power or to ensure their own safety.

Our knowledge of the life of the prisoners within the tower becomes less; of the royal servants Turgy only remains and the friendly and articulate commissioners have disappeared from the scene. It would be false, however, to suppose that the prisoners lived a life of cloistered calm, for their apartments were invaded daily by a host of menials and functionaries, by waiters, cleaners, wood-carriers, laundry maids, lamplighters, commissioners and, of course, by Antoine Simon, the general factotum, the arbiter of all things, the ever-watchful guardian posted at the fulcrum of revolutionary politics by his mysterious protector. And round and about the tower circulated soldiers, tradesmen, contractors, labourers, porters and the commissioners who came and went. More than 6000 passes to the Temple were issued every month.

A special pass was issued in May to Citizen-Doctor Thierry to attend the boy King who was suffering, reported the Queen, who asked for the children's own physician, Dr Brunier, from 'a stitch in the side which prevented him laughing', and a violent headache. The boy's illness was feigned, the Commune was informed by Hébert, who had been at the Temple that day. He had seen him at 5 p.m. 'playing and jumping and appeared to be very well'. That night he fell ill with a fever and the Queen kept him in bed for two weeks, until May 29th, when she asked the Commune for the novel *Gil Blas* with which to amuse her son. This simple request was discussed at length, one member remarking that the child who 'being very bright and intelligent' (whereby no doubt he spoke from his experience following his duty as a commissioner) would only learn naughty tricks from the morality expounded by that book, and he advocated *Robinson Crusoe* instead. 'His mother has inculcated him with her principles; and you won't spoil him any more,' retorted a colleague and *Gil Blas* won the day.

In April the Commune increased the precautions for guarding the prisoners. The wall surrounding the tower was heightened to thirty-six feet, and a lattice screen was erected round the parapets where they were allowed to walk, all drawing materials were confiscated and the Tisons were prohibited from receiving visitors. This led to an explosion for, when their daughter Pierrette was refused admission, Tison flew into a violent passion, venting his fury upon certain commissioners whom he declared were too friendly to the prisoners, and Madame Tison went mad. Tormented by remorse at her denunciation of Toulan and Lepitre she threw herself at the Queen's feet crying, 'Madam, I ask for your Majesty's pardon. I am a wretch, for I am the cause of your death and that of Madame Elizabeth,' and, seeing Turgy who had entered the room to set the table, she cried, 'Turgy, pardon me, I am a miserable woman. I am the cause of your death.' She became seized with convulsions and she had to be dragged away by four men who had great difficulty in holding her. Next day she was declared insane and she died shortly after this incident, which made Madame Royale laugh. Her mother, and Madame Elizabeth, she says, could not have been kinder to the woman, though they had no reason to be grateful to her.

In order to make up for the loss of their servitor Turgy offered to ask to be allowed to be shut up in the Tower, but the Queen pointed out that it was through him that all their information came and that if Turgy became a prisoner too 'we should in future be entirely in the dark'. Should she be rescued, Marie Antoinette invited Turgy 'to join us wherever we may be, with your wife, your son, and your whole family'. The kindness shown to Madame Tison by the Queen so impressed Tison, says Turgy, that he repented of his conduct in the past and desired to give some proof of his sorrow. This he did on the first opportunity. One day the little King's seat at the dinner table, the chair with the cushion on it, was occupied by a commissioner on duty, no less a person than the ex-priest Pierre Bernard who had volunteered to witness the King's execution. The boy was forced to sit on a chair that was so low that he could hardly reach the food on his plate, but no one dared to disturb the boorish Bernard. Tison tried to come to the rescue; bringing forward another chair, he asked the commissioner to give the child the seat he generally used. Bernard roughly refused, saying 'I never saw a table or chair given to prisoners; straw is good enough for them', and he refused to budge. Bernard, it is pleasant to report, was guillotined on July 29, 1794.

Louis Charles fell ill again in June. He had injured himself whilst playing and the Queen demanded the services of the famous truss-maker Hippoy le Pipelet, who was allowed to visit the patient and bandage him for hernia. Chaumette and his crony Hébert came to watch the treatment, and Dr Pipelet, who had been told by the Commune that 'he would be paid only as for an ordinary prisoner', and not as a former Court Doctor, was ordered to undress the boy and place him upright on a chair near the window, and 'to state that the child had in his blood a poison which condemned him to death'. Chaumette and Hébert attributed the boy's ailment to his mother's immodesty. The boy, stated Pipelet in 1823, was 'perfectly sound' and he had injured himself 'whilst riding astride a stick as children do', and no trace of the indisposition would remain. Chaumette's and Hébert's vile slander became, as we shall learn, the principal charge made against the Queen at her trial.

Hardly had the boy recovered when the blow fell. On July 3, 1793, the Committee of Public Safety decreed that the young Capet should be placed in the charge of a teacher and secluded 'in a separate apartment, the most secure in the Tower'. The selection of the child's gaoler-guardian was left to the Commune and it chose Antoine Simon for the post which carried a salary of 9000 francs a year. Simon was an ignorant dolt, yet his advancement had been rapid. Born in the year 1739, which made him fifty-four in 1793, he had failed to earn a living as a shoemaker and, after failing again as an eating-house proprietor, he reverted to his old trade with no better success, falling into such a mire of debt that, when his first wife died, he was forced to sell her few belongings to pay the cost of the funeral, and to drown his grief in a prodigious drinking bout. Overwhelmed by liabilities that amounted to 5000 livres and possessing only twenty sous, he married again, this time a charwoman named Marie Jeanne Aladame who had been bequeathed 2000 livres by her employer, who owned the house in which the widower lodged. The Revolution began in the year following Simon's second marriage and we do not hear of him again until August 1792, when he became one of the elected representatives of The Théâtre Français Section, one rich in remarkable men, and he was appointed as one of the four special Commissioners of the Commune to supervise the transfer of the Royal Family to the Temple prison.

From September 29th onwards Simon was in charge of the prison finances, a position of responsibility, and he became President of the Temple Council. Yet he could neither read nor write or keep accounts. He, and no one else, had the free run of the apartments on the second and third floors and he could come and go as he willed. In his minor way Simon was one of the greatest beneficiaries of the Revolution, a man of the people who was honoured and trusted. He has been described as robust in build and hard of hearing and the sketch by an unknown artist of 'Simon, Concierge du Temple' shows him to have been a man of 'brutal and besotted features' (as he has been described) with the wide-eyed look of animal cunning. His colleagues found him 'a poor wretch without either education or instruction, but not so wicked as historians have wished to paint him' (Goret); a man with 'a good foundation of sensibility, honesty and even generosity, but not very clever', and 'full of enthusiasm for liberty and equality' (Verdier).

Marie Antoinette seems to have liked Simon and she thought her family were fortunate to have 'the good M. Simon who gets everything we want'. Simon certainly knew how to make himself indispensable and he was ever ready to run errands to the shops when the prisoners wanted anything. He was also self-important; when the Queen, seeing he was hot, invited him to take a glass of wine, he answered, taking the glass, 'I do not drink like this with everybody'. His pomposity drew the ridicule of his colleagues at the Commune who believed, on one occasion as we may recall, that the simpleton was easily hoaxed, whereas the truth may be that Simon had stumbled on the plot to abduct the boy King, which certain people in authority preferred should be kept quiet.

Simon, it had been inferred, served as the puppet of a powerful protector, a conspirator who required to keep an unsuspicious underling at the Temple to safeguard his interests and he has been identified as Chaumette, the all-powerful Procurator of the Commune who supervised all matters relating to the Temple and the imprisonment of the Royal Family. Hébert, who was Chaumette's henchman, made Simon the instrument of his villanies, says Dr Verdier; he lavished praise on the ex-shoemaker and convinced him he was the foremost of patriots. Simon idolized the sly and cunning Chaumette who boasted that he was the son of a provincial shoemaker.

Chaumette and his fellow revolutionaries were fascinated by the inmates of the Temple, and by the boy King; to these cynical power-hungry men, Louis Charles represented salvation if the great experiment in Liberty, Fraternity and Equality collapsed. The politician who possessed him could escape the penalty of his crimes if, and at several moments it seemed probable, the royalists and their allies triumphed. The young Capet was a valuable hostage who might be bartered for personal immunity. Both parties in the State, the extremists, the Jacobins, and the more moderate Girondins, were prepared to proclaim Louis XVII, if needs must. A British spy, whose identity has never been solved, disclosed the secret plottings of the members of the Committee of Public safety to his employer, the British Minister at

Genoa, Sir Francis Drake, who passed on the information to his chief at the Foreign Office, Lord Grenville.

This spy insinuated himself into the innermost circles, the inner 'cabinet', of the Committee. Monsieur 'X', as we may call him, was a Frenchman, who Sir Francis Drake reported 'hid his true sentiments under the outward show of the most exalted Jacobinism', and in whom he had every confidence. He gathered and transmitted information which was unsuspected by historians until the startling discovery, in 1885, that his reports had been preserved in the private papers of Lord Grenville which were published by the Historical Manuscripts Commission (Dropmore Papers).

Despairing of the permanence of the Revolution, the cynical rulers of France were considering the question 'of proclaiming young Capet King' and they strove for the possession of the valuable boy, each faction accusing the other of the intention to restore him while protesting their own revolutionary fervour, and each was fearful of being deprived of him. 'If we do not forestall them, they will forestall us,' was Chaumette's secret fear. At the Commune, Hébert dared to say, 'The King never dies; he is in the Temple', and he cloaked his true sentiments by the words 'let this little serpent and his sister be cast upon a desert island; we must rid ourselves of them at any price'. Another member, Couthon, accused Hébert of being 'that secret partisan of royalty'. The subject of the child was mentioned daily at the meetings of the Commune.

The isolation of the phantom King was the first step in the plot. In June, 1793, Chaumette controlled the Temple and the child within it. 'I shall remove him from his family in order to make him lose the idea of his rank,' he told François Hue, who had called to enquire about the prisoners, and to ask that he might be allowed to serve them again. Anxious about the safety of the magic talisman, Chaumette betook himself to the Tower, where he inspected the parapets within which the family were allowed to take the air, with a view to raising them 'so that the prisoners could see nothing save the sky above their heads', but, instead, the parapets were blocked to prevent them from being seen from outside. 'Who instigated all these precautions, some of which might be superfluous,' wondered Goret, and he thought that 'an occult and powerful party had a hand in all that, unknown to the Council'. Dr Cerdier suspected that only those who were initiated into the mystery 'had a close view of the horrors which were happening'.

And 'horrified' is the word employed by Madame Royale to describe her mother's feelings when she was informed of the cruel order separating her from her son. On July 3rd, at ten o'clock at night, the six commissioners on duty, Eudes, a stone-cutter, Gagnant, a painter, Véron, a perfumer, Cellier, a Counsel, Devèze, a carpenter, and Arnaud, a secretary, came to the Queen's apartments and read to her the decrees. Madame Royale describes the scene:

'As soon as my brother heard this he started screaming and threw himself into my mother's arms begging not to be parted from her.

'My mother would not give up. She defended his bed against the municipals. But they insisted on taking him and threatened to use violence and to send for the guard to carry him off by force.

'An hour was spent in discussion and argument, insults and threats by the municipals and tears and opposition from all of us. At last my mother consented to give up her son. We got him up and when he was dressed my mother handed him over to the municipals after bathing him in tears, as if she foresaw that she would never see him again.

'The poor little fellow kissed us all tenderly and departed in tears with the men.'

Next day the commissioners reported to the Commune:

'After various earnest entreaties, the widow Capet at last determined to deliver her son, who was then led into the appointed apartment and placed in the hands of Citizen Simon who is in charge of it. We would observe moreover that the separation took place with all the sensibility which one would expect under the circumstances in which the magistrates of the people showed every deference compatible with the severity of their duty.'

In her daughter's laconic words, 'My mother felt she had reached the height of unhappiness in being separated from her son. However, she thought that he was being looked after by an honest and educated man. Her misery increased when she knew that the shoemaker Simon, whom she had known as a municipal, was in charge of her unhappy child.'

Although the Queen implored the Council for permission to see her son, it was not granted. For two weeks she and the Princesses heard the boy crying in the room below, in the apartments which the King had formerly occupied. He was taken into the garden every day by Simon and 'the only pleasure my mother had', says Madame Royale, was in watching him through the loopholes of the battlements where the women were still allowed to go: 'Sometimes she waited there for hours to get a glimpse of her darling child.' The Queen got a little news of him from the commissioners and from Tison, who 'went down on washing days, saw Simon and heard from him how he was'. Tison, who tried to make amends for his bad conduct, gave the Queen some news, but 'not much'.

Madame Royale goes on to say, 'Simon treated my brother very badly, when he cried at being separated from us, till at last the child was so frightened that he did not dare to weep,' and she states that her brother was taken into the gardens in order to refute the rumour that he was no longer in the Temple.

'Every day we heard him singing with Simon the Carmagnole, the Marseillaise and many other horrid songs.

'Simon made him wear a red bonnet and a carmagnole jacket and he forced him to sing at the windows so as to be heard by the guard and to utter fearful blasphemies against God and to curse his family and the aristocrats.'

The first step to the implementation of the plot had been taken: the boy-King had been stolen from his mother. It remained to eliminate the ex-Queen.

On August 2nd, at two o'clock in the morning, General Hanriot, the Commander of the National Guard in place of Santerre, who was with the army in the Vendée, accompanied by four commissioners of police, came to the apartment on the third floor, roused the women, and read to the Queen the decree ordering her to appear for trial before the Revolutionary Tribunal and committing her meantime to the Conciergerie prison. Hanriot's manners were rough and he used bad language, says Madame Royale.

'My mother heard this order without flinching. My aunt and I immediately asked to be allowed to go with my mother, but as the decree did not say so they refused.

'My mother packed up her clothes in a bundle. The municipals did not leave her and she was obliged to dress in front of them. They asked for her handbags which she gave them. They went through them and took out whatever was inside, though there was nothing of any importance, made a parcel of the contents which they said would be opened by the tribunal in the presence of my mother. They only left her a handkerchief and a bottle of smelling salts in case she felt unwell.

'At last my mother went after having embraced me and told me to be brave and to look after my health. I did not reply. I was quite sure that I would never see her again.

'My mother had to stop at the bottom of the tower because the municipals had to draw up a paper for her discharge from the Temple.

'As she went out she knocked her head against the lintel of the door, which was lower than she thought, but she did not hurt herself very much. After that she got into a carriage with a municipal and two *gendarmes*.'

One of the gendarmes had the grace to enquire if the prisoner had hurt her head. Looking back at the tower which loomed dark and sinister in the hot, stifling night, Marie Antoinette answered, 'No, there is nothing now that can hurt me any more.' The hired fiacre rattled over the cobbles, disturbing the silent, sleeping city. At 3 a.m. the escorting gendarmes beat on the great doors of the Conciergerie with their muskets. Preceded by guards bearing flaming torches, the Queen was taken through the long corridors and lodged in a small cell.

12

THE SECOND VICTIM

The cell at the Conciergerie prison which is shown to visitors as
that occupied by the unfortunate Queen is not the low wide
room in which Marie Antoinette was placed and where she
lived for several weeks before being transferred to another cell
in which she spent her last days on earth, although it may lie in
approximately the same position, for the buildings facing the
Women's Courtyard were reconstructed in the nineteenth century. The room in which she was first lodged had previously
been a council chamber and some of its former glory remained,
for its peeling wallpaper still bore the stamp of the royal fleur-
de-lis. It had been disused for many years and it was damp and
dark, for its heavily barred windows brought in little light. Its
floor was of brick and a wooden partition divided the room into
two, with a gap which was blocked by a four-foot wooden screen.
The guards occupied the outer part of the room and the Queen's
part was furnished with an ancient folding bedstead and straw
mattress which had been mended by rope and was covered with
torn blankets. There was a basin, a small table, and two cane
chairs, one of which contained a night stool which was emptied
each morning by a convict. Marie Antoinette laid herself on the
bed and mopped her perspiring face with a handkerchief, for it
was very hot.

It had not been definitely decided to put the Queen on trial;
the decree ordering it was intended as a threat, to convince the
foreign powers and particularly Marie Antoinette's nephew, the
Emperor of Austria, that the revolutionaries held a valuable
hostage whose life was in danger.

The news from the war front, and from within France, was
bad: the Prussians were advancing through the Rhineland, the
Austrians, Dutch, British and Hanoverians were besieging the
key fortresses on the northern frontier, which were expected to

fall, the Spaniards were pushing through the Pyrenees, and the naval base of Toulon was besieged by the British. The greater part of France was in revolt against the rule of Paris and the Vendéan royalists dominated the west. Plots were rife to rescue the Queen; her abduction, even failure to bring her to trial, would release the fury of the Parisian mob. The revolutionaries despaired; their leaders sought personal safety from the dilemma. They feared that, if they failed to execute the Queen, the mob would tear them to pieces; on the other hand, if they handed her over to the guillotine they would lose their hostage, their only chance of staving off the vengeance of the royalists, which would be fearful.

The revolutionaries were frightened men. Of all the terrible dangers they faced, the threat from the mob seemed the worst. 'You must first satisfy the *sans-culottes*,' warned Hébert; 'they will kill all your enemies, but you must keep up their excitement by the death of Marie Antoinette.' He had promised the mob her head and he would cut it off himself if there was any delay. If the Republic collapsed they would all die, he told his friends, for 'it could not be otherwise. That being the position, 'we have nothing to live for except revenge'. Only by a colossal purge could the revolutionaries save their own lives. All France must be devastated, and all the French people must be made co-partners in their crime. Thus was created the Terror, the 'weapon of terror' as Danton named it, by which to suppress revolt at home and to warn the foreigners that, if they continued to advance, they would find nothing and no one to rescue.

A mad girl from Normandy gave the Jacobins their excuse. Actuated by mistaken zeal for the revolution which she believed had been betrayed, Charlotte Corday stabbed Marat while he sat in his medicinal bath on July 13th. The old revolutionary was the darling of the mob and it demanded vengeance. The Law of Suspects was hurried through the Convention; by its terms anyone could be arrested and guillotined after a perfunctory examination. Within one year 300,000 people were imprisoned. In Paris alone, between March 11, 1793, the date of the inception of the Revolutionary Tribunal, and July 17, 1794, the end of the Terror, the Sansons executed 2632 people, at an average of 5·24 persons a day. Another 20,000 died in the provinces. It was not necessary even to be a 'suspect'. A lawyer visiting his client in a

Parisian prison was herded on to the tumbrel and was guillotined along with fifty others.

A *levée en masse* of the entire population and the resources of France was called, the first time in modern history in which a threatened state mobilized its entire forces. Commissioners from Paris were sent to join the armies, to bolster morale and to spy on their Commanders. Although the revolutionaries did not fully realize it, they had little to fear from the Allies: the Prussians and Austrians hoped to prolong the war in order to keep the greedy eyes of the other from the partition of Poland. The British had only selfish interests, the destruction of the French fleet and its bases, and the establishment of a bridgehead on the continent at Dunkirk, which the Duke of York was diverted to besiege. The Emperor of Austria was indifferent to the fate of his aunt and he did nothing to save her, accuses Madame Royale.

Marie Antoinette's imprisonment in the Conciergerie lasted for seventy-five days and day and night she was annoyed by the coarse talk of the two gendarmes who never left her cell and who filled it with tobacco smoke, and by their mere presence. She was allowed no privacy when she dressed and undressed and used the night-stool, and she was condemned to complete inactivity. Sometimes in her intense weariness at doing nothing, beyond reading the *Voyages of Captain Cook* which the gaoler's wife had provided, she went and watched the guards playing cards. She had only the clothes she wore at her arrival until Michonis, the Commissioner of the Temple of whom we have heard already, brought a parcel of underwear from Madame Elizabeth. The gift proved a problem, for the Queen had nowhere to store the extra clothes. The maid, Rosalie Lamborlière, supplied a cardboard box which the Queen welcomed 'with as much pleasure as if it had been the most beautiful piece of furniture in the world'. Rosalie, the maid to Madame Richard the gaoler's wife, served the Queen with heroic devotion and she did everything she could to make the Queen's imprisonment bearable; when she was in the room she tried to screen her from the gaze of the guards, and she cooked and served the excellent food that Madame Richard provided.

Marie Antoinette spoke to Rosalie of her misfortunes without showing any emotion or depression, but she wept when she thought of her deserted children. Madame Richard did her best to help the Queen, says Rosalie. One day she brought into the cell her youngest child, who had fair hair, very pretty blue eyes, and a charming face that was much more refined than was common in his class of life. He was known as 'Fanfan'. When the Queen saw this fine little boy she was obviously moved. She took him in her arms, covered him with kisses and caresses, and bursting into tears began to talk about her son, who was of about the same age. She thought of him night and day. This incident was most painful to her, and after they had gone upstairs Madame Richard told Rosalie that nothing would induce her to take her little boy into the cell again.

Another young girl also rendered the Queen remarkable service. Mademoiselle Fouché came daily to the prison to bring comfort to the many priests and nuns who were held there, and early in August she asked Richard if she might be allowed to visit the Queen. For a long time he refused to listen to the request, repeating 'Impossible, absolutely impossible', but Mademoiselle Fouché detected a hint in his voice that his *no* might become *yes*. Pressing some pieces of gold into the gaoler's hand, she repeated her request. 'Pay attention to what I say,' said Richard, 'there are four gendarmes entrusted with the guarding of the prisoner: two of them are devils, but the other two are good lads. They relieve each other at midnight. Come at half-past twelve, and— we shall see.' Mademoiselle Fouché was overwhelmed with delight.

Richard kept his word and she was taken to the Queen's cell. Marie Antoinette was not in bed and the visitor was struck by her blanched hair, hollow cheeks and faded colouring. Mademoiselle Fouché explained that she hoped to bring a priest to console her. The Queen eyed her without speaking and the visitor understood that she feared a trap to compromise her. 'As you will,' at last she answered. On her next visit, Mademoiselle Fouché brought the Abbé Magnin, who had dressed in lay clothes and called himself M. Charles to overcome Richard's fears. Magnin states in his own deposition that he received the Queen's confession and gave her the Sacrament on two occasions while Richard was still the gaoler at the Conciergerie. Mademoiselle Fouché also brought the Queen some fine chemises to replace the coarse linen with which she had been provided, and she planned to bring her a new dress, to replace her worn and tattered costume, until she realized that its appearance would arouse the suspicions of the commissioners who would conclude on their daily inspection that the prisoner was in touch with outsiders. She brought some inconspicuous and warmer stockings instead. The Queen, who was touched by the girl's kindness, forbade her to bring writing materials for 'if you were surprised with a single word of mine in your possession, your death would be a certainty'. She did, however, give her a little ebony box which contained a porcelain cup mounted in silver which she asked to be given to her daughter, to whom Mademoiselle Fouché sent it in 1804.

The dampness of her cell and the state of her nerves affected the Queen's health and she became ill; she refused medical aid, states Rosalie, 'since no doctor could remove the cause of her illness'. Her clothes became mildewed, and her shoes encrusted with dirt from the decayed brick floor. Rosalie tried to clean them with a knife. To her astonishment, one of the gendarmes took the shoe and scraped it with his sword. The women in the markets, where she went to shop, says Rosalie, always sold her the best they could find 'for the Queen', and they gave her a melon and peaches for the prisoner.

Towards the end of August, says Rosalie, 'a most unfortunate thing happened, which did the Queen a great deal of harm'. This was the 'Affair of the Carnation', as it became known. Commissioner Michonis, whose position as an officer of the Gendarmerie gave him the right of entry into the prison, and whom the Queen knew to be a loyal friend, visited her cell, bringing with him a short statured man whose clothes were bespattered with mud. Marie Antoinette recognized the Chevalier de Rougeville, a one-time Colonel of the Grenadiers whom she knew to be a man of reckless courage and complete loyalty. What could his presence mean? The Queen nearly collapsed. Foreseeing the danger, de Rougeville whispered, 'I am going to save you. Pick up the flower,' indicating the red carnation he held in his hand. While Michonis gave Marie Antoinette news of her children, de Rougeville slipped behind the partition, which hid him from the gaze of the guards, and dropped the carnation to the floor. As soon as her friends had gone Marie Antoinette picked it up. Within its petals she found a tiny piece of paper on which she read a message telling her to be ready to leave her cell on the night of September 2nd, at midnight when the guards were changed. On a subsequent visit de Rougeville left a sum in gold for the Queen to bribe the gendarmes in the cell and he told her that the guards in the corridors and at the gates had been bought. To put the escape plan into operation, all that was required was a note from the Queen stating: 'I will come.'

The conspirators were unaware that the Queen lacked writing materials and they failed to warn Richard and his wife that the Queen would be sending a message. Marie Antoinette pricked out the required words with a pin on a scrap of paper and she bribed a guard to take it to Madame Richard. She, not knowing who de Rougeville was, decided to give it to the first Commissioner who came on duty, and, by a stroke of luck, Michonis turned up. He put the note in his pocket, warning Madame Richard to say nothing about it.

On the night planned for the rescue someone blundered. Either the conspirators failed to bribe the right men or the Queen in her anxiety left her cell at the wrong time. She bought her way out and walked unhindered through the empty corridors until she reached the main gate. The guards stationed there knew nothing of the plot and they took her back to her cell. In the alarm that followed, the guard whom Marie Antoinette had bribed to carry the note reported that he had given it to Madame Richard, who was forced to tell that she had handed it to Michonis. He was asked to explain the incident. He had once before fallen under suspicion, due to the alarm raised by Simon. Then he had bluffed his way out of danger and now, once again, he tried to brazen it out. He produced the note, or more probably a piece of paper which had been pricked by a pin (it is exhibited at the Conciergerie prison) and he said it had come from a crazy prisoner. His impudence and audacity failed to save Michonis and he was condemned to the guillotine. De Rougeville escaped.

After the affair of the carnation the Queen, says Rosalie, 'seemed to be more anxious and much more alarmed than before.' She did not expect to be tried and she still hoped that her relatives would insist on her being given up to them. The Committee of Public Safety sent a Commission to the prison to hold an enquiry; the Queen's person and her cell were searched and the last of her jewels were taken away, and even the little gold watch that had been given to her by her mother. But she managed to secrete under her stays the little locket which held a picture of her son. The Richards were ordered to be imprisoned and their place was taken by Bault, the gaoler of La Force, and on his arrival Marie Antoinette was transferred to another room, which had formerly been the pharmacy, the barred windows of which overlooked the *Cour des Femmes*, from where the sentinels could see into her cell.

'At first sight Lebean [as she called Bault],' says Rosalie, 'seemed hard and stern but he was not a bad man at heart', and he and his wife were as pliable as had been the Richards. Rosalie kept her job, though she was no longer allowed to go outside the prison, and she states that Bault was made answerable for the Queen's person with his life. He alone possessed the key to her cell and even he was not allowed to enter unless he was accompanied by an officer of the Gendarmerie.

Surprisingly, following the imprisonment of the Richards, she and her husband, stated Madame Bault, who wrote after 1814 when it was wise to express such sentiments, did their best to help the Queen. 'For heaven's sake, don't do anything imprudent, Rosalie, or I am lost,' Bault told the maid. He refused to obey the Commissioners' orders to serve only the coarse prison food to the prisoner, on the pretext that an attempt might be made to poison her, and he tacked a piece of old carpet on the wall behind her bed to keep out the damp. When the Commissioners expressed their disapproval he told them its object was to deaden the sound and prevent anything from being heard in the next room, an ingenious explanation which satisfied them so completely that Bault was told 'you did right'.

For some inexplicable reason Rosalie was forbidden to leave a glass of water in the Queen's cell. One day when she was carrying a half-empty glass through the corridors she encountered an American visitor, M. de Saint Leger, who asked, 'Did the Queen drink the water that has gone from this glass?' Rosalie answered that she had. With a quick gesture M. de Saint Leger uncovered his head and drank the water that remained, with every indication of respect and pleasure.

Mademoiselle Fouché knew and respected Bault and, taking advantage of his good-will, she and the Abbé Magnin visited the Queen, and the Abbé again celebrated Mass and gave her Communion, admitting Mademoiselle Fouché and the two gendarmes to the divine banquet. These two men, relates

Magnin, fell under the executioner's knife. It is possible that the Queen received another clandestine visitor, the English Lady Atkyns, of whom we shall hear again in connection with the plots to abduct the Dauphin.

On October 12th the Queen was informed that she would be brought to trial at once.

Early in October Fouquier-Tinville, the public prosecutor, had informed the Committee of Public Safety that the evidence amassed against the Queen was unlikely to gain a conviction for treason before the Revolutionary Tribunal, for it constituted nothing more than a rehash of the ancient grievances against the monarchy. Hot on the heels of this discouraging report came Antoine Simon. 'Citoyen and Citoyenne Simon have learned certain facts from the child's mouth,' he solemnly declared. He had caught young Capet in practices 'injurious to his health' and upon being reproved he had made accusations against his mother. Chaumette and Hébert hurried to the Temple, bringing with them Mayor Pache (who had succeeded Chambon), four commissioners, one of whom was named Denis Etienne Laurent, and a doctor. They ascended to the second floor where they found Louis Charles and Simon.

The boy, we recall, had injured himself in play in June. The Queen had treated her son on the doctor's instructions and, left to himself, he had continued the practice and, upon being reproved by Simon, he claimed parental authority. He talked about the repugnant subject without embarrassment and in complete ignorance of its meaning. Laurent took down his answers, and the boy signed the paper, or may have been forced to sign it, for the signature 'Louis Charles Capet' on the famous document, which is exhibited at the Museum of the Public Archives, is clumsy even for a boy of that age. The terms of the alleged statement, and the expressions used, suggest that its scurrilous implications were obtained by twisting the boy's words. In reply to further questions, Louis Charles incriminated certain Commissioners of the Temple who had had secret communications with the prisoners.

The statement obtained from Marie Antoinette's son was not enough for these monsters. Next day, October 9th, they reappeared at the Temple and ascended to the third floor, where the two princesses, having just finished doing their rooms, were dressing for afternoon dinner. Pache, the Mayor, begged Madame Royale to come down to the second floor, whereupon Madame Elizabeth insisted upon accompanying her niece. Her request was refused and she was told by Chaumette that the girl would be returned upstairs. There was nothing for it but to obey and Madame Royale, aged fifteen, went downstairs, being very embarrassed at finding herself alone for the first time with a dozen men, and ignoring Chaumette's unctuous compliments.

Madame Royale had not seen her brother for three months and she embraced him tenderly, but Madame Simon dragged him away, and pushed her into another room where she was interrogated by Chaumette. 'This concerns neither you nor anybody,' he began. 'It does not concern my mother?' Chaumette explained that certain citizens had not done their duty, and he named, amongst others, Toulan, Lepitre, Moelle and Michonis, whom he said had conversed with the prisoners. Madame Royale said she did not know any of these commissioners and she was ignorant of anything that might have happened when they were on duty.

Her brother was brought in and seated on a chair and 'he swung his little legs, which did not reach the ground,' Goret was told by one of the men who was present. At Chaumette's request Louis Charles repeated the indecent statement he had made the day before, and in reply to his sister's horrified denials, he announced, 'Yes, it is true.' 'I heard this son accuse his mother and I said "I don't believe a word of it," ' states Commissioner Daujon, who acted as Secretary that day.

Madame Royale refused to put her signature to the report and she states :

'I was interrogated on a thousand hideous things of which they accused my mother and my aunt. I was overwhelmed with such horror and so indignant that, despite my fear, I could not help crying that it was infamy. Ignoring my tears they insisted. There were certain things that I did not understand, but what I did understand was so horrible that I wept with indignation.'

The princess, before she was returned upstairs, asked Chaumette the favour of being reunited with her mother, to which he replied, 'I can do nothing.' 'What, Sir,' she remarked, 'you cannot obtain it from the General Council?' Chaumette said he had no authority there. Upon her niece's return, Madame Elizabeth was taken downstairs and the boy was again made to repeat his accusation. Nothing that came from such despicable men could surprise her, she said and 'that such an infamy was too much beneath her to permit her to reply to'. When her nephew protested that he was not lying, she snapped, 'Oh, the monster.'

Daujon told Goret that the child's replies had been suggested to him. 'Everything showed it, his uneasiness, his bearing', and Madame Elizabeth was not deceived and her exclamation had been caused by surprise.

Whatever the truth of the horrible charges that were put into the boy's mouth, and the answer seems simple, Chaumette and Hébert carried the statement to the public prosecutor whose savage penstrokes can still be seen on the document.

As a result of the child's accusation, Toulan and Lepitre and the other commissioners he had named were arrested, but Toulan only was executed.

On Saturday, October 12th, at six o'clock in the evening, 'the Widow Capet' was taken by a court usher, with an escort of four gendarmes, to the Grand Chamber of the Hall of Justice which adjoined the Conciergerie. The day's sitting was over and the huge room was dark and empty, save for the President of the Tribunal, Herman, the prosecutor Fouquier-Tinville and the clerk, Fabricius, who sat at desks illuminated by two candles. Marie Antoinette who was dressed in her shabby black dress and a white bonnet over which she had draped a widow's veil, sat on a bench. Herman put questions and Fabricius scribbled notes. In the obscure depths of the room shadowy figures moved. The Queen strained her short-sighted eyes to try to identify these privileged spectators who were watching her so intently.

At the conclusion of these formalities, the Queen was told that she could employ counsel and on her statement that she knew no lawyer to whom to entrust her defence, two advocates, Tronson-du Coudray and Chauveau-Lagarde, were named by the court.

The accused Queen appeared before four judges and twelve jurymen (an ex-deputy of the National Assembly, a musical instrument maker, a surgeon, a coffee house keeper, an auctioneer, a barber, a printer, a musician, a wooden shoe maker, a carpenter, and two whose occupations were not named), at eight o'clock in the morning of Monday, October 14th. The crowd of spectators at the back of the hall jostled each other in their eagerness to get a better view as the white-faced, pallid woman, dressed in widow's weeds, was led to an armchair which had been placed in front of the judges. When she seated herself, people at the back of the Court shouted, demanding that the accused be made to stand so that nothing of the spectacle of her humiliation should be lost. 'Will they never be tired of witnessing my fatigue?' Marie Antoinette murmured as she took her seat at the judges' bidding, and during the reading of the indictment her fingers were seen to tap the arm of the chair 'as though on a piano'. Marie Antoinette sat attentive and calm as the clerk read the accusation:

'Antoine Quentin Fouquier-Tinville, Public Prosecutor to the Revolutionary Criminal Tribunal, makes known that after examination of all documents transmitted to him, it becomes manifest that, like Messalina, Brunehaut, Frédégonde and Médicis, who in the past were termed Queens of France, and whose names are forever odious, Marie Antoinette, widow of Louis Capet has, since her residence in France, been the scourge and bloodsucker of the French people.'

The ex-Queen was charged with having had political dealings with the enemies of France, with having spent in shocking manner the finances of France (the 'fruit of the people's sweat') 'to satisfy her dissolute pleasures and pay the agents of her criminal intrigues', and having sent her nephew, the Emperor of Austria, millions 'that he has used and still uses to carry on war against the Republic'. The indictment was filled with unprovable accusations. She had taught her husband 'that art of dissimulation whereby he for so long deceived the noble French people'. The people *had* been most criminally deceived, the Queen agreed, but 'not by my husband or by me'. Her reply offered a chance to make the prisoner incriminate herself, thought Herman, the President. Jumping to his feet he demanded, 'By whom then have the people been deceived?' 'By those in whose interests it is to do so,' prudently answered the Queen. She did not know their names.

The accusations multiplied and each was a shameless distortion of facts. Occasionally Marie Antoinette interrupted to deny the vague charges. A National Guardsman spoke about August 10th. After the Queen had left the Tuileries he had found under her bed empty bottles with which, he concluded, she had intoxicated the *chevaliers du poignard*. There followed a stream of witnesses, former palace servants, *femmes de chambre*, gaolers, gendarmes, even dressmakers. The hearing of witnesses went on until dusk and continued next day. 'I have nothing to say,' repeated the Queen. No witness had produced any positive fact, she claimed.

Finally, the prosecution produced its star witness, Antoine Simon. He repeated the vile calumny and Hébert, his lips curling lasciviously, read the boy's loathsome statement against his mother. When he finished there was complete silence; a member of the jury rose: 'Citizen President, I call your attention to the fact that the accused has not answered the charge brought by the citizen Hébert on the subject of what has passed between herself and her son.'

The Queen rose in outraged remonstrance: 'If I have not answered it is because Nature refuses to reply to such an accusation,' and turning to the spectators she cried, 'I appeal to all mothers here to-day. Is there not one who in her innermost heart would not have shuddered at such a crime?' From the women in the packed gallery rose a murmur of sympathy that turned quickly into a piercing cry. Several had to be taken out and the President was forced to hammer for silence. 'The fool. He will save the woman yet,' exclaimed Robespierre when he heard of Hébert's monstrous allegation.

Sitting down, Marie Antoinette asked the officer of the guard, Lieutenant de Busne, for a glass of water. He obtained the drink, an act that nearly imperilled his life. The Queen had sat in the hall for fourteen hours on the first day and it was now six o'clock in the evening of the second day. Her two advocates addressed the Court, each speaking for two hours. Following a violent diatribe delivered by the President of the Court, the jury retired to deliberate their verdict. At one o'clock in the morning, Marie Antoinette was taken to a cell adjoining the hall, and Rosalie Lamorlière was ordered to bring her some broth which she had kept in reserve, foreseeing that the Queen would need sustenance. As Rosalie approached the cell, a superintendent of police, a little man with a broken nose, snatched the bowl from her hand and gave it to the greatly overdressed young woman with him, telling Rosalie, 'this young woman is extremely anxious to see the Widow Capet and this is a grand opportunity for her to do so'. Whereupon the woman entered the cell carrying the soup, half of which she spilled in her excitement.

The jury returned at 4 a.m. It was bitterly cold in the hall, and many of the spectators had left, telling their friends that they expected that the Queen would be banished. The accused was brought back into the Court and ordered to stand. The jury announced its verdict: 'Guilty on all counts'. Fouquier-Tinville demanded the death penalty. Marie Antoinette listened impassively as the President decreed that sentence. She gave no sign of fear, but seemed stunned by surprise, noticed Chauveau-Lagarde:

'She came down the steps without a word, without a gesture, and crossed the hall as though she neither saw nor heard; then, when she reached the barrier and faced the crowd, she raised her head with the utmost dignity. It is plain that until that terrible moment the Queen had continued to hope; and yet, without hesitating, she displayed the finest kind of courage, for it is impossible to show any greater courage than that which survives even hope itself.'

Walking through the dark corridors on her way back to her cell, Marie Antoinette told Lieutenant de Busne, 'I can hardly see where I am going.' He took her arm to guide her, a thoughtful act for which he was censured by his chief, who complained that he held his hat under his arm, instead of wearing it as he had been ordered to do in the ex-Queen's presence.

When she reached her cell, Marie Antoinette asked for writing materials and when these were brought she wrote a letter to her sister-in-law, which Madame Elizabeth did not receive;

'It is to you, my sister, that I write for the last time. I have been condemned, not to a shameful death, for that is for criminals, but to rejoin your brother; like him, innocent, and I hope to show the same courage in these last moments. I am calm as one is when conscience had no reproach to make. I bitterly regret abandoning my children. You know that I only lived for them and for you my good and sweet sister, you who have sacrificed everything to remain with us. In what a position I leave you.'

She had to speak, she said, of what was painful to her heart, the appalling accusation which she believed Hébert had put into her son's heart:

'I know how much pain the child must have caused you. Forgive him, my dear Sister; think how young he is and how easy it is to make a child say what one would, even what he does not understand.'

About seven o'clock Bault told Rosalie to go to the Queen:

'Two candles, still alight but nearly burnt out, were on her little table, I presume they had been left there for her all night. The Queen was lying on her bed in her clothes; she was still wearing her long black dress. A constabulary officer was seated in the farthest corner of the room, and seemed to be asleep.

'Her face was turned towards the window, and she was supporting her head with her hand. "Madame," I said to her tremblingly, "you ate nothing yesterday evening, and hardly anything during the day. What would you like to have this morning?" The Queen was weeping bitterly. She answered, "I shall never need anything again, my girl: everything is over for me." I took the liberty of persisting. "Madame," I said, "I have kept some broth and some vermicelli on the range: you require support: let me bring you something." The Queen, weeping still more bitterly than before, said to me, "Rosalie, bring me some broth." I went to fetch it. She sat up, but could hardly swallow a mouthful or two.

'When it was daylight, that is to say about eight o'clock in the morning, I went back to Madame to help her dress. Her Majesty went into the little space that I usually left between the folding bed and the wall. She herself unfolded a chemise that had probably been brought to her in my absence, and having signed to me to stand in front of her bed so as to hide her from the gendarme, she stooped down behind the bed, and slipped off her dress in order to change her underlinen for the last time. The officer of the Gendarmerie came forward instantly, and standing by the head of the bed watched the Queen's proceedings. Her Majesty quickly threw her fichu over her shoulders, and with the greatest gentleness said to the young man: "In the name of decency, monsieur, let me change my linen without being watched."

' "It is impossible for me to allow it," answered the gendarme roughly; "my orders are to keep an eye on you, whatever you are doing."

'The Queen sighed, slipped her chemise over her head for the last time as cautiously and modestly as possible, and then dressed herself, not in the long black dress that she wore before the judges, but in the loose white gown that she usually wore in the mornings. Then, unfolding her large muslin fichu, she crossed it under her chin.

'When she was completely dressed she glanced round her room with an expression of great anxiety, as though seeking something that she feared she would not find. I was trying in vain to guess the cause of her anxiety when I saw her carefully fold up the soiled chemise she had just taken off, wrap it closely in one of her sleeves, and then with a look of intense satisfaction slip the little bundle into a hollow space that she had caught sight of in the wall, behind a strip of the canvas.'

Rosalie left the room, not daring to say a word of farewell or even to curtsy, for fear of compromising the Queen.

The turnkey, Louis Larivière, entered the cell and he was there when the judges arrived with the registrar, Fabricus.

'Her Majesty, who was on her knees beside her truckle-bed, rose to receive them. The president said: "Pay attention: your sentence is about to be read to you", and they all four uncovered their heads, which was never their custom on occasions of this kind. It seemed to me that they were almost startled by the Queen's air of majesty and goodness.

' "It is needless to read it," said the Queen in a clear voice. "I know the sentence only too well." "No matter," answered one of the men; "it must be read to you again." Her Majesty made no answer, and the registrar began to read.'

Just as he finished an immensely tall young man entered the cell. He was Henry Sanson, the son of the chief executioner.

'He came up to the Queen and said, "Hold out your hands." She recoiled a step or two, and answered in a troubled voice, "Are my hands to be bound? Louis XVI's were not bound." The judges said to Sanson, "Do your duty." "Oh, my God!" cried the Queen distractedly. As she spoke Henry Sanson roughly seized her hands and bound them tightly behind her back. I saw the Queen raise her eyes to heaven with a sigh, but though her tears were ready to flow she restrained them. When her hands were bound Sanson removed her cap and cut off her hair. She turned round with a look of deep emotion, and saw the executioner taking possession of her hair and putting it in his pocket to carry away.' [It was burnt in the great vestibule after the execution.]

The drums had been beating since 5 a.m. and by seven o'clock the people of Paris were afoot to secure places round the scaffold. Cannon were mounted on every bridge and in the chief squares and at every road junction between the Conciergerie and the Place de la Révolution. At ten o'clock mounted patrols scoured the streets and the traffic was diverted from those through which the Queen would pass, the very streets through which she had ridden twenty-three years before on her triumphal entry into Paris as the beautiful bride of the young Dauphin. Now she was an old woman, half blind, her white hair peeping from her coarse linen cap, dressed in a shabby gown and wrapped in an old shawl.

At twelve minutes past eleven, Marie Antoinette was brought into the prison courtyard, and she mounted the steps to the executioner's cart, the same as was used for any condemned prisoner. She sat herself on the rough plank seat and Sanson stood behind her holding the rope that secured her hands. The single white horse drew the cart through the streets, lined by a vast, silent throng. The Queen looked indifferently at the people, show-ing, says an eye-witness, 'no sign of dejection or of pride'. She took no notice of the occasional cries of '*Vive la Republique*'. and 'Down with the Tyrant'. Her only sign of emotion came when the cart entered the Place de la Révolution, and when she saw the Tuileries.

The cart drew up at the scaffold. Marie Antoinette alighted easily and ascended to the platform. She submitted to the executioners, shaking her cap from her head herself, and step-ping accidentally on Sanson's foot. 'Pardon, Monsieur,' she in-voluntarily exclaimed. His assistants seized her; 'Make haste,' she cried. It was all over in four minutes, and at 12.15 Sanson held up the Queen's head.

With the killing of the Queen the Revolution reached new depths of infamy: the French hated Marie Antoinette, 'the

Austrian woman' as they called her, for she personified their grievances real and imagined. There was no valid revolutionary reason for her execution, which Napoleon called 'something worse than regicide'.

On the day she was put to death, October 16, 1793, the Revolution was saved by the minor victory of Wattignies, which relieved the fortress of Maubeuge, besieged by the Austrians.

13

THE GAOLER

The prisoners in the Temple were not told of the Queen's death; whatever they may have suspected, Madame Elizabeth and Madame Royale knew no more than that she had been taken to the Conciergerie and, other than on October 7th, they did not again see the boy, whose transfer to Simon's custody had caused a sensation in Paris where it was whispered that certain members of the Convention wished 'to restore the throne of the tyrant, whom you have punished, in favour of his son'. Rumours of a monarchial restoration were rife, and the public named Chaumette as the instigator of the plot. These rumours were seditious, declared Robespierre from the Tribune of the Convention, and the Committee of Public Safety sent four of its members to the Temple to check the presence of the prisoners. They found, stated the *Moniteur*, 'Capet's son in the first apartment, quietly playing draughts with his mentor.'

Her brother, Madame Royale learned, probably from Tison, asked for his mother and demanded 'that they show him the law which ordered the separation'. The boy, who was now eight years and five months old, continued to be treated by Dr Pipelet, and Dr Thierry, who told Madame de Tourzel, whom he met at this time, that 'he was deeply touched by the situation of the Royal Family', to whom he had formerly acted as court physician. In his account, which he sent to the Commune, Thierry listed sixteen visits to the young Capet, between July 1793 and January 1794, the period when he was under Simon's guardianship, and he reported that he treated him only to prevent a recurrence of the 'verminous affliction' from which he had been suffering for some time, due no doubt to the condition of the prison, and 'he got rid of a prodigious quantity of worms'. On July 4th, the day following the separation, and on each of the next twenty-two days, the boy was treated with 'a medicinal brew made in a water bath with veal, the thighs and backs of frogs, the juice of plants and *terre foliée*'. On the 26th, 29th and 30th, he was given enemas made of 'Corsican Coralline, lemon juice and olive oil', and the apothecary Robert supplied also 'a syringe with an ivory barrel' at the cost of fourteen livres.

Apart from these minor ailments, Louis Charles was generally in good health and he was under the care of reputable doctors who would have remarked the terrible deterioration in his health and the rough treatment that royalist legend attributes to the period of Simon's guardianship. Nor was he made to eat 'the coarsest food', as Madame Royale states, for at the meeting of the Commune held on September 1st it was stated that 'the prisoner's table is still served with the same profusion', and even following the 21st of that month, when the condition of the women prisoners was made more severe, it was decreed 'that no modification should be made in the régime of the little Capet'. A billiard table and a cue-rack were installed in the apartment on the second floor, a little girl named Clouet, whose mother brought the laundry every ten days, was allowed to play with Louis Charles and Simon gave him a dog which the boy named Castor and of which, states Madame Simon, 'he was very fond'.

And Simon, whom legend depicts as the monster who undermined the boy's health by his ill-treatment and cruelty, provided his charge with an oak aviary which contained thirty-two perches and which was installed by a carpenter named Le Marchand, who built it within one of the window embrasures in order 'to give the birds light', which required the removal of some of the planks by which the casement was blocked. Other accounts paid by the Commune show that one of the turret rooms was turned into a pigeon-cote and 'seeds for the little Capet's pigeons' were supplied for several months. Simon went even further to provide for the child's well-being: he found in the rooms within the Temple precincts occupied by Mathey, the door-keeper of the tower, 'a marvellous contraption', which no doubt had belonged to the Prince de Conti, a former resident, which is described as 'a gilded cage made entirely of silver with moulded gilded garlands and crystals and chimes and a bird organ to instruct the birds', and 'an infinity of drums, springs, fusees, bellows and triggers by which the birds on alighting on one of the perches to eat, made the bird-organ play'. Simon brought the cage to the second floor of the tower where its mechanism was repaired by the clock-maker Bourdier who owned a shop in the Quai de l'Horloge du Palais. The cost of the repairs, 300 francs, was paid for by Simon himself.

The Simons fulfilled their responsibilities as the child's guardians. They bathed the boy, using a thermometer to test the temperature of the water, and the laundry bills prove that his linen was frequently changed. They did, however, take away the mourning clothes he had worn for his father since January, dressing him instead in gaily coloured garments which he possessed or which were specially made for him by the former court tailor, Bosquet, who supplied in September a nankeen jacket, waistcoat and trousers, a silk-lined frock-coat of Louviers cloth, a small dress-coat, and a waistcoat and trousers of the same material, the cost of which was paid by the Commune. If Simon occasionally dressed his charge, as Madame Royale states, in a *carmagnole* (a short tight jacket) and a red phrygian cap, the uniform of the *sans-culottes*, it was probably done in fun, to match his own garb or to demonstrate his own revolutionary fervour. The sketches that were made at this time and which show Simon walking in the Temple gardens with the boy-King depict Louis Charles wearing a broad-brimmed hat, a dress coat and a wide sash.

The authentic records refute the royalist charges against Simon; the cruel beatings, the drenchings with water, the broken toys, the crushed bird, the cowed and weeping boy, his dreadful blasphemies against God, his starvation and mental torture. Simon had been charged 'to democratize the royal child', not to kill him, for he was far too valuable. No doubt the boy learned bad language from his rough mentor; Simon taught him to revile the aristocrats and tried to educate him as a *sans-culotte*, and went too far it seems for some of the Councillors of the Commune for, on September 5th, Chaumette found fault with the schoolmaster Leboeuf who, he said, had dared to reprimand the patriot Simon for teaching the young Capet indecent songs, and Leboeuf was arrested and his house was searched. Simon's supposed brainwashing of the boy also scandalized Commissioner Daujon who, though an opponent of royalty, was not a rabid revolutionary. One day when Daujon was on duty a noise was heard from the women's apartment on the floor above and Simon's apt pupil cried out, 'Aren't those damned bitches up there guillotined yet?' which so horrified Daujon that he left the room in disgust and 'by way of protest'.

No doubt Louis Charles's character deteriorated under Simon's care; he was surrounded by rough people who, however kind they may have been, reduced him to their level of behaviour as Gagnié, the chief cook at the palace, testifies. Visiting the apartment in the tower, Gagnié found the boy playing in the billiard room with several commissioners who 'passed him from one to another and blew puffs of smoke in his face', until finally he was rescued by Gagnié who told him, 'I am sorry to see you in this state, Monsieur Charles,' whereupon the excited child replied, 'What you instruct me? You call me Monsieur? So you are not up to date. To punish you, drink a glass of water.' When the commissioners applauded this joke, Louis Charles gave Gagnié a glass of water which he drank dutifully, saying 'Thank you, Monsieur Charles.' 'What, Monsieur again?' scolded his tormentor. 'Oh, I see clearly that you are not up to date. Drink another glass of water.' Gagnié bowed out of the joke by claiming that 'I don't drink as much water as that,' and the commissioners laughed uproariously in order to stifle their true feelings perhaps for, though the date of this incident is not expressly stated, it seems to have occurred on October 16th, the day on which the boy's mother was guillotined.

Other than on October 7th, the day of the dreadful confrontation, Madame Royale did not meet her brother following the separation on July 3rd, and she knew of his presence in the tower only from the sounds she heard from the floor below and from the occasional glimpses she gained from the battlements when Simon took him into the garden. The two Princesses were permitted to go up to the roof every day and Madame Royale says that, despite the vigilance of the three commissioners who were perpetually on duty, she and her aunt succeeded in getting some information from outside their prison. They learned in September that the Queen had been accused of having kept up a correspondence with the foreign powers, and 'we immediately threw away all the written papers we had with us, our pencils, and everything we had hitherto concealed, as we were afraid lest we should be forced to undress before Simon's wife'. They had preserved some ink and paper, pens and pencils, notwithstanding the close search that had been made both of their rooms and their furniture.

On September 21st, Hébert came to the Temple, accompanied by several municipal officers, for the purpose of executing the decree of the Commune by which it was directed that the women prisoners should be confined more strictly than hitherto. Aunt and niece were confined to one room and Tison, who continued to do the coarse work, was kept in one turret. Hébert ordered what Madame Royale describes as 'a turning box' to be constructed in the door to the room, through which food was to be passed and he ordered that no one whatsoever, with the exception of the water-carrier and the wood-porter, should be allowed to enter the room. These orders were not carried out and the commissioners continued to enter the room three times a day, making a careful inspection of the bars at the window and searching drawers and cupboards. 'We made the beds ourselves and were obliged to sweep the room, which took us a long time to do at first, until we got accustomed to it,' recounts the young Princess, who remarks that Hébert told them that thereby they would learn that equality was the first law of the Republic.

This greater severity of treatment resulted in the removal of the arm-chair in which Madame Elizabeth had been accustomed to sit, and even of necessities; 'When our meals were brought, the door was instantly clapped to, lest we should see the persons who brought them. We had now no opportunity of hearing anything, except through the porters, and the information we thus obtained was very rare and trifling, although we listened with avidity to everything. We were prohibited from walking on the turret, on the pretext that we should attempt to escape through the windows, notwithstanding they were secured by bars. The very linen that was given us was of the coarsest and filthiest description.'

Four commissioners, who were 'completely intoxicated', states Madame Royale, made a special visit at four in the morning and for four and a half hours they searched the women's rooms and took away their plate and porcelain, checking the items against the list of articles that had been supplied over a year before, and 'accusing us of having stolen some of it, whereas the fact was that their colleagues had made away with it'. The searchers found a purse containing gold coins that had been hidden by Princess de

Lamballe behind a commode, and they confiscated such trifling things as bonnets, playing cards and books, other than religious books which they left, 'but not without uttering a thousand blasphemies'. And Simon accused the Princesses of counterfeiting money. The young Capet, he told the Commune, had heard from the floor above the sound of knocks and steps which he had not heard, 'being somewhat hard of hearing', but his wife supported Charles Capet's statements. Once again Simon incurred the jeers of his colleagues, who expressed their opinion that the noises 'were caused by wood which the Princesses were arranging, by the fagots they were making and unmaking', a reasonable explanation for, as is reported by several people, it was quite easy to hear small sounds within the tower from one floor to another, a fact which renders the complete silence that enveloped the second floor after January 21, 1794, so inexplicable.

On October 1st the establishment of the Temple was reduced from thirty employees to fourteen and the rest of the old placeholders were expelled, the supply of pastry and poultry was stopped, and it was ordered that the women prisoners should be given for their dinner only 'a single soup, boiled beef and some other dish with a bottle of wine a day'. The three ex-royal waiters were dismissed and on his last day on duty Turgy was forced to omit setting the table and to serve each Princess with a piece of beef, a loaf of bread, and to provide each with a pewter spoon and an iron fork. Gagnié, the chief cook, was allowed to keep his employment because he had contrived to put the tradesmen with whom he dealt so much in his debt that they were unable to reimburse him. Even Simon's movements became restricted, for permission to come and go as he wished was withdrawn and he was allowed to visit the gardens with his charge only under the surveillance of one of the commissioners.

'The winter,' says Madame Royale, 'went by without any important incident,' except that she and her aunt learned from the cries of the newsvendors of the execution of the Duc d'Orléans. They were subjected to many inspections and searches 'but they let us have wood for the fire', which at first had been refused. They passed the time in 'tolerable tranquility'.

The next entry in Madame Royale's diary of her imprisonment requires careful consideration for it marks the last occasion on which she heard any sound from the floor below and from which she drew a particular conclusion.

'On January 19th we heard a great noise in my brother's room and from which we conjectured that they were removing him from the Temple, and we were confirmed in this belief when we saw them, through the keyhole, [in another MSS she says through the hole in the sun blinds] carrying away a bundle of things. We also heard, on the succeeding days, the frequent sound of the opening of his door, and of persons walking in his room, so that we remained persuaded of his departure. I have since, however, learned that it was the removal of Simon that caused this bustle.'

She and her aunt believed that her brother had been replaced by some German or other foreign prisoner whom they baptized 'Melchisedec' to give him a name.

Simon and his wife left the Temple on January 19, 1794, and they did not return there, yet from that date until June 8, 1795, the rooms on the second floor of the tower were occupied by a boy. Whether or not the bustle on January 19th was caused by the removal of the boy King or by that of the Simons, from that date begins the enigma of the Temple, the question of the identity of the boy who died there eighteen months later, a problem to which we shall need to return, after we have followed the fortunes of Madame Royale.

The sudden removal of Simon from his responsible and well-paid post smacks of subterfuge and intrigue. On January 3rd the Commune suddenly decided that it was incompatible with the principles of equality for its members to hold two jobs, that of an elected representative of the people of Paris and simultaneously a position of profit, such as Steward of the Temple or mentor to the young Capet. Coru at once resigned his stewardship and he was followed by Legrand, who relinquished his job as Registrar, showing an example that Simon had either to follow or resign his membership of the Commune. He announced at once that he would leave the Temple in order to devote himself to the interests of the people of the Théatre Français Section and he thereby relinquished his annual salary of 9000 francs, a considerable sum for which he could hardly have been recompensed by the position of Inspector of Carriages which, apparently, did not carry the stigma of plurality of employment.

The question of plurality of offices was only an excuse to get rid of Simon, for the Commune immediately appointed other men to succeed Coru and Legrand, but not Simon as the boy's guardian, though it ordered 'that a list of candidates should be drawn up with that object in view'.

Simon and his wife had moved on January 5th to a room within the Temple precincts 'above the stables' where they were fed 'at the expense of the house', and Simon does not seem to have returned to the Tower until the 19th, when at nine o'clock at night he entered the council chamber and informed the commissioners who were on duty that he was about to leave. The four commissioners, Cochefer, Lasnier, Lorient (a doctor), and Legrand (a lawyer) stated in their report, which they all signed, 'He exhibited to us the person of the said Capet, prisoner, being in good health, asking us kindly to take charge of the said Capet and grant him a provisional release until the Council had granted a definite release from the said supervision which ended today, which provisional release we have granted; and we have taken over the custody of the said Capet.'

Contrary to the usual practice, these four commissioners were not relieved next day and they remained on duty for forty-eight hours, when they were relieved by four new men, two of whom, Warmé and René Bigot, were not members of the Commune, from whose ranks the Commissioners of the Temple had been drawn for sixteen months.

Simon did not leave the vicinity of the Temple and he and his wife secured a lodging nearby, as well as occupying two rooms and a kitchen in a house in the Rue Marat in which they had formerly lived. He continued to visit the Tower as a commissioner when his turn came to serve, and Madame Simon also went there at will, entering the enclosed area around the prison, not by the main gate but by the side door near the stables, where it was only necessary, states one of the commissioners, to knock with a stone 'placed for a signal agreed upon by the doorkeeper Piquet and the people of the neighbourhood'.

Simon continued to meet his friends at the Café Desnoyers which was frequented by Hébert, and by two municipal officers named Pierre Sault, an artist, and Jacques Lasnier, a rent collector, and one of the commissioners to whom he had relinquished his charge. To Lasnier Simon spoke of the little Capet 'with tears in his eyes', and he remarked that the latter had asked him, 'Simon, my dear Simon, take me with you to your shop. You can teach me to make shoes and I will pass as your son.' Simon told his friends, 'I would give an arm for this child to belong to me, so lovable he is, and so attached am I to him.'

According to royalist tradition, on January 21, 1794, the boy on the second floor of the Tower was 'walled up' like a beast and subjected thereafter to the process of slow torture and callous barbarity from which he subsequently died. It is certain only that there was a child living in the Tower, a strangely quiet and silent child.

The partisans of more than one pretended Dauphin claimed that the boy King had been smuggled out of the Temple in a basket of dirty linen on January 19th by Madame Simon, and within forty-eight hours his place had been taken by a deaf and dumb boy for whom was later substituted another boy who was dying of scrofula; questions to which we shall return later.

14

THE THIRD VICTIM

The gap in Madame Royale's diary, now our only direct source of information about the women prisoners, from January to May, 1794, provides an opportunity to catch up with events. Toulon, which had surrendered to the British in the previous August, was retaken in December, thanks chiefly to the enterprise of the artillery commander, Napoleon Bonaparte, and in the fluctuating war on the frontiers the Austrians and Prussians had been repulsed. In the provinces the Vendéans had been badly beaten and large areas had been 'liberated' from the counter-revolutionary forces. The revolutionary politicians were, however, as yet unaware of the extent of their military successes and they were fully occupied with the Power Game in which he who did not kill might himself be killed. In April, Chaumette, Hébert and Danton were guillotined, along with Madame du Barry the faded courtesan of the *ancien régime*, who was dragged to the scaffold screaming for mercy. Rather than face the guillotine, Pétion took his own life. The Terror mounted to its peak; the Parisian prisons were packed with victims; Fouquier-Tinville worked overtime, and people were taken to the guillotine in batches. They were drawn from all classes, rat-catchers, washerwomen, bankers, aristocrats, in fact anyone who was suspected of treason or seditious intention, or who was merely someone's enemy. The aged de Malesherbes, his sister, his daughter, and his grand-daughter died, and thirty-two young people of Verdun who had too eagerly welcomed the invaders in 1792 were condemned to death: two only were executed, and the rest were ordered to be tied to the guillotine for eight hours.

During the winter the two women prisoners were treated with 'coarse vulgarity'. They refused to be annoyed and, when Madame Elizabeth was denied 'fasting fare' during Lent, she omitted breakfast and ate only bread for dinner. Her niece, she said, had not arrived at an age that required her to abstain, but she herself would touch nothing that was forbidden and she scrupulously performed all the duties prescribed by her religion. Candles were withdrawn and the two Princesses went to bed directly it became dark. Nothing of importance occurred until May 9th.

That night, as they were going to bed, they heard knocking on the door. Madame Elizabeth called out that she was putting on her gown and the door was pushed with such violence that it burst open. The men who entered, four commissioners, a representative of the Revolutionary Tribunal and two officers, told her, 'Citizen, you will accompany us downstairs.' 'And my niece?' She would be taken care of, she was told. She embraced the girl who was trembling in every limb and tried to calm her agitation, telling her that she would soon return. 'No, Citizen,' said one of the men, 'you will not return; put on your bonnet and come downstairs.' Madame Elizabeth embraced the girl again and complied 'being overwhelmed with insults and coarse buffoonery', says Madame Royale. The door of the prison clanged, and she was gone.

Madame Elizabeth was taken to the Conciergerie and next day she was judged and condemned to death. On her way to the scaffold she was told by another woman, 'Madame, your sister-in-law has met the same fate as we ourselves are about to suffer.' The wanton execution of the King's sister, who had taken no part in the governance of France and who was regarded as a saintly person, horrified the Parisians. She was thirty years of age and her life had been a model of virtue. Under no circumstances could she have been considered a danger to the State and the only reasonable explanation for her execution seems that the presence in the Temple of an intelligent and suspicious adult was an embarrassment to the men who had plots to hatch. Only a few days before her execution, the British spy informed his masters, 'They do not doubt that, in the present state of affairs, Robespierre has one of two plans; to carry off the King to the Southern Provinces if the armies [of the foreign powers] approach Paris, and that is the Committee's project; or take the King to Meudon and make his personal treaty with the Power that draws the nearer to Paris, and that is the plan of which Robespierre is accused.'

Robespierre had by the April executions become the inheritor of the magic talisman, the guarantee of personal safety. Certain apparently enigmatic jottings which he made in his note book at this time show that he understood the importance of the prisoners of the Temple: 'a new cook to be appointed'; 'arrest the old one' [? Madame Elizabeth], 'opium', 'a doctor', 'replace members of the Council', and, significantly, under the date of May 10th, 'report'.

Gagnié, the chief cook, was relieved of his duties, being replaced by Meunier, the *rôtisseur*, and on May 10th, the day following the arrest of Madame Elizabeth, 'there came', states Madame Royale, 'a man who I believe was Robespierre; the municipal officers treated him with great respect. His visit was kept secret from the people of the Tower, who either did not know who he was, or did not wish to tell me.' She gave her visitor the letter she had written; 'My brother is ill. I have written to the Convention for permission to nurse him. The Convention has not yet answered. I repeat my request.' Robespierre surveyed her with an air of indolence, looked at her books and, after joining the municipals in their search, went away.

The revolutionary leader's visit to the Temple about this time is confirmed by the British spy who believed that the boy prisoner was removed from the tower by Robespierre and returned within a few days.

Whatever is the substance of this possible abduction and return, Madame Royale heard nothing and she was not told of her aunt's death. She spent a cruel night comforting herself with the hope that Madame Elizabeth had been sent out of France but, when she recalled the manner in which she had been taken away, her fears returned. To her entreaties for news next day, the commissioners replied that her aunt had gone 'to take the air'.

The fifteen-and-a-half-years-old girl was left in loneliness, to exist in dreadful silence which was broken only by the daily inspection of the commissioners who told her nothing. She had lived through a series of astonishing calamities; she had seen her father taken to execution, her mother and her aunt had disappeared, and she had been separated from her brother, whom she believed was ill. Condemned to a monotonous existence, she mended her clothes, re-read her books a thousand times and walked briskly to and fro for an hour every day. Cut off from fresh air and sun, she had only her thoughts and they could hardly have been comforting. The commissioners redoubled their severity, taking away her knives and even her tinder box, on the excuse that if she lighted the fire she might fall asleep and burn herself. Except when she was directly interrogated, she never said a word, even to the man who brought her meals. She asked for nothing that was not absolutely necessary, and even that was refused in the roughest and most insulting manner. She contrived to keep herself and her room clean; she had soap and water and she swept her room every day. The privation of light affected her less as the days lengthened.

Such was her situation, says Madame Royale, when on July 27th, she heard the drums beating and the tocsins ringing. On that day, the day of 9th Thermidor, though she did not know it, fell the triumvirs, Robespierre, Saint Just and Couthon, victims of their own ambitions and intrigues. They had carried the Terror too far and the middle classes struck back. Next day, they were guillotined along with eighty-three members of the Commune, amongst them Antoine Simon, and their place was taken by Paul Jean Barras, who became the inheritor of the magic talisman. The Red Terror, the rule of the *sans-culottes*, was replaced by the White Terror, by the return to power of the prosperous middle classes who, with some of the aristocrats, had created the Revolution.

Next day, at six o'clock in the morning, Madame Royale was awakened by sudden noise and tumult; the guards were called to arms, the drums beat and within the tower there was a constant opening and shutting of doors. She heard the bolts of the door of the room below withdrawn, the first sound from the second floor she had heard since January; she jumped out of bed and hurriedly dressed. A delegation from the Convention, composed of men wearing tricolour plumes and sashes, entered her apartment, at its head Barras. He asked her name, expressed surprise at finding her up and dressed so early and left again. Unknown to Madame Royale, for it was not carried out, Barras ordered on July 28th that 'the two children of the King of France shall be allowed to walk daily in the prison courtyards'. It is significant that Barras's first act on assuming power was to visit the Temple and inspect its prisoners.

Following this incident, the guards at the tower were doubled and the three commissioners on duty remained for eight days.

Three nights later Madame Royale was roused from her sleep by loud knocking and upon opening her door she was spoken to by a new commissioner, who told her he had been entrusted with the guardianship of herself and her brother. This man, Christopher Laurent, who was aged twenty-four, entered the room and asked politely if she wanted anything. Thereafter he came three times every day, always treating the girl with politeness and civility, and never showing familiarity or disrespect. But in answer to her questions about her brother, and her request to be restored to her mother, he replied in evident embarrassment, saying that these were matters with which he had no concern. Laurent, the registers of the Temple state, had been appointed 'Keeper of the Tyrant's children', and we shall hear more of him in connection with the boy who now became his special charge.

Laurent, says Madame Royale, 'was very attentive to me'. She had no reason to find fault with his conduct during the time he was on duty at the Temple, 'but quite the contrary', an enigmatic phrase that suggests that the young man and teenage girl struck up a sort of friendship, in contrast to the attitude of the other commissioners who advised no more than that she should have patience and rely upon the justice and goodness of the French nation. Laurent restored her tinder box and he gave her candles, but he would not speak about the boy.

Towards the end of October a strange, and to Madame Royale an inexplicable, incident occurred. At one o'clock in the morning she was roused by knocking; she hastily arose and opened the door, trembling with fear. Outside stood Laurent and two other commissioners. They stared at her and went away without saying a word. This nocturnal visit can be explained possibly by an alarm of a plot to rescue the prisoners, which may have had something to do with the revolt of the *sans-culottes* at that time, when Barras called in the military to defend the Convention. General Bonaparte dispersed the crowd with grape-shot, thus establishing a state of affairs whereby, as time went on, the politicians needed to rely more and more on the army.

On November 9th, Laurent was joined in the performance of his duties by a man named Gomin and, as the winter progressed, Madame Royale had every reason to be satisfied with her guards both of whom were civil and polite, bringing all the wood she required and helping to light the fire. Then on March 31st

Laurent was replaced by Etienne Lasne whom she calls 'an honest man'. A glimpse of the girl during that winter is supplied by the *ci-devant* baron, Jean Baptiste Harmand, the deputy for La Meuse, who wrote after the Bourbon restoration and before his own death from hunger in 1816. In his respectful account of his visit to the second floor of the tower, Harmand says;

'A very large fireplace and, in it, a very small fire appeared opposite the door of entry. On the left was a bed and, at the foot of the bed, the door of the other room. It was a bleak wet day, and the cold seized you as you entered the great room with its lofty, old-fashioned ceiling and walls of enormous thickness. The whole place seemed to me damp and chilly, though very orderly.

'Madame was seated in an arm-chair beneath one of these windows which, as I have described above, were blocked by large grilles and were several feet above the level of the head. It was the only one which lighted the room. A ray of light, broken and partially intercepted by the grille, descended perpendicularly without throwing any light around. Beneath the window the effect of this shaft of light was such as might be produced in a dark place by means of a mirror presented to the sun, and Madame, as she sat under this disc of light, seemed as though invested with an aureole of glory. Such was my idea of this scene, truly worthy of an artist's brush.

'Madame, who was dressed in a gown of plain grey cotton, was sitting huddled up as though she were not sufficiently clad and protected from the cold. She was wearing a hat which, as well as her shoes, seemed much the worse for wear. Madame was knitting. Her hands looked swollen and purple with cold, and her fingers were disfigured with chilblains. Madame knitted with difficulty and with an air of obvious discomfort.'

The man was a stranger and Madame Royale looked at him with uneasiness. Harmand opened the conversation; 'Madame, how is it that you are sitting so far from the fire when it is so exceedingly cold?'

'Because I cannot see near the fireplace.'

Taking courage, Harmand said he had been sent to take her orders for anything she might want, to which the girl, who was accustomed to such meaningless protestations, made no answer. Noticing the harpsichord, Harmand asked if Madame would like it to be tuned. 'No, Monsieur,' she replied, 'the piano is not mine; it is the Queen's. I have not played on it and I shall not do so.' Becoming more confident, she enquired for her brother. 'Madame,' answered Harmand, and indicating the commissioners who were with him, 'we had the honour to see him before we came to you'. To the girl's request to be allowed to see her brother, he replied in the affirmative says Harmand, but he left the Temple without arranging the meeting.

Despite these suggestions of deprivation and austerity, Madame Royale was well cared for. On November 20, 1794, she was supplied with five ells of linen at twenty livres the ell, nine ells of ribbon at six livres the ell, sixteen busks at ten sous a piece, eight ells of lace at five livres the ell, and four corsets at eighteen livres each. Two months later she was given four pairs of stockings, thread, needle, ribbons and a thimble and a pound of powder, thread, knitting needles, tea, syrup of orange, and liquorice. The laundry bill for the girl Capet from March 21st to April 19th comprised ninety-five items. During much the same period the food supplied to the prisoners, the girl, the boy and Tison, and for the commissioners and staff, included chickens, mushrooms, asparagus, cake, sweetmeats, and chocolates. On Fridays fish was served.

Unknown to the girl upstairs, the boy prisoner died on June 8, 1795. The commotion that preceded and followed his death, the visits by doctors, commissioners and guards, the sawing of the skull during the autopsy, and the removal of the corpse were unheard by Madame Royale, yet at other times she remarked, in the deep silence that enveloped the tower, the moanings of Tison who, for reasons that are unknown, was kept prisoner in his room on the third floor. The boy below, we recall, had heard the sounds of logs and fagots being moved on the floor above him.

Following the official announcement of the death of Louis Charles, the Comte de Provence, who was living in Verona, proclaimed himself King of France and titled himself Louis XVIII.

The sudden death of the 'little Capet' brought a marked change in the condition of the imprisonment of Madame Royale, who became called the 'Orphan of the Temple'. On June 13th, the Committee of Public Safety informed the Commissioners of Police, who had taken control of the Temple after the fall of the Commune, that they desired to provide the daughter of Louis

Capet with a companion and it asked for a list of names of women of irreproachable character and staunch republicanism. Three days later the commissioners submitted the name of a thirty-year-old woman, Hillaire Chanterenne, the wife of a police official, whom they described:

'She herself has been reared with care, in circumstances of moderate ease. Her manners are agreeable and ladylike, and she is of good appearance. Although she has lived much in the country she is fully able to adapt herself to the conditions of town life; the circles in which she has moved, though not brilliant, have always been select.

'She speaks French well, and writes it with ease and correctness. She also knows Italian and a little English. Her time has been spent in the study of languages, history, geography, music, drawing, and in those various pursuits and amusements with which the members of her sex are accustomed to beguile their time.'

Citoyenne Chanterenne, stated the commissioners, was a general favourite in the community in which she lived and her loyalty to the Republic had never been called into question. Her appointment was confirmed by the Committee which gave orders that the daughter of Louis Capet should be provided with whatever she requested, and the control of the Temple by civil commissioners was abolished. The guard was reduced to one officer and fourteen men, and of the security men only Lasne, Gomin, two turnkeys and two gaolers remained.

From many parts of France, and particularly from Orléans, whose citizens wrote a bold letter, demands reached Paris 'to loose the fetters' of Marie Thérèse Charlotte de Bourbon, 'the hapless girl who, born to a heritage of sorrow, bereft of all consolation and help, has been brought at length to mourn the loss of all she held dear'. The Convention applauded these sentiments and the Committee of Public Safety stated that 'it felt itself impelled' to release the girl to her Austrian relatives, conditional upon the exchange of eight French prisoners, the minister and four deputies who had been abducted by General Dumorieuz in 1793, Drouet, the postmaster of Saint-Menehould, who had recognized and stopped the Royal Family on their attempted escape to Varennes in June, 1791, and who had been captured by the

Austrians, and two ambassadors who had been made prisoner in Italy.

The negotiations for the exchange occupied several months and Madame Royale was not told either of their inception or of the decision to give her a companion. In belated kindness she was provided with better clothing, 'two morning gowns of coloured taffeta, and two of pekin and cottonnade with a lining of Florence taffeta, six pairs of coloured stockings, six pairs of shoes, two dozen chemises of the finest Dutch linen, and a green silk gown', and she was given paper, paint brushes and books. She was weary of solitary confinement, she says, and so low-spirited that, if granted the society of a person who was not quite a monster, she could not forbear to love her.

She was feeling depressed on June 21st when the door of her room opened and she did not look up from her book until she heard a faint creaking sound. A young woman, elegantly dressed, her eyes brimming with tears, stood before her. Madame de Chanterenne (as she related in letters that have been preserved in her family) explained her mission, telling Madame Royale that she would live in her apartments and act as her companion. She was an instant success and from all accounts the two women got on well from the start. She had been strictly told, stated Madame de Chanterenne, not to reveal to the Princess the fate of her relatives. Either she did so, or one of the visitors who were now allowed to come, informed the girl, for she certainly knew about her bereavements by September.

Madame de Chanterenne immediately obtained permission to take her charge onto the battlements and before long they were allowed to walk in the gardens and take the air, which quickly restored the girl's health and gaiety. The two women lived together, laughing, joking and having unaccustomed fun, as far as the girl was concerned, so much so that on July 28th Madame de Chanterenne reported to the Committee:

'Citizen Representatives,

'I have deferred writing you till now in order that I might give a fuller account of my actions in my capacity as the companion, appointed by the Committee, to the daughter of Louis Capet. From the very beginning of my residence here I have had every cause to congratulate myself on the success of my measures, a success which I can affirm with confidence now surpasses all my expectations. This result I owe to the happy disposition of my companion, who is responsive to the slightest encouragement on my side. She already possesses a strength of character far in advance of her years, and all that she requires is a proper field for the development and exercise of her talents and good qualities. Her kindness of heart is united to much strength and energy of mind, while the brooding and constrained air which she generally used to display has given place to a frank and engaging sweetness of manner. Everything that can be of use to her she has at her disposal. The unremitting attentions of her guardians supply her every necessity. Since she has been taking more exercise, and her thoughts have been diverted, by frequent change of occupation, from melancholy subjects, her health has quite recovered.

'I will only add, Citizen Representatives, how greatly pleased I am with my charge, and how deeply I am indebted to you for having afforded me the opportunity of giving you some proof of my zeal, and the occasion of justifying the confidence you have placed in me.

'You have been informed, Citizen Representatives, by one of the last reports of the Citizens of the Temple, that I was absent for a few hours the day before yesterday on some private business of my own. I shall, however, never be away more often than is absolutely necessary, my principal object being to carry out your wishes and designs.

Fraternal greetings,
Hillaire Chanterenne.'

Madame Royale's ex-governess, Madame de Mackau, and Madame and Pauline de Tourzel, were allowed to visit her in September, but François Hue's request for permission was refused. He contented himself instead by frequenting a room in a house near the Temple from which he could see the Princess walking in the gardens. During the summer, she spent a considerable time each day in the gardens, reading and sketching and playing with the little dog which she named Coco or Castor, of which her brother had been very fond and which had been given to her by Lasne and Gomin. The dog became attached to her and never left her side.

Of the meeting between the Princess and her former governess, the *Messager de Soir* reported on September 17th:

'The daughter of Louis XVI was visited by Madame de Mackau, and spent a part of the day with her. Madame de Mackau, who is very aged and has suffered greatly from the effects of her long imprisonment, appeared ill and very feeble, and the daughter of Louis XVI took her arm and passing it through her own supported her steps. Madame de Mackau carried in her hand a large white hat with which she intended to shield herself from the sun, which she found very trying, but the daughter of Louis XVI, took it from her and held it up with her unoccupied hand so that Madame de Mackau should suffer no inconvenience. Ever since this unhappy young lady has been allowed to leave the tower, she has been in the habit of walking in the garden from five o'clock till dusk. Madame de Mackau had not arranged to leave until seven o'clock, but she did not feel equal to remaining all the time out of doors. The prisoner therefore went into the tower with her and remaining at her side showed her every attention. It was just three years, one month, and one day, since Marie Thérèse Charlotte de Bourbon had last seen Madame de Mackau.'

Either Madame de Chanterenne was jealous of the renewal of old intimacies or she may have feared that the visitors might disclose the information she had been forbidden to reveal. Whatever may have been her reasons, and pique seems more probable than fear of disclosure, for that was certain to be the consequence of outside contacts, she wrote on September 12th to the Committee:

'Citizen Representatives,

'In accordance with the permission of the Committee, Citoyenne Mackau has visited Marie Thérèse Charlotte who received her with the liveliest demonstrations of pleasure, while, on her side, Madame de Mackau evinced a degree of feeling which leaves no room for doubt as to the depth of affection she entertains for her interesting pupil. The latter, Citizen Representatives, appears fully to appreciate the measures that have relaxed the stringency of her confinement, particularly with regard to the facilities afforded her for the reception and entertainment of her friends. But her feelings are now satisfied on that score, she has indeed told me as much and said that meeting any other people than those whom she now sees, would be almost a matter of indifference to her. I am therefore of opinion that it would be as well to avoid, as far as possible, any unnecessary repetitions of these emotional scenes, as they may be injurious to her health or at the very least have the undesirable effect of disturbing that serenity of mind which by appealing to her reason and her fortitude I have succeeded in producing in her. Your discretion will, of course, determine whether this suggestion, which I make in accordance with the results of my own observation, is or is not worthy of your consideration, and I have no doubt that any decision you may come to will fully conform to those kindly and humane principles, by which you are ever actuated, and of which Marie Thérèse Charlotte is so worthy an object. I cannot too often reiterate how eagerly this unfortunate young woman looks forward to the termination of her captivity, of which the kind actions of the government appeared to justify the hope. Her regard for me is equalled by the affectionate interest which I take in her, and which an acquaintance with her cannot fail to evoke.

Hillaire Chanterenne.'

Madame de Tourzel was accompanied by her daughter Pauline, who was the same age as the Princess, and she was told on her arrival by Madame de Chanterenne that 'Madame is aware of all her losses'. Yet, despite the implication of the word 'all', neither mother nor daughter seems to have been convinced that Louis Charles was really dead. They had doubted the authenticity of the official announcement and, at the Temple, Madame de Tourzel seized the opportunity, when the backs of Lasne and Gomin were turned, to inspect the registers, searching the entries relating to the boy's illness and death, before she was caught by Gomin, who flew into a violent passion, reproached her bitterly and threatened to report her action.

Madame de Tourzel commiserated with the Princess on the loss of father, mother and aunt, without referring to her brother, and Madame Royale spoke of the ill-usage he had undergone but not of his death. She appears to have disbelieved that her brother was dead and her uncertainty remained after the Bourbon restoration, when something like forty men claimed to be the lost Dauphin and the true Louis XVII.

Madame de Tourzel informed the Princess of the deaths of many of her old friends and servitors in the revolution, and she was astonished to find that the girl she had not seen for three years had become 'a beautiful woman, tall and strong, with an air of nobility'. Courageously, even at that time when the restoration of the monarchy was being openly discussed as the only remedy for France's ills, Madame de Tourzel smuggled into the tower a letter to the Princess from her uncle, Louis XVIII, and she sent her answer to Verona. The Princess was allowed to roam about the tower and she conducted the Dauphin's ex-governess up and down its winding stairs and along its corridors, showing her the rooms she and her family had occupied within both the Great and Little Towers.

Madame de Chanterenne was not alone in her jealousies, as Madame de Tourzel shows by her remarks;

'Madame de Chanterenne was not lacking in intellectual qualities, and had apparently been well educated. She knew Italian, and this had given pleasure to Madame, who had learnt it as a child. She was a skilful embroiderer, and gave lessons in the art to the young Princesses. But she had been brought up in a little provincial town where a great deal of attention had been shown her, and this had given her rather too much self-importance, and such an exaggerated idea of her own powers that she presumed to play the part of mentor to Madame, and to address her familiarly, though the latter was too good-natured to notice it. Pauline and I endeavoured by our own example to impress her with an idea of the respectful attitude she ought to adopt, but our efforts were in vain. So little notion had she of what was becoming, that she even thought she had the right to put on little airs of authority, which it pained us to behold. She was, moreover, very sensitive, and liked people to show her attention, so that she regarded us with great disfavour when it became apparent that we intended to limit our intercourse with her to the barest demands of good breeding. Madame had taken a liking to her, and nursed her with the most affectionate care during a nervous attack she had one day when we were at the Temple. She appeared to be fond of Madame, and in the circumstances it was fortunate that the latter had near her someone whom she appeared to like, and who undoubtedly possessed some good qualities.'

Madame Royale received another visitor in September, her self-styled cousin, an adventuress who called herself Comtesse Stéphanie Louise de Montcairzain, and who claimed to be the result of the *liaison* of the Prince of Conti and the Duchess de Mazarin, and who, it seems, resented the slight placed upon her by the republicans who had refused to execute her as an aristocrat. Somehow, she obtained permission to visit the Temple in order to see her 'unfortunate relative'. The Princess, who was certainly unaware of Stéphanie's existence and her claim to cousinship, greeted her with reserve until the visitor, who alone describes the meeting, made herself known. Then she kissed and embraced Stéphanie, telling her 'you have suffered many misfortunes' and announcing 'we must call you Mademoiselle Conti'. The improbability of these remarks and the certainty that Madame Royale was not deceived is indicated by Stéphanie's lament that on her return next day to the Temple she was refused admittance, and that subsequently a woman (not herself, she claims) named 'Stéphanie Louise de Bourbon' was adjudged insane and committed to the asylum of Sainte Pelagie.

Meanwhile the Emperor of Austria, Marie Thérèse's cousin, Francis II, had been calculating the advantages to be gained from procuring the girl's release in exchange for his French prisoners; her mother's dowry had never been paid; she owned, if the republicans could be induced to disgorge them, two large estates which had been the private property of Louis and Marie Antoinette, and the rich contents of the royal castles that had been requisitioned on the abolition of the monarchy. Her future husband would benefit from these riches, and Francis had a brother, the Archduke Charles. And he was not unmindful that Louis XVIII, who was hopelessly in debt, also had a nephew of marriageable age, the Duc d'Angoulême.

15

THE MARRIAGE PLANS

The negotiations for the exchange of prisoners fell into abeyance after June 30th, when it was first proposed to restore Maria Thérèse to her Austrian relatives, because the Convention lay in its death-throes. Its rump departed on October 5th and Bénezech, the new Minister of the Interior, revived the overtures to the Emperor who despatched 'ladies of the Court to the Swiss frontier to await Madame's coming'. Privately, he expressed his eagerness to receive the Princess 'who would cost him nothing'.

The Directory were equally keen to rid themselves of their embarrassing prisoner whose long confinement and terrible sufferings had awakened the sympathies of the French people, and had aroused royalist hopes: the Parisians were showing a dangerous loyalty to the tragic Princess. Concerts had been held for several weeks in a building overlooking the tower and a report, preserved in the National Archives, states 'fashionably attired men and women go to them in order to gaze at their leisure upon the girl Capet who betakes herself into the garden as soon as she is told that the royalist gathering is complete. Then the partisans of the late Court make signs of their humble devotion to her royal person'. The meticulous reporter of these manifestations of goodwill remarked that 'the daughter of Marie Antoinette' is said to reply to them 'sometimes a little haughtily', but her maid of honour 'was quick to make up for anything that might appear ungracious in the bearing of the Princess'.

Madame de Tourzel fell under suspicion and she was warned that all royalists would be treated with the utmost severity. She was detained in prison for three days and an enquiry was held, at which both Madame Royale and Madame de Chanterenne were examined; the latter was prohibited from leaving the tower, even to visit her family, a cruel injunction that brought from her a flood of protests. She informed Bénezech that she had undertaken a voluntary exile with no thought that her liberty would be curtailed. The government's displeasure, she said, had brought trouble and gloom to an abode where hitherto had prevailed, if not happiness, 'a feeling of tranquil hopefulness which was the result of my presence here, and the sedulous care I bestowed upon my charge', and she protested her loyalty to her companion 'whose affection for me is only equalled by my love for her'.

Whether or not the Directory feared a royalist rising, Bénezech visited the Temple 'in order to convey to Madame the official news of her coming release and to ask the names of the ladies she wished to accompany her'. This was a thorny problem, for both the French and the Austrians prohibited Madame de Tourzel from joining the party, and for the same reason; she was suspected of being an agent of Louis XVIII's. Instead, Maria Thérèse was offered Madame de Soucy, Madame de Mackau's daughter. Although she expressed the opinion privately that Madame de Soucy 'is entirely without brains and she speaks ill of many people', she accepted her, and stated, 'seeing how I am situated, that I am alone and utterly ignorant of the ways of the world, it is necessary that I should have someone to advise me, and there is, I think, no one better able to assist me in this respect than Madame de Sérent'. The sixty-year-old Duchess was no longer in France, she was informed. Marie Thérèse also recommended the appointment of François Hue, whom her father had commended to her, and of Gomin, 'as he it was who first mitigated the hardships of my captivity'. The names of Madame de Soucy's seventeen-year-old son; Catherine Verennes, a confidential servant; Baron, the turnkey at the Temple; and Meunier, the rôtisseur, were added to the list.

In addition to ensuring that she had suitable companions (the monarchial word 'suite' was carefully avoided) the Directory provided the Princess with a little trousseau and to prepare it in time the tower was invaded by dressmakers and seamstresses who worked day and night to make a muslin gown embroidered in gold, another of lawn with white embroidery, another of *moire satinée*, another of white satin, and another of pink velvet, the bill for which came to the staggering sum of 8,917,937 livres. At the suggestion of Lasne and Gomin, certain articles that had belonged to the late King and his son, which had been placed under seal in the Council Chamber, and the linen and gowns left by Marie Antoinette, were given to the Princess.

Marie Thérèse had become a valuable pawn in the game of European power politics. Her uncle, Louis XVIII (as it is convenient to call the Comte de Provence), viewed the plan to hand her over to the Austrians with suspicion and distrust. He had far greater need of her, for the marriage of the 'Orphan of the Temple', the young and innocent girl whose tragic fate had aroused universal sympathy, to his nephew and heir presumptive would strengthen the chances of the Bourbon restoration to the throne of France, which was not enhanced by his own unpopularity. The Austrians, believed Louis, had ulterior designs; they hoped that the Revolution had broken the Salic Law, which denied succession to a female, and they intended to marry the girl to an Archduke who would become, by right of his wife, King of France. Louis had no illusions about the Emperor, for Francis had refused to recognize his 'accession' and he had persuaded other powers to reject it. Louis could not prevent Marie Thérèse's transfer to Vienna: he could only advise and warn her of the dangers that lay ahead, and he could do that only by correspondence and through intermediaries, for he was stuck in Verona in Italy. He was as yet unaware that one of his agents, François Hue, had been denied access to the Princess, and that the other, Madame de Tourzel, would be forbidden to see her again.

In his first letter to his niece, written on July 8th and sent via Madame de Tourzel, Louis was cautious. The girl had been cut off from the world for three years, she was only seventeen and she had undergone harrowing experiences. 'Nothing,' he said, 'can repair the dreadful losses we have suffered, but I trust you will let me temper their bitterness,' and he assured her, 'regard me, I implore you, as your father, and be very sure that I love you, and shall always love you, as tenderly as if you were my own daughter.' Throwing caution to the winds, Madame de Tourzel, who brought this letter to the Temple on her first visit, encouraged the girl to answer it, though she was always watched, and she enclosed a note with Marie Thérèse's reply, 'my own life, and perhaps Madame Royale's liberty, is at stake if they should discover that she has written'. She brought Hue into the conspiracy and he wrote also, referring to the touching nature of 'this delightful meeting', and informing the King, 'that Madame Royale, who has been told of all her losses, bears them with a degree of courage and strength worthy of her august descent', which gave Louis some hint of the state of mind of his correspondent.

Marie Thérèse in her reply, commenced 'My dear Uncle', a form of address which has been taken to suggest that, on September 5th, she did not know of the death of her brother or disbelieved it, for, if Louis XVII was dead, she should have addressed her uncle as 'Sire', as she did later on.

She was touched, said Marie Thérèse, by her uncle's sentiments, and the phrase could not have been diplomatic for the reassurance of her principal relative's feelings must have come as a ray of light in the darkness of her life. Her letter reached Verona on the 18th, and all that day Louis remained closeted with his adviser, the Comte d'Avaray, and together they planned their campaign to keep up the correspondence to influence the girl for the good. They did not know the date of the proposed transfer and they were unaware that Madame de Tourzel had been banned from the Temple. As it might be necessary to intercept Madame Royale en route to Vienna, Louis sent d'Avaray to the Rhine, to join the Prince de Condé, the commander of the *émigré* forces, and he gave him letters addressed both to the Princess and to Madame de Tourzel, whom he imagined would accompany her. Though these letters did not reach their destination, they show the King's concern.

He hoped it would not be long, Louis told his niece, before he could confide to her ear alone, his words and wishes that are 'as precious as they are sacred', and offer her the care of a father. She owed her future liberty to the generous affection of the Emperor, and he no longer trembled for her fate. To Madame de Tourzel, Louis wrote more openly, for he relied upon her to impress his counsel upon his niece.

'I find it very difficult to believe in the entire disinterestedness of the Court of Vienna, and I cannot help suspecting that its apparent generosity hides ulterior motives, and a very definite plan to make me buy my niece's freedom very dearly some day. Moreover, after all that she suffered in France, it would probably not be difficult to inspire her with insurmountable aversion to her own country, which I desire above all things, to be her own country always. It is only too likely that this may happen to her in Vienna.'

He feared, Louis told his confidante, that the Emperor would try to persuade his niece to marry the Archduke Charles, a young man 'of limited mind and deplorable health'. He had begged the Emperor, he said, to confide the Princess to his own care, but his entreaties had been ignored. Louis omitted to mention that the young Archduke, though ugly, carried the glamour of considerable martial renown, dangerous qualities that might turn the head of a young girl who was unaccustomed to the proximity of marriageable young men. Normally, as reigning King of France, Louis could have scotched any dangerous romance by withdrawing his consent to marriage to a foreign prince, but, as the titular ruler of a tiny *émigré* court, his influence could be purely persuasive.

It was necessary to advise the girl where her duty lay, and, once again, Louis chose Madame de Tourzel to speak of it. To her he wrote on September 29th:

'I am counting upon you to defeat any schemes that the Court of Vienna may have formed, and to remind my niece perpetually that, grateful as she ought to be to the Emperor, she is a Frenchwoman; that she is of my blood and has no father but myself; that she, like the rest of my family, ought to share my lot, whether happy or unhappy; and above all that she should form no ties, nor even enter into any engagement, without my knowledge and sanction. I will say more: I have been thinking of her future happiness, of that of my whole family, and of my own, and I can devise no more certain means of attaining these various ends than by marrying her to the Duc d'Angoulême, my nephew. I know it for a fact that when the King and Queen had no other child but her, they desired this marriage. After their boys were born, it is true, my nephew was no longer a suitable match for her, and they changed their views. But I am very sure that, if they had lived and had lost their boys, they would have reverted to their first intention. I am therefore merely carrying it out.'

Louis begged Madame de Tourzel to explain his wishes to the Princess without delay, 'though it is a delicate matter to discuss with a young girl'; and he entreated her discretion, as well he might, for his reference to the wishes of Marie Thérèse's late father and mother was no more than a *ruse de guerre*, and had no substance in fact, as Louis admitted to d'Avaray. Whether or not this letter reached Madame de Tourzel, she was no longer in direct communication with the girl. Realizing that possibility, d'Avaray wrote to a friend in Paris, whom he hoped might gain access to the tower through Madame de Soucy; 'it is important to inspire the young Princess with the greatest dislike of Vienna, and to let her guess that there is an intention of marrying her to an archduke, which, over and above the unsuitability of the match, would give her an epileptic husband', and he urged, as a counter-attraction, she should be given the truthful portrait of the Duc d'Angoulême, the husband intended for her, and the only suitable match in Europe. The Princess should be encouraged, d'Avaray suggested, to demand vociferously to be taken to Rome to join her French aunts, rather than remain in Vienna with her Austrian aunts, 'whose authority she would dislike'.

Madame de Tourzel states that she made the King's views known to the Princess and that she revealed to her the late King and Queen's wishes about her marriage, but the ex-royal-governess wrote many years later, after Marie Thérèse's marriage, by which time the expression of her endeavours on the royal behalf were politic.

At eleven o'clock on the night of December 18, 1795, Lasne heard two gentle knocks on the outer door of the Tower and on opening it he found, as he expected, M. Bénezech, the Minister of the Interior, who gave him a letter saying, 'This will relieve you of all responsibility.' The letter, which Bénezech had written in his own hand, relieved Citizens Lasne and Gomin of the custody of 'the daughter of the last King', who had been handed over 'in perfect health'.

Marie Thérèse, who was accompanied by Madame de Chanterenne, was waiting in the Council Chamber when Lasne brought the news that her captivity was over. With her joy there were mingled tears, for it was the moment of parting from her 'dear Renète', as she called her companion. As she embraced Madame de Chanterenne, she stuffed into her hand the account she had written of her captivity. Ten years later, the recipient sent it to Madame Royale at Mittau and she made a few corrections and took a copy before returning it via Cléry to Madame de Chanterenne, who kept it until her death in 1836. The incomplete copy made by Madame Royale was published in 1817. The original manuscript passed to Madame de Chanterenne's grandson, who gave it to the Duchesse de Madrid, who allowed it to be published in 1863.

The two women were still embracing when Bénezech entered the Council Chamber and 'Madame took a step forward as if to pass out, then suddenly cast herself once more into Renète's arms'. Then with a brisk step she left the tower, and with Bénezech at her side walked across the courtyard and passed out of the gates. The guards stood motionless; the officer on duty saluted. For a moment Marie Thérèse hesitated, looking up at the Great Tower with tears in her eyes, and then taking Bénezech's arm, she stepped into the street.

The Minister and Princess entered the waiting carriage and were driven to the rue Bonday behind the Opera, where the travelling coach with its lamps burning awaited under the trees. Bénezech introduced the Princess to her escort, his secretary the fifty-year-old Captain Méchain, whom he said would pose as her father. Within the coach she found Madame de Soucy and Gomin took another seat. Hue, the servants, Madame de Soucy's son, and her dog would follow in another coach, Madame Royale was informed. A mounted courier stood ready to lead the way. M. Bénezech shut the carriage door, bowing, hat in hand. 'Farewell, Madame,' he called, 'and may you be restored to your own country; you and all those who are able to bring it happiness,' disclosing his secret royalist sentiments. It was midnight, and the girl's eighteenth birthday.

The great travelling berlin, drawn by six horses, lumbered through the streets of Paris and took the turnpike for Basle in Switzerland, where the exchange of prisoners would take place. Changing horses at the post-houses, the coach travelled slowly, halting for breakfast at Guignes and for dinner at Nogent-sur-Seine, where a crowd of spectators, warned by an officious traveller, an officer of dragoons, had collected to welcome the Orphan of the Temple, as Madame Royale informed Madame de Chanterenne in a letter describing the journey. Day after day, the coach travelled on, its passengers lodging at night at inns, avoiding large towns. A delay occurred at Troyes, for there were no fresh horses available; M. Carletti, the Tuscan Ambassador, travelling ahead had taken them, stated the post-house officer, who remarked that 'every nag in the place' had been taken by 'that confounded linen draper', the name he bestowed upon M. Carletti, whose carriage looked like a hawker's cart, loaded with packages. The royal coach caught up with Carletti at Vendeuvre, where he was forced to relinquish his horses.

At Chaumont the incognito was again revealed and the rumour that the Orphan of the Temple was lodging at the Hôtel de la Poste brought the excited townspeople flocking. The Town Council was at once convened and the Mayor was instructed to wait upon the Princess 'as a mark of respect and sympathy'. Méchain's protests that the girl was his daughter were of no avail and the crowd cheered the Princess, weeping with joy at her delivery from prison and with grief on her departure. When the coach rolled away, the proprietress of the inn, Madame Royer, put on exhibition the utensils the Princess had used for her breakfast. 'How different it all is from Paris, and oh, what joy and what pain it brings me,' Marie Thérèse told Madame de Chanterenne. Her heart was full and she asked, 'Why did not this change come sooner? I should not then have seen all my family perish and so many innocent ones besides.' Lest perhaps her dear Renète feel jealous of her new friends, Marie Thérèse lamented that she had been taken away from her, and 'this woman', meaning Madame de Soucy, had been forced upon her instead. 'I have need,' she cried, 'of someone in whom to confide, someone whom I love and to whom I can unburden my heart.' She did not know Madame de Soucy well enough to tell her all she felt. Gomin, she said, 'is most attentive. He puts himself to a lot of trouble and does not allow himself time to eat or sleep.' Captain Méchain was kind but nervous, and forever on thorns 'lest the émigrés should kidnap his Princess or the terrorists put her to death'. She disliked his familiarity in calling her 'daughter' and she on her part always addressed him ceremoniously as 'Monsieur'. The deception was pointless, for everywhere the people addressed her as 'Princess'.

Heavy rains, which churned the roads into quagmires, delayed the coach's progress and it did not reach Huningen on the Rhine, the last outpost on French soil, until December 24th, and the travellers bedded down in the Hôtel de Corbeau, in preparation for the final stage of the journey to Basle. Late that night they were caught up by the second coach, carrying the servants and the trousseau, which had left Paris ten hours after the royal conveyance. December 25th, Christmas Day before the revolutionaries had abolished the festival, was a day of hail and farewell. Hue presented himself at the Princess's door, holding the dog Coco in his arms and, as Marie Thérèse informed her friend Madame de Chanterenne in a letter she wrote that night, 'before his name could be announced', and unrestrained by considerations of etiquette, Coco jumped from Hue's arms, scrambled through the half-open door, and threw himself upon her, displaying such joy at being restored to his mistress that she thought he would die for want of breath. 'Coco, my beloved Coco, is sleeping in a corner near the fire,' she told her friend at the end of her letter. But not without an unhappy incident, it seems, for some unkind person (the British Minister, Mr Basil William Wickham, reported to the Minister of Foreign Affairs) called it a 'hideous little dog' and advised its mistress that it would be easy to get a nicer one, whereupon Marie Thérèse dissolved into tears and cried, 'I love him, he is all I have to remind me of my brother.'

Baron and Meunier brought news of Madame de Chanterenne whose grief at the parting had been terrible, and next day Gomin, on his return to Paris, carried the Princess's letter to her friend, in which she said 'There is talk about my marriage, which it is declared will take place shortly. I trust it will not be so. But I know not what I am saying. It is being said that I shall be married within a week.' Captain Méchain sent messages ahead to warn the French Minister, M. de Backer, that he was ready to carry out the transfer of prisoners. De Backer went at once to Huningen, where he found the Princess only slightly fatigued by her journey, regretful at leaving France, and seeming to be little attracted by the honours awaiting her in Vienna.

At the Princess's request, de Backer sent a seamstress who brought a selection of bonnets, gowns and fichus, from which she made a selection, distributing others to the female members of the party. She informed de Backer that she was not paying for them, as she had no money, and directed that the account should be sent to the government of France. De Backer did so, and he made final arrangements for the exchange of the prisoners on December 26th on Swiss territory, at the village of Richen, and thither the French prisoners and their servants, twenty people in all, were taken. The exchange required skilful handling, for it was necessary to prevent such confirmed Jacobins from meeting the Princess face to face, and the neutral Swiss demanded that both parties should be treated with equal deference. To overcome these difficulties, Boucart, the Burgomaster of Basle, persuaded the worthy merchant, M. Reber, to loan his country house for a few hours.

On the day appointed for the exchange, de Backer reached Huningen at six o'clock in the afternoon and the Prince de Gavre, the Emperor's special envoy, who was accompanied by the Austrian Minister in Switzerland, Baron de Degelmann, went to M. Reber's house, the gates of which were guarded by a detachment of mounted police to hold back any curious spectators who had been able to leave Basle before the city's gates were closed.

Escorted by Méchain and de Backer, and a contingent of French Dragoons, Marie Thérèse entered her coach, which drove to the frontier, where the French guards fell behind and a body of Swiss Cavalry took over. The coach proceeded to Reber's house and she was taken into the drawing room. De Backer formally identified the Princess, telling de Gavre, 'I am instructed to hand over to you Madame Royale of France.' The girl's eyes filled with tears and she exclaimed, 'I shall never forget that I am a Frenchwoman.' Stepping forward, the Prince de Gavre told her that 'he was authorised to assure her in the name of the Emperor of the kind sentiments entertained towards her by the House of Austria and the cordial welcome awaiting her in Vienna'. I am fully sensible,' replied the Princess, 'of His Imperial Majesty's kindness, which doubtless the blood of our common ancestry has prompted in him', a spirited and perhaps carefully composed remark that contrasted with the Emperor's callousness in abandoning Marie Antoinette to her fate.

The ceremony was completed shortly after 7 p.m. and the Princess was taken to another room, where she was given refreshment, while the French prisoners were relieved of their parole and handed over to de Backer without Marie Thérèse becoming aware that one of them, the postmaster Drouet, was he who had betrayed her father on his flight to Varennes in 1791. Captain Méchain took the Frenchmen to Huningen where the five Jacobin deputies were greeted; 'we lose an angel and they give us five monsters'. (They were fortunate men, for in 1795 they were the only prominent politicians to keep their heads on their shoulders.) On reaching Paris Méchain was rewarded with 10,000 francs in cash for 'the zeal and prudence with which you have carried out your mission'. The turnkey Baron returned to Paris and Gomin to the Temple, where he collected the salary due to him. He disappeared until 1815, when Madame Royale appointed him concierge at the Château Meudon.

The Prince de Gavre escorted the Princess to her carriage, on to which had been loaded her luggage and the packages containing her Parisian trousseau. She asked Hue to have these packages removed, and she told de Backer, 'I am grateful to M. Bénezech for his kindness but I am unable to accept anything.' The Princess's last minute refusal to accept the trousseau placed de Backer in difficulty. How could he explain the rejection of the gift. He surmounted it with diplomatic subtlety: strict Austrian etiquette, he informed the Directory, dictated that a foreign princess be stripped of her attire, even down to the chemises she wore, on arrival at the frontier.

Marie Thérèse entered the Austrian carriage at 9 p.m. She was driven through Basle, where the people had gathered on the beautiful moonlight night to wave and acclaim the Princess on her way to freedom; at the Porte Saint Jean a French *émigré* leapt on to the carriage step and tried to speak to the Princess, but he was forced to relinquish his hold as the coachman whipped up the horses.

The *cortège* bringing the precious prize entered Austrian territory on December 30th. The French *émigrés* who tried to pay court to their Princess en route were repulsed and at Innsbruck Marie Thérèse met her cousin, the Archduchess Elizabeth ('the sternest, the most awe-inspiring, and the most intellectual of the Princesses', according to the Baronne du Montet) who, to her surprise and indignation, at once touched upon the subject of her marriage to the Emperor's brother. More happy was her reception by her great-uncle, the Elector of Treves, and his sister, Princess Cunegonde, who undertook to transmit a letter privately to Verona.

His niece's opening statement, 'I am impatiently awaiting any orders that my King and uncle may be good enough to give me with regard to my future conduct', must have brought relief to the anxious Louis whose joy would have been increased as he read, 'I assure my uncle that, whatever may happen, I shall never dispose of my future without your knowledge and consent'. Her next paragraph may not have been so pleasing: 'I ask my uncle's forgiveness for the French who have gone astray, and entreat him to pardon them', for Louis had not a forgiving character.

In one sense his niece's letter came as a shock to Louis, for her statement showed that she had not received the advice he had transmitted via Madame de Tourzel. It was too late now to tread cautiously and in his reply Louis made his wishes clear. He would, he said, send a copy of her letter to his brother (the Comte d'Artois) and his son (the Duc d'Angoulême) 'who have long made me the confidant of their wishes and hopes in respect of you', and he asked to plead his nephew's cause for, being bashful, 'he will not perhaps see as clearly as we the engagement to which you pledge yourself in your letter'. In her answer, he begged his niece to say something 'to prove that you will feel no repugnance in accepting the husband whom your father and mother chose for you, and whom they would choose again to-day'.

Despite his confidence in his niece, Louis thought it wise to caution her about the Emperor 'who cannot be ignorant of your parents' wishes', yet 'may be intending another marriage for you'. Should such a proposal be made, he charged her to state, 'I was pledged to my cousin the Duc d'Angoulême by my own desire and in accordance with the wishes of the King, my uncle, in whose hands I have deposited my promise'.

Marie Thérèse on Austrian territory was as much a captive as she had been in the Temple. The Emperor had callously abandoned her mother to her fate without raising a finger to save her, and the Austrians had confidently predicted her marriage to the Archduke. On her arrival in Austria she was lodged in the late Emperor's luxurious suite in the Hofburg Palace, and her companions, Madame de Soucy and François Hue, were removed to an hotel and were not allowed to see her privately. The French émigrés were excluded from her presence, even Louis's representative at the Austrian Court, Cardinal La Fare. She was surrounded by Austrian relatives, all eager to influence her. Cléry only succeeded in evading their vigilance to bring her uncle's letters. 'I am closely watched,' she warned her uncle in a letter that was smuggled out of the palace by Cléry. It was a difficult situation for a young girl, one which she surmounted by strength of character alone.

His niece had indeed fallen amongst wolves, understood Louis, and he and his confidential adviser d'Avaray devised a plan to cloak her in impenetrable armour. Marie Thérèse must be induced to want to marry the Duc d'Angoulême, not solely from duty, but by desire, and to achieve that happy result they composed a romantic version of the young man's feelings; his long felt sympathy in her horrible imprisonment, his exasperation at the delay in her release, his profound unhappiness until his dear Thérèse was quit of France, his own hopes, his constancy, his regret that military service kept him from her, the object of his affection. And it was necessary to work up the young Prince's feelings which, said d'Avaray, was 'no easy matter', for he was 'of naturally cold character and temperament'. His heart needed to be fired, stated d'Avaray in his memorandum.

Louis could not be certain that his niece had received his letters and he wrote again on January 17th, giving the letter to Cléry for delivery. 'The husband I offer you,' said Louis, 'is my nephew, the Duc d'Angoulême. I know him well, I have studied his character carefully, and I am sure that he will make his wife happy.' 'Do not doubt me,' the girl replied, 'I shall always remain faithful to the wishes of my father and mother with regard to my marriage, and I shall reject the Emperor's proposals for his brother. I shall have nothing to do with them. I shall obey my uncle's orders in everything.' And she stressed, 'God will never let me be false to the illustrious blood that flows in my veins.'

'Our eyes filled with tears,' states d'Avaray, 'when we read and re-read this masterpiece that the soul and heart of Marie Thérèse had produced.' Louis was equally astonished; 'A mere child, an orphan, with no support and no weapons but her sorrows, actually proposes to frustrate the wishes of a powerful sovereign and the intrigues of a cabinet renowned for its astuteness, and to prove, before the astonished eyes of Europe, the source of the blood that flows in her veins. I have given you advice—forgive me for it. I did not really know your heart.'

Louis made an astute move. Marie Thérèse and the Duc d'Angoulême were first cousins and consequently came within the prohibited degrees of consanguinity, from which only the Pope could free them. Fearing that the Emperor might take a similar step in respect to the Archduke Charles, who was also the girl's first cousin, Louis wrote, asking for the necessary dispensation, knowing well that His Holiness would not grant two such reliefs in respect to the same woman. But Louis was sufficiently astute to realize that the Pope might prefer to please a reigning Emperor in preference to a deposed King: he entreated the good offices of the Bourbon King of Spain. The Holy See granted Louis's request, which strengthened the French position that had been further jeopardized by the expulsion of Madame de Soucy from Vienna. She was replaced as lady-in-waiting to the Princess by an Austrian subject, Madame de Chancelos who, though wholly devoted to the Imperial family, won Marie Thérèse's affections. She was given a household of her own, with the Prince de Gavre as her Grand Master; he secluded her from her French friends and she, on her part, shut herself off as much as she could from her Austrian relatives. The Empress, a Bourbon from Naples, was eccentric and the Imperial family, according to Goethe, were 'merely so many middle-class Germans'. Francis had fourteen children and his father had begotten sixteen; Marie Thérèse was surrounded by cousins, princes and princesses who led gloomy and joyless lives. She was forced to live in the sombre royal palace, in which every move was dictated by strict etiquette. Her cousins filled her with despair, she told her uncle; she forebore to inform him of her opinion of the Archduke Charles, other than to say that 'he is very kind but plain. I have only seen him twice', and she told Hue 'to write to the King to put his mind at rest', and to report that the Emperor 'has not mentioned a word of the matter to me'.

The Emperor had renounced the idea of the Austrian marriage, Cardinal La Fare assured Louis, and he was given permission to visit Marie Thérèse on March 6th, and on the following day he reassured his royal master, 'Madame is a French-woman, a subject, and a Bourbon.' French, she might be, but nevertheless, Marie Thérèse rejected the overtures of the émigrés, deeply paining the Duchess de Tarente, her mother's old friend, and Madame de Tourzel, both of whom she forbade to come to Vienna.

Louis had a new fear; the Emperor intended to retain his niece and refuse to give her up, and might force the odious marriage upon her as the price of her freedom; gloomy thoughts that were dispelled by the batch of variously dated letters he received from his niece in March, in the earliest of which she pledged herself to marry the Duc d'Angoulême 'with all my heart'. She preferred that marriage to any other, even to her imperial cousin if it was offered. Her second letter said that Madame de Soucy, before she left Vienna, had seen the Emperor in private. She had told him that the Princess's parents had wished her to marry the Duc d'Angoulême and he had replied that he much approved of the match. Nonetheless, Marie Thérése blamed Madame de Soucy for her presumption in discussing the delicate matter. 'The approval of the Emperor pleases me, but it does not surprise me,' replied Louis, now finally relieved from his anguish. His last suspicions gone, he wrote to the Emperor, expressing his desire to celebrate the marriage of 'this precious child', and requesting her release to her loving uncle.

The wedding was delayed for three years. In April 1796, the French brought pressure to bear on the Venetians to expel Louis from Verona, and he was forced to wander until, on May 4, 1799, the Czar Paul I granted him asylum at Mittau in Courland (one of the Russian Baltic provinces), where Louis was able to set up an imposing little Court. He called his nephew to him and he sent for Marie Thérèse. The journey across eastern Europe took her a month and she arrived on June 3. She married her cousin, the son of Comte d'Artois, who was three years her senior, seven days later in the great hall of the palace. The Cardinal who conducted the service was assisted by the Abbé Edgeworth, who had attended Louis XVI to the scaffold, and amongst the guests was Cléry, the bride's father's faithful attendant. The ghosts of the Temple were well represented at the ceremony which improved the chances of the Bourbon restoration.

After the nuptial contract had been signed, Louis wrote to the Emperor requesting the belated payment to her daughter of Marie Antoinette's dowry. The Austrians refused to pay the sum on the grounds that it had been paid, and they produced a receipt. Louis declared it was a forgery and he complained that 'in the position to which Madame Royale is reduced it is ignoble and unjust to make use of such a plea to rob her of her patrimony'.

The loss of the dowry was a small recompense to pay for the great advantage Louis had gained. With the Orphan of the Temple at his side, Louis XVIII would be able to ascend the throne of his ancestors.

16
THE ENIGMA

We heard last of the boy prisoner on the second floor of the tower on January 19, 1794, when Madame Royale detected sounds which she thought indicated that her brother was being moved and which were occasioned by the removal of the Simons. Madame Royale heard no more from the floor below and she was not told of her brother's death on June 8, 1795, yet a boy lived in the tower for seventeen months. Who was he? The boy King or a substitute? That is the enigma of the Temple.

On January 19th, when Simon relinquished his charge, the boy was in good health, had been well treated, was Louis Charles, and he was the coveted magic talisman, whose possession could ensure personal safety if the Republic collapsed. The boy who died seventeen months later was of no consequence to anyone, and he appears to have been an older boy who may have been dumb. The problem of the identity of the prisoner is made more complicated by the suggestion that there were two substitutes. Louis Charles was abducted on the night of January 19th, 1794 and replaced by a dumb boy who in turn was replaced by one dying of scrofula, believes G. Lenôtre, the chief exponent of the 'substitution' theory.[1] Before proceeding it is advisable to state that few modern historians support the theory that Louis Charles was abducted from the Temple.

In 1814, Madame Simon who, following the execution of the ex-cobbler, spent eighteen years as an inmate of the hospital for incurables, confessed that 'her little Prince', as she called Louis Charles, was not dead, and that on January 19th, 1794 she and her husband removed him and another boy had been put in his place. She told her story to four nuns whose testimony was taken by the Lady Superior, a woman who, as Lenôtre remarks, 'published a methodical course of canonical law and a dictionary

[1] G. Lenôtre, *The Dauphin*, 1911.

of civil and ecclesiastical law, which does not indicate a superficial mind, easy to deceive and likely to act thoughtlessly'.

Madame Simon stated:

'On January 19th, 1794, she and her husband had brought to the Temple for their removal a vehicle containing a wicker work hamper with a double bottom, a pasteboard horse and several toys for the Prince. From the pasteboard horse they took out the child substitute for the Dauphin and enwrapped the latter in a bundle of linen which they loaded on to the vehicle with the hamper. When going out the guardians wished to examine the cart, but Simon flew into a passion and hustled them, shouting that it was his dirty linen, and so they let him pass.'

Madame Simon did not know what had become of the Prince but she was convinced he was still living.

The nuns who testified to this statement declared unanimously that, in their opinion, Madame Simon was neither insane, imbecile or a lunatic but rather 'that she possessed good sense and a good heart, that she was clean and had never been seen drunk, that she did not believe in dreams, was sincere, frank, and of good faith, that she took Communion at least six times a year, and that nobody had influenced her, because, before 1814, she never saw anybody; yet she had never erred or varied her statements'.

Madame Simon had told much the same story in 1811 to Dr. Rémusat. Hearing one of the patients complain of the regime of the hospital, he rebuked her, which drew her remark 'Ah, if my children were only here they would not leave me without assistance.' When the doctor again rebuked her, she said, 'Oh, you don't know of what children I am speaking. I mean my little Bourbons, whom I love with all my heart,' and she explained, 'Yes, I was the governess of the children of Louis XVI.' 'But the Dauphin is dead,' exclaimed Dr Rémusat. 'No, he isn't,' the woman answered. Recalling the conversation later, Dr Rémusat said, 'the Dauphin had been abducted on January 19, 1794. I am not quite certain whether it was in a bundle of linen or otherwise. I put other questions to her but that was all I learnt.'

On his descent to the ground floor, Dr Rémusat asked the Chief Medical Officer who that woman was, and he replied, 'She is the widow of the gaoler of the Temple.'

Madame Simon repeated her astonishing confession on yet

another occasion. When on December 13, 1814, seven months after the Bourbon restoration, the Duchesse d'Angoulême, the former Madame Royale, visited the hospital, she was not told of the widow Simon's presence and the patient was locked up in a private room until after the Princess had left. 'What a misfortune,' Madame Simon cried, 'I had a great secret to communicate to her.' Later the Duchesse returned incognito. She visited Madame Simon and listened to her story, to which she now added the statement that 'her dear Charles' had come to see her in 1802. 'How were you able to recognize him?' enquired the incredulous Princess. 'Madame, as I recognize you, notwithstanding your disguise. You are Madame Marie Thérèse.' That this interview actually occurred is attested by the Comte de Montmaur, who was then making confidential enquiries for the Duchess about a man who claimed to be the lost Dauphin, who stated that he accompanied the Duchess to the hospital.

The strange story that was being told by the woman in the hospital for incurables came to the ears of the Minister of Police who was determined to scotch it, for it was calculated to undermine the legitimacy of Louis XVIII. On November 16, 1816, Madame Simon was taken to the Ministry where she was subjected to angry denunciations. Before she became frightened and uncommunicative, she said that she would recognize the young Prince again by the scar he bore at the bottom of the jaw, where he had been bitten by a rabbit at the Tuileries. She was ordered to say nothing more in the future under pain of imprisonment. She returned to the hospital crying, 'My life is at stake', and she told the nuns that 'they had sought to intimidate her'. Madame Simon appears to have recovered from her fright, for she again repeated her assertions, telling the partisans of the pretender Charles Navarre that she had no doubt whatever but the Dauphin had been abducted and replaced by a rachitic and deformed child who had been taken from the School of Surgery. Finally, on her death-bed, on June 10, 1819 she declared, 'I shall always say what I have said,' which the nun at her bedside (whose recollection was collected by the grand-daughter of Pauline de Tourzel) interpreted to mean; 'In the presence of the sacraments and death she wished to confess the testimony which she had never ceased to render to the Dauphin's escape and to his existence'.

It is easy to dismiss Madame Simon's testimony as the babbling of a solitary old woman who after many years of confinement desired to make herself prominent, but it is a remarkable fact that she first spoke of the Prince's abduction in 1811, three years before the Bourbon restoration, when such views were highly dangerous, and she repeated it in her death-bed confession, after she had taken the sacrament. The only apparent discrepancy in her story lies in her statement that she and her husband removed their belongings from the Tower on January 19th, which conforms to Madame Royale's recollection of the noise she heard, whereas the Simons had given up residing there on January 5th. This probably has no importance for they may not have removed their possessions until the 19th, when Simon was given the discharge from his duties.

Thus, according to a self-confessed participant in the plot, Louis Charles was abducted from the Tower on January 19, 1794, and another boy was substituted for him. But if plot there was, whose was it? Chaumette and Hébert were then in undisputed control of the Temple, and of its inmates. Hébert, on his arrest on March 16th, was accused of planning 'to annihilate the sovereignty of the people, and French liberty for ever, to re-establish despotism and the monarchy', and Couthon, one of the Triumvirs, revealed in the Convention 'that they [Chaumette and Hébert] had attempted to pass into the Temple a package containing fifty louis in gold, with which to facilitate Capet's escape; for the conspirators, having formed a plan to establish a regency council, the child's presence was necessary on the occasion of the Regent's installation'. On March 14th, the *Courrier Republicain* reported that 'the Regent' had been identified. That night Chaumette was arrested, and four days later he and Hébert were replaced in their positions of supreme authority at the Commune by two other men who were nominated by the Committee of Public Safety, one of whom, Payan, was a protégé of Robespierre's. The reconstituted Commune congratulated the Committee 'on the rigorous measures taken to foil the plans of the conspirators'. On April 5th, Danton was convicted of having attempted 'the re-establishment of the monarchy'. But, apparently, according to the *Moniteur*, the plot had not been fully scotched for, when Chaumette was brought to trial on the 10th, it reported the prevalence of the conspiracy 'to assassinate the members of the Committee of Public Safety and other patriots and to place the little

Capet on the throne'. Chaumette's behaviour while awaiting trial suggests that he hoped to be saved, and the *Moniteur* reported that, in various Parisian prisons, seditious and revolutionary movements had raised cries of 'Long Live the King'. Chaumette was condemned to death for the crime of conspiracy 'to re-establish the royalty and giving a tyrant to the State', and prosecutor Fouquier-Tinville declared he 'was recognized to be the author and accomplice of this conspiracy'.

If Chaumette and Hébert conspired to re-establish the monarchy, it is logical to conclude that they plotted to secure the person of Louis Charles, and that they may have carried out the abduction. Whether or not the boy King had been removed from the Temple, by April 1794 Robespierre and his friends had become the inheritors of the magic talisman.

Dangerous as it is to base a hypothesis upon a hypothesis, there seems to be some corroborative evidence to suggest that the boy inhabiting the second floor of the Temple after January 19th was not Louis Charles. No new guardian was appointed to succeed Simon, and the life of the imprisoned boy became enshrouded in silence. No reference was made to him at the meetings of the Commune, whereas, previously, he had been the subject of almost daily comment.

So impenetrable did the silence become that it gave rise to the royalist tradition that, following Simon's removal, the boy prisoner was walled up in his room and condemned to live in the solitary isolation that resulted in his death from neglect seventeen months later. But, as M. Lenôtre observes, there is no trace in the Archives either of an order to 'wall up' the boy, or of any record that such work was carried out, or that he was ill-treated. Four commissioners came daily to the tower and many of them had served there before, and had been charmed by the intelligent little boy; yet no municipal representative protested against such vile treatment of an innocent child. Nor did any of the guards who stood duty in the tower. Between January and May 1794, Antoine Simon served as a commissioner on five occasions without protesting against the treatment of the boy whom he had declared he loved like a son.

And the boy himself? Up to January 1794, Louis Charles is said to have been robust, outspoken, vivacious, and playful, and expert and attentive doctors had been called in to treat his slightest ailment. Would not the terrified child have protested, cried, wept, and hammered on the door, if he had been suddenly subjected to complete isolation and condemned to light his own fire and live in filth and degradation? In the sonorous tower, his cries would have been unmistakable, yet neither Madame Royale nor anybody else appears to have heard them.

The boy was not entirely sequestered. On February 15th and 29th, workmen entered 'the little Capet's room', to fix a piece of white glaze, twenty-two inches by twelve inches, in the frame of the partition above the stove, to clean the stove and to replace the stove pipes 'inside the whole length and outside the whole height of the tower'. 'Besides,' remarks M. Lenôtre, who examined detailed plans of the interior of the tower, 'sequestration in a single room was impossible.' If the boy was imprisoned in Cléry's old bedroom, where tradition places him, he must have used the corridor to gain access to the water-closet in the southern turret, and if he was given the use of the whole floor, the famous wicket by which the gaolers communicated with him must have pierced the outer door on the staircase. How then did the eight or nine-year-old boy light and replenish the porcelain stove in the ante-room?

'We are led to this deduction,' remarks M. Lenôtre, 'either the sequestration was not as absolute as pretended, or else its object was to hide the fact that the victim of so rigorous a measure was no longer the Dauphin.' If the boy was buried in a dark room, it was because they dare not show him. 'And thus arose the belief in some substitution or other; for the parties who were quarrelling over the little King had too great an interest in publishing his presence in the tower of the Temple to hide him in that way and thereby authorize suspicions and doubts which would diminish the value of the hostage they all coveted.'

The boy who was held prisoner in the Tower after January 19th was not the Dauphin, concludes M. Lenôtre. Chaumette and Hébert, with the help of the Simons, had spirited him away in order to make him King. They abducted him and hid him so secretly that no one could find him.

After their deaths, the prisoner on the second floor of the tower was enshrouded in silence until May, when a municipal representative named Crescend was denounced by his colleagues for having 'offered himself very often for duty at the Temple, although his turn had not come, and had been moved to pity by the lot of Charles Capet, pretending that this child had been badly brought up'. Crescend, who had seen and talked with the boy, did not remark any deplorable condition of his imprisonment.

Robespierre was now master of France and of the Temple, and one of his first acts was to visit the tower and inspect the prisoners. He held the trump card, for he possessed the little King, the talisman which could save him from destruction, the hostage with which to win the co-operation of the foreign powers who threatened France. And Robespierre, according to the British spy, planned to possess himself of the King, and make his personal treaty with the powers. The spy states that 'on the night of May the 23rd to 24th, Robespierre went to the Temple to fetch the King to take him to [the Château de] Meudon.' An abduction that may have necessitated the use of 'opium', the word that Robespierre, we recall, scribbled in his note-book. 'Later,' says the spy, who had infiltrated himself into the secret councils of the Committee of Public Safety, 'the King was brought back to the Temple on May 30th.'

Robespierre abducted the boy and within the week returned him to the Temple. Why? Because, thinks M. Lenôtre, he discovered that he wasn't Louis Charles. Robespierre had been forestalled by Chaumette and Hébert, who died without disclosing their secret. From that moment Robespierre went into political decline. He deserted the meetings of the Committee of Public Safety and abandoned his duties, foreseeing the collapse of his regime, because he had lost the magic talisman.

On July 28th, the day preceding Robespierre's fall, according to the *Moniteur*, Dorigny, the municipal representative of the Popincourt Section, told his fellow citizens 'you would be very astonished if, tomorrow, a King were proclaimed to you.' Robespierre died speechless; the injury to his jaw resulting from his attempt to take his own life prevented him, if he had so willed, from disclosing the secret of the Temple—that the boy prisoner was not the little Capet. During the night of 9th Thermidor, the rumour spread through Paris that the young Prince had escaped. The inheritor of the magic talisman did not lose a moment in ensuring that the boy King was still in the Temple. On July 30th, at six o'clock in the morning, General Barras went there, demanding that the son of Louis XVI be shown to him. Significantly, it was Barras's first act as the new Master of France.

Barras, in his own memoirs (the version edited by M. Georges Durny) states 'I was at the Temple and found the young Prince in a cradle-shaped bed in the middle of his room. He was in a sound sleep and woke with difficulty. He was wearing trousers and a grey cloth jacket. I asked him how he was and why he did not sleep in the big bed. He replied: "My knees are swollen and pain me at times when I am standing. The little cradle suits me better." I examined his knees and found them very swollen, as well as his ankles and hands. His face was puffed and pale. After asking him if he had what was necessary and having advised him to walk, I gave orders to the commissioners and scolded them for the neglected state of the room. I proceeded to the Committee of Public Safety. Order has not been troubled at the Temple, but the Prince is dangerously ill. I ordered that he should be taken for a walk and summoned Doctor Dussault. It is urgent that you should consult other doctors, that they examine his condition and give him all the care his condition demands. The Committee gave orders in consequence.'

But nothing was done to alleviate the boy's condition and neglected state. We do not know if Barras recognized the prisoner as the son of Louis XVI. If he had been in any doubt he could have asked the boy's sister, whom he visited that day, to identify him. Barras may have been deceived. Whatever he may have thought, he changed the regime at the Temple. The Commune had been dissolved and no fresh commissioners arrived to relieve those who remained on duty for three days, until July 31st, and on that day Christopher Laurent was appointed as the children's guardian.

This twenty-four-year-old Creole from Martinique, who held the appointment of Clerk of the Court of the Temple Section, had on 9th Thermidor shown his loyalty to the Convention and to his chief, Botot the magistrate of his Section, who was Barras's secretary. Laurent was Barras's 'nomination' and he was wholly devoted to him. Yet, he did not carry out the orders that Barras says he gave. Brother and sister were not reunited, as Barras had promised, no doctor was called and Laurent would not allow the servants to enter the neglected rooms on the second floor in order to clean them. Two days after his arrival at the Temple, Laurent, on his own authority, ordered that seals be placed on Simon's papers, which had been deposited in the Council Chamber. Within this time, Laurent, believes M. Lenôtre, had discovered that his charge was not the Dauphin, and he at once informed Barras. Laurent's interference with the late citizen Simon's papers is otherwise inexplicable, claims the principal exponent of the theory of the Dauphin's abduction.

To Barras the news came as an astonishing revelation; he had been forestalled. He ordered Laurent to remain day and night in the tower, and he only held the keys and had the right to visit the prisoners. A new steward, Andre Liénard, was appointed on July 31st to replace Lilièvre, who had been arrested.

Laurent saw Madame Royale daily, and she states that 'He gave my brother baths and washed away the vermin with which he was covered', that he procured him a new bed, which he brought down from the floor above, and her brother was 'always alone in his room' and 'remained thus during the whole summer'. Laurent visited the boy three times a day, but did not dare to allow her to meet him. Laurent could not have feared compromising himself, for Barras had given that order. He could not allow the girl to see the boy because he was not her brother, concludes M. Lenôtre. No one but Laurent saw the boy, and he kept his prisoner in such close seclusion that the people of his section complained that he had lost their confidence and they considered it 'impolitic and even dangerous that such a man should remain entrusted with the custody of Capet's son'. These remarks so angered Laurent that he reported to the Committee of Public Safety, that if injustice was done him, he would resign the post 'which he had in no way sought'. Laurent redoubled his vigilance with the result that the soldiers on guard complained that they did not know 'whether they were guarding stones or anything else'.

Faced with the discovery that the boy King had been abducted, and that another boy had been substituted for him, Barras made secret enquiries throughout France to discover his whereabouts, in the hope of finding him before the scandal became known, and, believes Lenôtre, in order to cover up the original and clumsy substitution, he determined to replace him with another substitute, one still more taciturn than the first. And that he did sometime prior to August 31st, because on that day the Temple was visited by two delegates of the Directory, André Dumont and Goupilleau de Fontenay, who came to inspect the Temple to ascertain if 'its tranquility and safety had been in no way troubled' by the explosion of the Grenelle powder-magazine which had shaken all Paris. According to Laurent, who reported their visit to the Convention, 'they ascertained the existence of the two children of Capet', and gave orders to double the guard, and Laurent benefited by their inspection to demand an authorization 'to introduce trustworthy men into little Capet's apartment, in order to clean it and rid it of the vermin occasioned by neglect'.

Goupilleau inspected the prison again two months later, and he was accompanied by his colleague, Reverchon, who came again on December 19th in company with Harmand. These men saw the boy prisoner and they would have been struck with the dissimilarity if they had seen the original substitute. After December 19th, Laurent was given an assistant and M. Lenôtre concludes that the second substitution therefore took place before August 31st, while Laurent was alone on guard.

Difficult as it is to stomach the idea of two substitutions, or even the necessity for the second one, to cast doubt on it, claims M. Lenôtre, 'it would be necessary to reject a document the authenticity of which it is difficult to contest, and which is no other than the report of a secret meeting of the Directory (published in full by the *Revue Historique*) in the course of which we see the Directors, Carnot, Rewbel, La Revellière, Lepeaux, Letourneur and Barras, talking of the abduction of the Dauphin as an established fact and approved by all'. At this secret sitting the Directors spoke of a banker named Petitival, who had backed them financially to overthrow Robespierre, and who had been entrusted by Louis XVI, through M. de Malesherbes, with the care of collecting sums due to the Royal Family. In return for his financial assistance, Petitival had extracted the promise that the Dauphin should be sent to live with him at the Château de Vitry-sur-Seine, and Barras and his friends had consented, on the condition that the child should always remain at the disposal of the Convention and that precautions be taken to prevent his abduction. In other words, Petitival and his banker friends had demanded the boy King's deliverance as the price of their aid, and their condition had been accepted for, as La Revellière said, 'it was contrary to the republican principle to imprison the children of Louis XVI and they ought not to make these children suffer for the faults of their parents'. Their imprisonment could not last for ever and they were under no obligation to bring it to an end. 'I have a strong dislike to the persecution of women and children,' declared Rewbel. The Directors clearly intended to transfer publicly the royal children to a more salubrious abode. Yet, in their memoirs, which were published after the Bourbon restoration when such sentiments and such a decision would have been applauded, neither La Revellière nor Carnot made any reference to the momentous decision taken at this second meeting of the Directory. Did they keep quiet because the transfer of the Dauphin to Petitival proved a fiasco?

Was a boy handed over to Petitival, and did the banker recognize that he was not the Dauphin? If so, he may have thought that he had been tricked by Barras, but agreed to hush up the scandal. He appears to have believed that a substitution had taken place for on January 22, 1795, his client, Cambacères, declared in a speech before the Convention that he had been charged, 'in consideration of the payment of the sum of 95,000 livres to occupy himself with the son of Louis XVI and to prove the substitution judicially, and to restore to the little King his legal existence', and after the official announcement of the Dauphin's death, Petitival, according to the *Revue Historique*, 'endeavoured to obtain the cancellation of a death certificate which he declared was a forgery'.

During the night of April 21, 1796, all the inmates of the Château de Vitry were murdered; Petitival's skull had been shattered, his mother-in-law's throat had been cut, two women guests and two lady's-maids had been killed by sabre cuts, and Petitival's valet had been struck down on the steps leading to the front door. Altogether 'eight or nine persons had perished' reported the newspapers. Several servants, one of them carrying a young boy, Petitival's son, escaped, passing through the band of assassins who had stolen nothing. The incident was barely reported in the newspapers, and it came up for discussion at the meeting of the Directory that was held on April 28th, when the Directors agreed unanimously that Petitival had been murdered by representatives of the Convention who killed him to hush up their swindles. 'Petitival' it was said 'has been killed, not only in order to avoid the payment of debts due to him but also in order to seize documents he possessed and prevent revelations.' Powerful men had decided on the banker's death, it was agreed.

Barras told his colleagues 'the lady's-maid who looked after the *child you know* had her head cut off.' The Directors were unconcerned with the fate of this child, and, if he was the boy who had been brought from the Temple, it is probable that Petitival sent him away when he discovered the deception. Who murdered Petitival and his family is a mystery.

That either the Dauphin, or his substitute, was abducted from the Temple about this time, or at least that plots were hatched to rescue him, is corroborated by the story of the English Lady Atkyns who, it is thought, may have visited the Queen at the Conciergerie and promised to save her son. Charlotte Walpole, who was born in the county of Norfolk in 1758, became an actress at Drury Lane Theatre and married the Baronet Sir Edward Atkyns in 1779. With him she visited France where she fell under the spell of Marie Antoinette and, after her execution, she spent a fortune, as much as 80,000 pounds it has been suggested, in trying to deliver the Dauphin, recruiting into her conspiracy two devoted royalists, Comte Louis de Frotté, the promoter of the insurrection in Normandy, and Baron de Cormier. One of the conspirators penetrated into the Temple in order to secure the assistance of Laurent who, however, refused to be bribed; escape routes were planned and ships were hired to stand by on the Normandy coast to carry the boy to England.

Lady Atkyns was informed that the expenditure of further money was unnecessary. 'I must write to you in haste,' Cormier told her in October, 1794. 'I believe I am able to assure you, declare to you positively that the *master* and his *property* are saved. I can give no details.' This letter was followed by one from Frotté who wrote, 'Cormier tells me that you are the only one to whom I can speak frankly. I speak to you as a friend whose loyalty and sacrifices I know. Everything is arranged; in short, I give you my word that the King and France are saved, and we ought to be happy'. Then, after an interval, Cormier wrote again; 'We have been deceived. That is unfortunately too certain'.

At the bottom of the letter, Lady Atkyns wrote, 'I was opposed to putting another child in the King's place. I pointed out to my friends that that might have grievous consequences and that those who then governed, after having touched the money, would abduct the august child and say afterwards that he had never left the Temple'. Lady Atkyns remained convinced, says M. Frédéric Barbey, that 'a higher power than mine took possession of him', which indicates her belief that she had been forestalled.[1] That Barras was aware of this conspiracy is suggested by his reply to his colleague, La Revellière, who asked 'Who tried to corrupt Laurent?' It was a lawyer named Lalliment 'who played in this intrigue the part of a simple commissioner'. 'They offered,' states Barras, 'a fairly large sum to Laurent who refused it, and this sum was offered to him when the child had already left the prison.' M. Barbey alleges that Laurent admitted 'our little deaf mute has been smuggled away into the palace of the Temple and well concealed', but this letter he quotes is only a copy. The conspirators either learned, it seems, that the boy had been rescued or they took possession of a deaf-mute.

The little Capet was mentioned at the meeting of the Convention on September 28th, when deputy Jourdan referred to him as 'a rallying point for the aristocracy', and other deputies called him 'the Capet foetus', and proposed that he be 'vomited' outside French territory, a suggestion that may have caused concern to those who, it is claimed, knew he was no longer in the Temple, and which led Laurent to write asking for the appointment of an assistant 'as precautions cannot be carried too far', and 'if some event should happen at this moment, I could not inform you of it myself'.

Special fears for the security of the boy prisoner were entertained in October, 1794, for two members of the Convention's Security Committee, Reverchon and Goupilleau de Fontenay, were suddenly ordered to go to the Temple and to verify the presence of the two prisoners, clearly the occasion at dead of night when Madame Royale awakened to find Laurent and two men standing at her door, who looked at her and left without saying a word. Following this visit, the Committee requested the commander of the Army of Paris to give the most severe orders 'to prevent even the appearance of the possibility of an escape'.

A succession of civilian commissioners, no one of whom was to be on duty more than once a year, was sent to the tower, and Laurent obtained his assistant, the 'tried republican' Gomin who

[1] Frédéric Barbey. *A Friend of Marie Antoinette*, 1906.

was thirty-eight years of age and had been commander of a battalion of the Fraternité Section. Madame Royale called Gomin 'a very honest man' and she says that 'the state of his little prisoner caused him so much pain that he wished to send in his resignation immediately', but he remained 'to alleviate the torments of the wretched child', whom he sought to amuse daily for a few hours. Gomin, she asserts, 'had him come to his room below, in the little drawing room, which pleased my brother very much because he liked a change of place'.

If Gomin spoke the truth, Madame Royale's statement implies that after December 19th, 1794, the boy was moved into the Little Tower, into M. Berthèlemy's drawing room which the Queen had once occupied. This move may account for the impenetrable silence that descended upon the second floor of the Great Tower, below which there was no room that could conceivably have been called a 'little drawing room'.

Harmand, the deputy from La Meuse, who was accompanied by two members of the Convention's Security Committee, Mathieu and Reverchon, visited the Temple on December 19th, although writing twenty-two years later, he mistook the date for February, 1795, and, as well as seeing Madame Royale, he went to the room occupied by the boy, which from his description appears to have been the room in the Great Tower formerly used by Louis XVI.

Harmand's description of the boy with whom he tried to converse suggests that the boy he found on the second floor of the Tower was either deaf and dumb, or was determined not to speak :

'The key turned in the lock noisily and on the door opening we saw a small and very tidy ante-room without any other piece of furniture in it than a china stove, which communicated with a neighbouring room by an opening in a partition and which could not be lighted except in that ante-room. The Commissioners pointed out to us that this precaution had been taken so as not to allow the child access to the fire. The other room was the Prince's. It was fastened from the outside and had also to be opened.

'The Prince sat beside a small four-cornered table on which were scattered a number of playing-cards; some of these were folded so as to make little boxes or pockets; others were built up in the form of a castle. He was busy with these cards when we came in and did not stop his game.

'He was wearing a sailor-suit of a slate-coloured material; his head was bare; the room was clean and well-lighted. His bed consisted of a little framework of wood; the mattress and linen seemed quite good.

'I approached the Prince. Our movements seemed to make no impression on him. I told him that the Government had been too late informed of the sad state of his health as well as of his refusal to take any exercise or to answer either the questions which were put to him or the proposal that he should take certain medicines and be examined by a doctor; that we had now been sent to him to obtain confirmation of these facts; and to repeat these proposals to him in the Government's name; that we hoped that he would assent to them, but that we took the liberty of advising him, even of warning him against keeping silence longer and taking no exercise; that we were empowered to give him the opportunity of extending his walks and of offering him whatsoever he might wish to distract him and help him to regain his health; and that I begged him to give me his answer, if he so pleased.

'While I was in course of making this little speech to him he gazed blankly at me without changing position; he was openly listening to me with great attention, but he gave no answer.

'I therefore repeated my suggestions as though I thought he had not understood me aright, and I explained them to him somewhat as follows: "It may be that I have expressed myself badly, or that you, Sire, have not understood my meaning, but I have the honour to ask you whether you would maybe desire a horse or a dog, a bird, or a toy of any sort, or one or two companions of your own age, whom we would present to you before they took up their abode here. Would you care now to go down into the garden or up the tower? Would you like sweetmeats, cake, or anything of that sort?" I endeavoured in vain to suggest to him all the things which a boy of his age might covet, but I got not a single word or answer from him, not so much as a sign or movement, although he had his head turned towards me and gazed at me with a most astonishing fixedness, which seemed to express complete indifference.

'I therefore allowed myself to take a more emphatic tone, and ventured to say to him: "Sire, so much obstinacy at your age is an unpardonable fault; it is all the more astonishing since our visit, as you see, has the purpose of making your residence more agreeable and of providing care for the improvement of your health. If you continue to give no answer, and do not say what you desire, how can we attain our end? Are there any other means of making these suggestions to you? Be so good as to tell us and we will arrange ourselves accordingly."

'Always the same fixed gaze and the same attentiveness, but not a single word.

'I began again: "If, Sire, your refusal to speak only touched yourself, we would wait not without concern but with resignation until it pleased you to break silence, since we must draw the conclusion that your situation displeases you less than we supposed, as you do not wish to leave the Temple. But you have no right over yourself. All those who surround you are responsible for your person and condition. Do you wish to compromise them? Do you wish to compromise ourselves? For what answer can we give the Government, whose agents we are? Have the kindness to answer me, I beseech you, or we shall be compelled to order you."

'Not a word. Always the same immobility. I was on the verge of desperation and my companions also; that look in particular had an extraordinary expression of resignation and indifference, as though it seemed to say: "What does it matter? Leave your victim in peace."

'I repeat, I could not go on; I was near to breaking out in tears of the bitterest sorrow; but I took one or two paces up and down the room, recovered my calm, and felt myself impelled to see what effect a command might have. I made the attempt, set myself quite close beside him on his right hand and said to him: "Be so good, Sire, as to give me your hand." He gave it to me and I felt it up to the armpit. I found a kind of knotted swelling on the wrist and another at the elbow. These swellings apparently gave him no pain, since the Prince seemed to feel nothing. "The other hand, Sire." He gave me that, too, but there was nothing there. "Allow me, Sire, to examine your legs and knees as well." He got up. I found similar swellings on both knees and in the hollows behind the knees.

'In this condition, the Prince showed symptoms of rachitis and deformation. His thighs and legs were long and thin, and the arms also. The upper part of the body was very short, the breast-bone very high, the shoulders high and narrow; the head was very handsome in all its details, the hair long and fine, well kept and light-brown in colour.

' "Now, Sire, have the goodness to walk a little." He complied at once, walked to the door which lay between the two beds, came back again at once and sat down. "Do you consider, Sire, that that is exercise? Do you not rather see that this apathy is the cause of your sickness, and of the ills which threaten you? Be good enough to believe in our experience and our zeal. You cannot hope to restore your health if you do not follow our wishes and advice. We shall send you a doctor, and we hope that you will answer his questions. Give us at least a sign to show that you consent." Not a sign, not a word.

' "Be so kind, Sire, as to walk about once again, and for a little longer." Silence and immobility. He remained sitting on his chair with his elbows propped on the table; the expression on his face did not alter for an instant. There was not the slightest move-ment to be seen in him, not the slightest surprise in his eyes, just as if we had not been there and I had not spoken.

'My companions had kept silence; we were looking at one another in astonishment and were just about to exchange our opinions when his dinner was brought in. Another pitiful scene followed; one must have seen him to have an idea of it.

'We gave orders in the ante-room that the disgusting diet should be altered in the future, and that from that day some dainties, such as fruit, should be added to his meals. I wished that he should be given some grapes, as they were rare at that season. As soon as the order had been given we returned. The Prince had eaten up everything. I asked him whether he was pleased with his dinner? No reply. Whether he liked fruit? No reply. Did he like grapes? No reply. A moment later the grapes were brought and set on the table before him. He ate them with-out saying a word. "Would you like some more?" Still not a word. "Do you wish, Sire, that we should go away?" No answer. After this last question we went out.'

The three delegates spent a quarter of an hour in the ante-room, 'exchanging their reflections' and coming to the conclusion that, for the honour of the nation and of the Convention which were ignorant of the matter, they would not make a public report, but one to their Committee only. Before leaving the Temple, Harmand ordered that the children should be re-united, and although 'the government showed the greatest zeal in carrying out the promises we made in its name and made that decree the same evening' the order was not obeyed. Harmand, who says he was entrusted with its fulfilment, was appointed Commissioner to the East Indies and left France within a few days, which may have been a way of silencing him. Even in 1814 Harmand employed veiled terms to describe the condition of the boy whom he may not have wished to suggest was other than the young Prince, for such a suggestion might have been interpreted as a threat to the legitimacy of Louis XVIII.

Harmand's description of the boy with whom he failed to converse harmonizes with the statement made in 1814 before the Tribunal of the Seine (in connection with a pretender's claim) by Lasne, who succeeded Laurent on March 31, 1795, that 'the Prince showed an extraordinary impassivity; he uttered no complaint and never broke the silence'. On another occasion he stated that the prisoner spoke once, during the last days of his life. Gomin, on the other hand, said in 1834 that the prisoner spoke daily and always on serious and lofty subjects and that 'these conversations left a profound impression upon my memory'. One of the two ex-gaolers was clearly lying.

The symptoms exhibited by the boy that were observed by Harmand imply a long-standing condition, the development, perhaps, of the swollen knees, ankles and hands, and puffy face noticed by Barras on July 30th. Then the boy could talk; on December 19th, he either could or would not. Six months after Harmand's visit he was dead.

If he was the boy King, how could those who stood to gain so much from his possession, and to lose so much from his death, have allowed the health of the precious talisman to deteriorate so quickly? It seems, rather, that M. Lenôtre may be correct in his opinion, that the boy who was seen on July 30 and December 19, 1794, was not Louis Charles, although his theory of the double substitution seems an unnecessary refinement. Is it not more probable that the original substitute, if substitution there was, may have been returned by Petitival when he discovered the deception?

There is nothing in the evidence to suggest that Louis Charles had been ill-treated, and it seems improbable that he would have been allowed to die from neglect. It is fair to conclude, therefore, that, on balance of probabilities if not beyond reasonable doubt, the boy who inhabited the tower durng 1794 was not the boy King, a conclusion to which the events of 1795 seem also to point.

17

THE DEATH AND BURIAL

During that winter Louis Charles became more valuable than ever before, for the Spanish Bourbons offered to make peace with France and to recognize the Republic on the condition that he and his sister were delivered to them. Yriarte, the Spanish plenipotentiary, made the position crystal clear; 'The desire at Madrid to see the prisoners of the Temple free, weighs more than any other consideration in seeking for peace. On our side it is a duty, a religion, a creed, fanaticism if you like. If we had the choice between the children of Louis XVI and the offer of a few departments bordering our frontier, we should choose the former. My instructions refer to appanages and pensions: but that is not the real question. We would receive the prisoners without condition if necessary.' And he assured the Frenchmen; 'Besides, one could, in order to reassure France, insert in the treaty a public or secret clause by which Spain undertook not to allow the children of Louis XVI to leave its territory and never to permit them to become a centre disquieting to the French Government.'

The French people were tired of the nightmare war and the Directory was eager to make peace. Several delegates to the Convention had urged the expulsion of the prisoners from French territory and the boy's deliverance would satisfy the Vendéan royalists who were still in revolt. But, apparently, the Directory was not in the position to provide the one condition essential to peace. It made the lame excuse that the boy had suffered greatly under Robespierre's control and was not yet in a fit condition to be handed over.

François Hue had his ear to the ground, and he heard that members of the Convention were saying openly, 'If, on the occasion of some popular movement, Parisians were to go to the Temple we should show them a little boy whose stupid air and imbecility would oblige them to renounce the plan of placing him on the throne.' And Frotté informed Lady Atkyns that a member of the Convention had told him; 'I must tell you the truth, because I think I may count on your discretion. Your sacrifice would be useless; you would be a victim of it and unable in any case to be of use to the son of Louis XVI. Under Robespierre they so changed the physical and moral nature of that unfortunate child that one has become entirely brutalized and the other cannot permit him to live. Consequently, give up this idea in which, in your own interest, I should very much regret seeing you persist, as things are, because you have no idea of the degeneration and brutishness of the little creature. On seeing him you would feel only sorrowful and disgusted and it would be sacrificing yourself uselessly, for you will certainly soon see him perish and, once in the Temple, *you might never come out again.*'

Whereas several people seem to have been aware of the condition of the boy, no one wrote about him at this time and we know only that in March and April, 1795, he was apparently eating well, for the steward Liénard supplied for the boy and girl, on March 21st and April 10th and 17th, two fowls, two pounds of jam and chocolate, bundles of asparagus, mushrooms, fish, and the little Capet was given four pairs of cotton stockings and a bushel of vetch for his pigeons.

On May 6, 1795, the boy was seen by one of the civilian commissioners: this man, a tradesman, told an English traveller in 1814 that he had been permitted by Lasne and Gomin, 'on the express condition not to speak to him', to enter the room where the child was in bed and in which he lay for an hour without moving. Then he asked in a weak voice who the visitor was. The commissioner made no reply, whereupon the boy raised up, put his legs out of bed and sat on the edge 'in an astonishing position', which made the visitor wonder what his stature would be if he stood up. The boy's face was covered with ulcers and pimples. He got back into bed and covered himself up, keeping silent, though several times he moved his lips as though he wished to speak, but no sound came. 'He was the most pitiable creature I have ever seen,' stated the narrator of the anecdote.

Whatever his condition had been before, the boy became seriously ill in May for on the 6th Lasne and Gomin reported to the Convention; 'The child Capet felt an indisposition and infirmities whch appeared to assume a serious character,' and in consequence, the Convention's Committee ordered Dr Pierre Joseph Desault, the chief physician at the Hospice de l'Humanité, to visit the boy, 'but only in the presence of the jailors'.

Dr Desault visited the tower several times, prescribing for the patient an infusion of hops, and ordering the massage of his joints with alkali. He made his last visit on May 29th, and he died suddenly next day on his return home after having dined with members of the Convention, a circumstance that has been given a sinister implication it may not deserve. Dr Desault's report on the boy's condition can hardly have been alarming for he was not replaced until June 5th when, by the decree of the Committee, Dr Pelletan visited the Temple. Writing in 1817, when it was wise to express sentiments of tenderness and solicitude, he related that on entering the former apartment of Louis XVI, which appeared 'clean and convenient', he found the boy surrounded by toys, such as 'a small printing plant, a little billiard table' and books, and he says that Lasne and Gomin 'lavished almost paternal care on him'. Dr Pelletan noticed that the grating of the locks and bolts on the door appeared to distress the patient and he advised that the noise should be deadened, and that the prisoner should be carried to the doorkeeper's room overlooking the garden, by which term he must have meant the drawing room in the Little Tower as that was the only room which overlooked the garden.

Retrospectively, Dr Pelletan said that 'he found the patient's stomach very enlarged and he was suffering from chronic diarrhoea', and he stated his opinion that 'unfortunately all assistance was too late and no hope was to be entertained'. That was certainly not his view in 1795, for he prescribed only a mild diet; 'The patient must breakfast at ten o'clock on chocolate or bread and currant jam. At dinner he must eat meat, soup, and sometimes vegetable soup, a little boiled, roast or grilled meat, vegetables such as asparagus, spinach, etc. In the afternoon for his *goûter*, apple, currant, apricot or grape jam, etc. For his supper, he may eat a little roast or grilled meat but especially vegetables; finally, he may be given a little salad made with lettuce, endive, chervil, cress or watercress. He may drink a little wine at his meals. He must be put to bed at nine o'clock and rise at 6 a.m.' The only medicine he prescribed, to be taken every morning, was three cupfuls of the decoction of hops 'to which must be added a table-spoon of anti-scorbutic syrup'.

The patient's removal to the room overlooking the garden by Lasne and Gomin was a success, stated Pelletan; 'the child displayed gaiety and gave himself up more freely to the interest they took in him'. Unfortunately, the doctor did not say if the boy showed gaiety by words or actions, but he appears to have been able to play with his toys and to read books, statements that little conform to the picture of the mute boy dying from neglect.

The President of the Security Committee told Pelletan, that the Committee would be pleased if no rumour or gossip concerning the boy's illness reached the public and he warned the doctor to maintain the greatest secrecy and to avoid the slightest imprudence.

Dr Pelletan came again on June 7th; he did not change the boy's diet, except that he recommended 'white bread made from pure wheat' and broth 'made with beef and chicken', though 'care must be taken that it is not acrid through too short boiling'. He prescribed also powdered rhubarb, six grains extract of quinine, four grains mixed, to be taken in a tablespoon of liquid, four *chopins* of white codex mixture, and orange flower water. Having written this prescription for Lasne and Gomin to obtain, Pelletan left, manifesting no great concern for his patient's life.

That night, Dr Pelletan received an urgent summons from Lasne and Gomin, which failed to disturb him, for he replied, 'the patient's condition cannot be made very alarming by the circumstances you have detailed to me. Although I am extremely tired with my day's work and it is eleven o'clock at night, I would leave immediately for the child's bedside if I knew I could be of the slightest use to him. Night time not being favourable for the application of any kind of remedy, I think you must confine yourself to giving the patient half a grain of discordium diluted in a tablespoonful of wine.' He would visit the patient next day, June 8th, at 11 a.m., bringing with him Dr Dumangin, the surgeon at the Charité Hospital, Pelletan said.

Nineteen years later, Doctors Pelletan and Dumangin disagreed violently about their responsibilities and the happenings within the tower. Pelletan got his blow in first, telling Antoine de Saint-Gervais, the author of *Vie du jeune Louis XVII*, that he blamed the sailors for not having removed the bolts and bars from the door and windows and that, while he was unburdening himself with warmth on this subject, the young Prince signed to him to speak in a lower voice and said, 'I am afraid that my sister will hear you and I should be very sorry if she learnt I was ill, because that would pain her.' Pelletan also said that, when his end approached, the patient, momentarily coming to himself, offered his hand which he brought to his lips, moistening it with his tears.

On the publication of the book, Dumangin wrote to Pelletan; 'Your narrative, Monsieur, has sensibly afflicted me on your account, for you appear alone, whereas common duties *constantly called us together* to the Temple. Why, sir, have you forgotten to mention me? Our bulletins, *signed by us both*, must be in the archives. I confess that, if I had been present at the time of the wording which is before me, you would have had great difficulty in detailing your reproaches to the jailors, in making your speeches, and in bestowing the kiss which I did not see you place on the hand of the dying King.' Pelletan replied reminding Dumangin that he had called at his house on June 7th and that they had agreed to visit the boy together for the first time next day. The incidents he described, he said, took place in his *confrère's* absence.

Whatever is the truth of this obvious attempt to win the sympathy of the restored Bourbons, Pelletan and Dumangin undoubtedly saw the boy on the morning of June 8th, for they ordered the continuation of the white decoction, alternating it with buttermilk, broth every quarter of an hour, and enemas evening and morning. Before the doctors left at 12.30 p.m., Pelletan reported to the Security Committee: 'We found Capet's son with a weak pulse, and an abdomen distended and painful. During the night and again in the morning he had several green and bilious evacuations. His condition appearing to us to be very serious, we have decided to see the child again this evening. It is indispensible to have a female nurse by his side.'

In his version of the day's events, Damont, the civilian commissioner on duty, relates that he entered the boy's room, and thought he was so ill that he advised the attendance of a nurse, whereupon Gomin set off to procure one, being passed on the way by the mounted courier who brought the authorization 'to place by the bedside of Capet's son an intelligent and honest woman whom the doctors would choose', an order that could not be put into effect until they returned.

Lasne and Damont remained at the bedside of the child to whom they gave the prescribed remedies. Suddenly, at about two o'clock, he came out in a cold sweat and it looked as though he was going to die. Panic stricken, Lasne and Damont sent a messenger galloping to Pelletan with the note; 'Citizen, the patient has just been seized with a most violent attack and it is of the utmost necessity that you should come to his side immediately.' Damont left the room and Lasne stayed with the boy alone for nearly an hour, during which time he was again seized with suffocation, making a sign that 'a call of nature required satisfying'. Lasne raised him up in bed, and according to Damont, 'he gave a great sigh and passed away at eleven minutes short of three o'clock'. Gomin, on his return, entered the room at that precise moment, and he was followed by the turnkey, Gourlet.

Faced with the sudden death of their prisoner, Damont, Lasne and Gomin reached two decisions, one that was entirely correct and the other equally strange. They wrote a letter which was taken by Gomin to the Security Committee, announcing the boy's death and asking for orders, and they kept his death secret from the other people in the tower. They carried on as they had done while he was alive, sending to the chemist for medicines and calling for the broth every quarter of an hour, taking the precaution to relieve the waiters of the cups at the door of the apartment, and answering their enquiries by saying 'he is doing well' and 'will pull through'. To round off the charade they entreated the waiters and the guards to keep quiet in order not to disturb the sleeping boy. They decided to do that, Lasne wrote in the register, 'in order to remove all suspicion'.

When Dr Pelletan reached the tower at 4.30 p.m., Lasne told him that he could not leave again until the Committee had decided what measures should be taken; an order that brought Pelletan's protests but not his liberation. Consumed with anger he wrote at once to the Secretary of the Committee, stating that 'he was detained by the jailors of the boy Capet'. Gomin returned from the Tuileries to say that the Committee members had decided to postpone the announcement of the boy's death until next day. He was accompanied by the Secretary of the Committee,

M. Bourguignon, who brought with him a decree which instructed Lasne and Gomin 'to inform Doctors Pelletan and Dumangin that they must call in two of their most well informed *confrères* to proceed to open the body and ascertain its condition'. Pelletan was allowed to leave, and Dumangin, who called later, was sent away, having been ordered to keep absolute silence. Lasne, Gomin and Damont kept up the charade; in turn they descended to the Council Chamber where they joined the other commissioners and guards for supper. One consideration puzzled them: what were they to say when Damont's relief arrived next day at noon? They asked for instructions from the Committee which replied that 'the service must be continued as usual unless otherwise deliberated upon'.

Next day Pelletan and Dumangin arrived at 11.15 a.m., bringing their chosen colleagues, Professor Lassus, the chief of the department of legal medicine at the École de Santé, and Professor Jeanroy, of the Paris Medical School. They entered the room in which lay the dead child, and they asked Lasne and Gomin, 'Is this child the son of Louis Capet? Is he the child given you to guard?' Both men affirmed that he was, whereupon Dumangin stated that he was indeed the sick and living child he had examined on the previous day, and he said he recognized him from having seen him at the Tuileries. The turnkey Gourlet stated that 'he had known the little Capet since his arrival at the Temple in August, 1792'. The identification was reinforced at noon by the arrival of the new commissioner, Darlot, to whom the reason for Damont's continued presence was explained. Darlot was taken up to the ante-room on the second floor, where he found 'four citizens busy writing', the four doctors writing their report, who rose on his appearance and took him into the bedroom and showed him the body. Darlot, 'who was greatly struck by the appearance of the face, which was not yet in any way disfigured', attested (and later confirmed in writing) his opinion 'that he remembered this dead child very well through having seen him walking in the Tuileries gardens, with all the pomp of the son of Louis Capet, and in the little garden where there were rabbits'.

Five people, none of whom had known Louis Charles before January 19, 1794, stated that the dead child was he. The one person who could have identified him with absolute certainty and who lived only a few feet away was not invited to view the body and she, Madame Royale, was not even told of her brother's death. Neither Baron, the turnkey, or Meunier, the cook, who had both been on duty at the Temple since August 1792, were asked to identify the body.

The news of the death of the little Capet was announced from the Tribune of the Convention about noon by Achille Sevestre, a member of the Security Committee, who stated tersely that the boy, who had been indisposed for some time, had died on the previous afternoon. The deputies remained 'dumb with astonishment', stated the *Moniteur*.

The autopsy on the dead boy was conducted by Pelletan on a table in the ante-room. He opened the body, sawed through the skull 'on a level with the socket', replaced the viscera, sponged, plugged and tightened the bandages, and, in the absence of his colleagues, surreptitiously removed 'a few precious remains'. He placed the heart in a napkin and slipped it into his pocket. He then stitched together the loose skin on the skull and wrapped it in a cloth. Damont picked up and pocketed some of the dead child's hair. The body was replaced in the bedroom at 4.30 p.m. and the doctors left, after all four had signed the following report:

'We arrived, all four of us, at eleven in the forenoon, at the outer door of the Temple, where we were received by the commissioners who led us into the tower. In a room on the second floor, we were shown the dead body of a boy who appeared to be about ten years old and who, we were told by the commissioners, was the son of the late Louis Capet. Two of us recognized the child as one to whom we had had to give attention during the previous day. The child's death must be ascribed to a scrofula of long standing.'

Damont states that the boy's death was concealed until noon next day, when two fresh commissioners arrived in order to execute various decrees concerning the boy Capet. They examined the registers and ordered that 'the event must be given the greatest publicity', though too much importance was not attached to it. They assembled the staff of the Temple, the six officers of the guard, and led them to the death chamber where they were shown the body and asked if they recognized the son of the tyrant. They said they did so and all six signed an attestation to that effect.

Following this inspection the news of the boy's death spread quickly through the Temple quarter; a report made by the police on June 12th says:

'The population of the Temple quarter say quite openly that the arrangements for the funeral of the little Capet were only a blind and that he is not dead, but has been allowed to escape and is now far away in safety.'

On the same day, the *Courrier Universel* informed its readers: 'Some contend that this death means nothing, that the young child is full of life, that it is a very long time since he was at the Temple. The authenticity of the secret and natural death of a child whom, notwithstanding all demagogic declarations, one cannot regard as an ordinary child, since, instead of running about at liberty in the streets, like the son of *sans-culottes*, a considerable armed force guarded him day and night, ought perhaps, I will not say for the honour of the Convention, but for public tranquility, to have been solemnly and publicly ascertained.'

'What astonished people,' stated a secret police report, 'was the suddenness of the decease,' for nobody knew that the Dauphin was indisposed; 'Suddenly all those people learned that he was dead. This appeared suspicious, and popular imagination was given free course.' The commissioner who arrived to replace Darlot at noon on the 10th, Querin, remarked that 'the news of the death not having been preceded by any announcement of illness, a fact which might give place to vexatious conjectures', which the two jailors, Lasne and Gomin, 'sought to divert the effect by every means which prudence suggested to them'.

Orders for the burial of the little Capet 'in the ordinary place and according to the usual forms in the presence of the number of witnesses as specified by law and supplemented by two members of the civilian Committee of the Section', reached the Tower at 4.30 p.m. Voisin, the conductor of the funeral ceremonies, who had been called, went to see Citizen Bureau, the doorkeeper of the Sainte-Marguerite cemetery, from whom he ordered 'a coffin for a young girl'. Bureau supplied a coffin of size one metre, forty-five centimetres, or four and a half feet long, or slightly less than the size (one metre, seventy-six) supplied usually for a ten-year-old child.

At 7.30 p.m., Robin, the Registrar of the Temple quarter, arrived at the tower, carrying his register, which was signed by Lasne and Gomin and by the officers on duty, who thereby declared that they recognized the deceased as the son of Louis Capet. Voisin, the funeral conductor, ascended to the second floor, picked up the corpse and carried it to the bottom of the stairs, in order not to disturb Madame Royale, where he placed it in the coffin on the top and bottom of which he inscribed in charcoal the letter 'D'. The coffin, he said in 1817, was about five feet long, 'the young monarch being tall for his age'.

Learning that a crowd of spectators had gathered, Dusser, the Commissioner of Police of the Temple Section, sent for two detachments of twenty to twenty-five soldiers and at 9 p.m. he gave the order for departure.

The coffin containing the body of the boy who had died was carried by four bearers, two of whom were relieved *en route*, and it was followed by Lasne and Gomin, two military officers, Garnier and Wallon, Quérin, the civilian commissioner on duty, Dusser, the Commissioner of Police and by another man, René Bigot, who had appeared at the tower before under inexplicable circumstances and whose presence at the prisoner's funeral is equally inexplicable, unless we accept an explanation which might perhaps solve the enigma of the dead boy's identity. At this stage, it is possible only to remind readers that this Bigot was one of the two men, who were *not* members of the Commune, who came on duty on January 21, 1794, two days after Simon left the Temple, when the substitution is claimed to have been effected. Now Bigot reappears at the boy's funeral and, after it had been accomplished, he signed the official death certificate at the Hôtel de Ville, describing himself as 'employee' aged fifty-seven, domiciled at 61 Rue Vieille-du-Temple, and declaring himself to be 'a friend of the deceased', a term that would seem to have been more applicable to Lasne and Gomin, neither of whom were asked to witness the certificate.

The crowd of curious sightseers was held back by the cordon of soldiers as the funeral *cortège*, which was preceded by eight soldiers led by a sergeant, turned into the street and marched to the cemetery of Sainte-Marguerite, which it reached at 9.30 p.m.

Speaking in 1817, Madame Betrancourt, the widow of the grave-digger, related, 'They buried him in the dusk, it was not yet quite night. There were very few people. I could easily draw near, and I saw the coffin as I see you. They put it in the common grave, which was the grave of everybody, the little and the big people, the poor and the rich. All went there because, so to speak, *everybody* was equal.'

But the common trench was not its final resting place, the widow stated. She said that early next morning her husband called her to the trench and made her descend into it, where 'thrusting his spade into several places he remarked that there was nothing underneath'. When she did not express surprise, he asked, 'Well, are you not curious? You don't even ask what has become of the coffin?' While she was hanging up her washing she saw her husband standing, leaning on his spade, 'in the attitude of one who is thinking', and later he told her that the night before he had taken the coffin from the common grave and reburied it 'in a grave dug against the foundations of the Church under the door of the left transept'.

In the official police deposition she made subsequent to this statement, Madame Betrancourt stated, 'My husband dug a separate grave, near the door of the Communion, along the wall of the Church and perpendicularly to the said wall. The grave stretched as much outside as in the wall and in its thickness, in such a manner as to be able to get half the coffin therein.'

Voisin, the funeral conductor, stated in 1817, 'I placed the coffin in a private grave which I myself had dug specially in the morning, a grave at least six feet in depth.' He filled the grave himself with earth, and some days later he went to see if the earth had been touched, but saw nothing altered. During the five further weeks that the cemetery was used, he dug only a few private graves, at a distance of about six feet from that of the young King, all of which were for people of the female sex, as far as he could recollect.

Bureau, the gate-keeper at the cemetery, stated that no special grave was dug and the Dauphin's coffin was placed in the common grave, and ex-Commissioner of Police Dusser testified in hospital that the coffin had been buried in a separate grave, and that, in consequence, he had been threatened for showing royalist sentiments.

Clearly some of these people lied, probably Voisin and Dusser who, in stating that the coffin was buried in a private grave, were actuated by the sycophantic desire to please the restored royal dynasty. Madame Betrancourt's remarkable statement seems preferable to theirs, for it would have been a strange story for her to have invented.

An enquiry was held at the cemetery in 1817 by M. Decazes, who acted on behalf of the pretender Charles Navarre, at which Voisin pointed out one site for the grave, Dusser deposed in writing to another, and Madame Betrancourt repeated her astonishing story. Further confusion was added by the declaraton of Touissant Charpentier, the head gardener at the Luxembourg Palace, who stated that he had witnessed the removal of the coffin to the Charmart cemetery three days after the original burial. Still another version came from General Comte d'Andigné, who had been imprisoned in the Temple in 1801 and who said he had unearthed in the garden 'the skeleton of a child who had been buried in quicklime', which he told the doorkeeper was evidently 'the body of M. le Dauphin'. 'Yes, sir', the doorkeeper had replied with evident embarrassment.

Permission was obtained to search for the coffin but on the day appointed for the exhumation, while the clergy of the church waited, a messenger from the Commissioner of Police of the district appeared and announced 'that there were reasons for postponing the operation'. The mortal remains of Louis XVI and Marie Antoinette were exhumed and re-interred at St Denis, but no official search was made for that of their son, and the first anniversary of his death following the restoration was unmarked by ceremonies.

This omission by the restored Bourbons to attempt to establish the identity of the boy by exhumation is considered suspicious by M. Lenôtre, who records the subsequent attempts to identify the skeleton unearthed at the spot that had been indicated by Madame Betrancourt.

In November, 1846, the Curé of Sainte-Marguerite, the Abbé Haumet who was consumed with curiosity about the famous burial in the cemetery, took advantage of the building of a shed against the transept of the church, to excavate at the spot where the grave-digger had told his wife that he had reburied the coffin. A few blows with a pickaxe disclosed a coffin which was carried into the presbytery and opened by M. Haumet in the presence of several doctors, and other priests, one of whom, the Abbé Bossuet, recorded his impression that, at first glance, everyone was struck by the strange disproportion between the arms, legs and trunk of the skeleton; the body being that of a child, while its members appeared to belong to a person of much more advanced age. The witnesses' doubts that it was the skeleton of the former Dauphin were set at rest by the appearance of the skull, which had been sawed in two above the level of the eye sockets and to which a few remnants of reddish brown hair still adhered.

The doctors present, Milcent and Récamier, drew up a report in which they stated their opinion that the bones were very probably those of a male, but which presented 'abnormal peculiarities'. 'The rib and clavicles are certainly those of a male subject. The head and bones of the trunk appear to indicate a more advanced age, about twelve years, while the members and teeth are those of an adult of fifteen to eighteen years.' They were clearly puzzled, and they concluded the report; 'It appears demonstrated that these bones are those of the child confined in the Temple and whose autopsy was made by Doctors Dumangin, Pelletan, Lassus and Jeanroy, but it is absolutely impossible that this skeleton could have been that of a child of ten years and a few months; it can only have belonged to a young boy of fifteen to sixteen.'

The bones were reinterred in an oak box at the site where they had been found.

Another exhumation took place in 1894, and these bones were examined by four doctors, Backer, the director of the *Revue Antiseptic*, Bilhaut, the children's surgeon at the International hospital, Magitot, a Member of the Academy of Medicine, and Manouvrier, a Professor at the School of Anthropology. They remarked that the skull had been sawn in two by 'an expert hand', the curvature of the ribs and the lack of development of the thoracic cage 'denoting a certain degree of rachitis', the lock of reddish brown hair, and they concluded that the skeleton was that of a boy of sixteen to eighteen who had reached the height of one metre, sixty centimetres.

The discovery of the skull that had been sawn during an autopsy suggests that the skeleton exhumed in 1846 and 1894 was indeed that of the boy who died in the tower on June 8, 1795, for it would be beyond the bounds of coincidence to conclude that two bodies, both of which had been subjected to an autopsy, could have been buried in the same cemetery on the same date. Yet, there is an apparent discrepancy between the widow Betrancourt's story and the record of the first exhumation. The grave dug by her husband was deep enough to run half beneath the church wall; the Abbé Haumet unearthed it with a few blows with a pickaxe. Did Betrancourt perhaps, suggests M. Lenôtre, as a precaution against discovery, bury another coffin on top of it, and did the searchers in 1846, in their haste and eagerness, exhume bones from two skeletons that had become mixed together? M. Lenôtre dismisses the possibility that Betrancourt could have drawn the wrong coffin from the common grave, because of the skull 'sawed by an expert hand'; and he recalls that Madame Simon stated that she and her husband took from the School of Surgery to the Temple a rachitic and deformed child to replace the Dauphin, such a child as seems to have been described by more than one subsequent visitor.

The exhumations serve only to deepen the mystery. The direct evidence appears to deny the theory of substitution; the circumstantial evidence supports it, for it would have been strange if the self-seeking politicians of the Revolution had allowed their magic talisman to pass from their hands. The enigma remains, unless it can be further elucidated by the claims of the various pretenders who after 1815 said they were the lost Dauphin, and possibly by Madame Royale's reaction to the question that then assumed such prominence—did Louis Charles escape from the tower of the Temple and, if he did, what became of him?

18

THE PRETENDERS

Madame Royale's marriage to the Duc d'Angoulême, says M. de Vaulabille (*Histoire des deux Restaurations*, 1825) 'was a bitter disappointment to the bride, a hollow fraud'. Her sickly husband was impotent, discovered Marie Thérèse, a fact she tried to disguise even after her death by prohibiting in her will the opening of her body, which was a custom of the Bourbon family. She and her husband (whose day, wrote a contemporary, was filled with 'Mass, vespers, benediction and hunting') stayed at Mittau with the King until 1801 when the Czar (who had become a passionate admirer of General Bonaparte) turned them out and in 1807, after various wanderings, the Royal Family took up abode at Hartwell in England, where Louis was forced to accept the humiliating status of a private gentleman. They lived there, in an atmosphere of gloom and piety, until 1812, the year that brought the first ray of hope, the news that Napoleon's army had perished in the snows of Russia. When the Emperor abdicated on April 6, 1814, and was exiled to Elba, the allied sovereigns invited Louis XVIII to ascend the throne of France.

He returned to Paris on May 3rd, driving through the city with the Orphan of the Temple at his side, the crowds staring in wonder at these survivors of a bygone age, Louis, a fat, shapeless man with slobbery mouth and hard eyes, the Duchess dressed in unfashionable English clothes and an ugly little hat, looking, thought Czar Alexander 'just like a governess', prematurely aged, with faded complexion and coarsened features; and seeming to say by her expression, 'I have forgiven nothing'. (I put on *that* face, you know the one,' Marie Thérèse wrote to her husband.) 'She showed in her face the hatred she felt for us', recorded Madame Cavaignac, an eye-witness to the Bourbon restoration, and she described the Duchess as 'a poor dried-up thing'.[1]

[1] Madame Cavaignac, *Memoires d'une Inconnue.*

Nonetheless, the Parisians were eager to welcome the woman in whose debt they felt themselves. Respect for her sufferings could have been turned into affection. Stiff with etiquette, Marie Thérèse sat erect in her carriage, watching the crowds with coldly observant eyes. 'The people fancied she hated them, and ended by hating her,' observed the Comtesse de Boigne.

A solemn *Te Deum* was sung at Notre Dame. Passing the Conciergerie, the Duchess swooned; to faint at such a spot twenty-one years after the deaths of her mother and aunt was considered tactless and an insult to Parisians. At the Tuileries had gathered twelve ladies, each drawn from one of the municipalities, carrying baskets of flowers; ignoring them the Duchess swept through the throng, flung herself into a chair and burst into stormy sobs. 'Why did she return at all?' wondered Madame de Cavaignac.

The Parisians had forgotten the passage of time; they expected to see the timid, heroic child of the Temple. They recoiled from the tall, masculine-looking woman, with weather-beaten complexion, bad teeth and hard eyes. She could not forget. That evening, the Comtesse de Chastenay, one of the playmates of her youth, was presented to her. The Princess tried to be gracious;

'Did your father die young?'

'Yes, Madame.'

'How did you lose him?'

'Alas, Madame, he perished on the scaffold during the Reign of Terror.'

The Duchess, stated the eye-witness, the Comtesse de Boigne, 'started violently and instantly made a gesture of dismissal. From that day forward she not only showed Madame de Chastenay no further kindness, but treated her with extreme rudeness, and avoided speaking to her whenever it was possible.'

Curt, brutal, forbidding, the Duchess dissipated the goodwill her reappearance offered the monarchy. Louis was equally ungracious. For him nothing was changed; he was King of France by Divine Right. Their airs and graces quickly bored the Parisians who were anxious to forget the past. The solemn ceremony of the reinterment of the bones of Louis XVI and Marie Antoinette was greeted by ribald jests. The Bourbons kept up the façade : it was shaken by a bolt from the blue.

On March 9, 1815, Napoleon landed on the coast of France; the Hundred Days had begun. Louis XVIII fled to Ghent, and the Duchesse d'Angoulême joined him there. Napoleon's bid to gain power ended at Waterloo. Again the Bourbons were restored. In 1824 Louis XVIII died, and was succeeded by his brother, who titled himself Charles X; the Duchesse d'Angoulême became Dauphine of France by right of her husband; during the reign of Louis XVIII, she had ranked second in the kingdom and now she took precedence after her husband. She found it humiliating to step aside and say politely 'After you, Monsieur le Dauphin'.

Like his brother, Charles refused to admit the days of hereditary monarchy and Divine Right were over. In 1830 he bowed to fate and abdicated; he and his son and niece crossed to England on the ordinary boat from Cherbourg. During the voyage, the Duchess enquired their destination from a sailor. 'Saint Helena,' he replied. She shuddered, raising her eyes in mute resignation. The sailor was not entirely correct, for the ship sailed to 'Saint Helens', a port on the Isle of Wight. The exiles did not remain long in England, whose people neglected to uncover in their presence. In 1833 they went to Prague, and there she nursed her uncle on his death bed, when in 1836 he died of cholera at the age of seventy-nine.

The middle-aged Duchess and her husband became good friends. They detached themselves from the preoccupations of the world, dawdling and yawning the days away, walking in the woods, reading, playing cards, eating their meals, talking a little, but never of the past. 'Not that,' she would say. 'Do not let us talk of sad things. We have enough sorrow as it is.' Occasionally she broke her reserve to speak of the Temple, but generally she took refuge in solitude. As she grew older, Marie Thérèse learned to forgive her enemies, or to forget the horrors of the past. When her husband died in 1844, she retired to live in a castle near Vienna, and there she died on October 13, 1851, aged seventy-two years. According to General Larochejacuelin, who made the statement in 1855, she declared on her death-bed, 'My brother did not die; that has been the nightmare of my whole life', and she implored him to seek out the Dauphin and restore him to the throne of his fathers.

Did the Duchess d'Angoulême believe that her brother had died in the Temple? During her lifetime, she neither wrote nor said anything tangible, other than on her death-bed, that expressed any doubt, but her actions suggest that her mind was in ferment, and she interested herself in the claims of several of the legion of young men who stated they were the lost Dauphin. The accusation that she steadfastly refused to consider the pretensions of these individuals, because she was determined to quash any claim, however strong it might be, in order to maintain the legitimacy of her uncle, is unjust. The Duchess was a woman of upright and inflexible character and if she had honestly believed that one of the claimants was her brother, she would undoubtedly have acknowledged him, however greatly her acceptance might endanger the regime to which her husband stood in succession. She was perplexed by the appearance of these impostors, as they seem to have been, for they all failed to satisfy the essential condition—a recital of the means of their escape from the Temple that fitted the known facts.

Yet, despite his inability to satisfy this condition, there are some strange facts relating to Jean Marie Hergagault, the first of these 'pretenders' to appear.

His father, René Hergagault, a tailor of St Lo in Normandy, married on February 24, 1781, at the Church of Saint Germain l'Auxerrois in Paris, Nicole Bigot, the mistress of the Duc de Valentinois, who bore a son by him in September, which the tailor adopted as his own, and five more children were subsequently born to them. This son, who was baptized Jean Marie, would thus have been fourteen years of age in June 1795, when the Dauphin officially died, aged ten years. Jean Marie left home in 1796 and after various wanderings reached, in the year 1798, the town of Châlons where he was arrested by the police who placed an advertisement in the newspapers enquiring for the relatives of a young boy 'who stated he was aged about thirteen and who did not appear to be any older'. The tailor Hergagault came to Châlons, recognized his son and took him home. Jean Marie again wandered off, and after further adventures, including several visits to prison, died in 1812, keeping obstinate silence about his origin and hinting only that he was the Dauphin. He claimed several parents, including the 'Prince of Monaco', which was one of the Duc de Valentinois's titles. If he was an impostor, Jean Marie was a circumspect deceiver, for he needed to be careful while the Republic endured. His charm won him many friends, hospitality and gifts of money.

If he was in fact seventeen in 1798 and had been born in 1781, he could not have been Louis Charles, interesting as his mother's name seems to be. A man named René Bigot, we recall, witnessed the death certificate of the boy who died in the Temple, acknowledging himself to be 'a friend of the deceased', and he had appeared there previously on January 21, 1794, under mysterious circumstances. Did he then substitute Nicole's son for Louis Charles, and continue to keep watch on the boy? Attractive as this speculation may seem, no relationship has been discovered between René and Nicole Bigot. Nicole came from peasant stock in Haute Saône, and René, his father and grandfather, were all Parisians. But René Bigot married in 1778 at the same church in which the marriage of René Hergagault and Nicole Bigot was later celebrated. Jean Marie Hergagault, we remark, was described in 1798 as appearing to be about thirteen years of age, the age that Louis Charles by then would have achieved. It is not therefore inconceivable that the boy who appeared at Châlons was Louis Charles, if Nicole's son had been substituted for him, and he may not have known the circumstances of his abduction.

The Duchess of Angoulême took an interest in the story of Hergagault, as she did in that told by another pretender, Charles Navarre or Mathurin Bruneau, as he called himself, who appeared in 1816. The ex-waiter Turgy, who had become her confidential servant, was despatched to Normandy to question him but Navarre had disappeared. 'What happened on January 21st when the firing of cannon was heard? What did your aunt say then and what did they do for you out of the ordinary?' Turgy was told to ask, a question that might have sorted the sheep from the goats, and which was not put to any of the other pretenders, some forty in all, who desired to win fame and fortune. Many were imprisoned for fraud, like the Baron de Richemont and Charles Navarre.

This army of impostors had retired by 1836 when perhaps the most impressive of the claimants appeared on the scene. Charles Willem Naundorff was a remarkable man, an inventor of genius who designed in later life an entirely new type of gun, the patent of which he sold to the Dutch Government, and an attractive person who won many friends, including the Dauphin's ex-nurse

Madame Rambaud, who, in company with M. de Joly, Louis XVI's ex-Minister of Justice, who had been at the Tuileries on August 10th, recognized him as the missing heir. Madame Rambaud declared she had observed certain marks, including the scar on the lip which had been caused by the bite of a rabbit. In reply to Joly's question, 'What did I give you when the Royal Family were taken to the National Assembly?' Naundorff replied, correctly, 'food'.

Naundorff stated that he had been carried out of the Temple in a coffin, after having been drugged with opium, on June 8, 1795 (the day of the child's death), a not inconceivable story if, as rumour has it, the substitute had been secreted in the attic on the unoccupied fourth floor of the tower. Naundorff stated that he had been taken by a Swiss lady to Italy, and after devious wanderings (the details of which he declared he would reveal only in Court), he reached in 1809 Frankfurt-am-Maine, where his life was saved by the intervention of Barras and the ex-Empress Josephine (Napoleon's first wife). He went to Berlin, where the Chief of Police, after consulting the King of Prussia, gave him identity papers in the name of Naundorff, and he became a watchmaker, an occupation that links him to Louis XVI, who was a keen amateur locksmith and repairer of watches.

Naundorff stated that he wrote to the Duchesse d'Angoulême in 1816 and received no reply. She steadfastly refused to see him, even in 1834, when he reached Dresden, where she was visiting. Nonetheless she had made some attempt to inform herself about the new claimant, sending the Vicomte Larochefoucauld to interrogate him in 1833. He reported to his mistress that Naundorff bore some resemblance, taking his age into account, to the most careful portraits of Louis XVII, and he possessed the general features of the Bourbon family. Following a second meeting early in 1834, Larochefoucauld told the Duchess, 'To be quite fair, I must add that the more one sees and observes the personage in question, the more one is tempted to see in him resemblances to the Royal Family and in more than one respect the mark of truth', and he urged his mistress to receive Naundorff. She rejected his advice and she refused to see Madame Rambaud, who had made a special journey to Prague to advance Naundorff's claim. In Dresden, the Duchess refused even to look at Naun dorff's children, who were said to strongly resemble the female Bourbons.

On June 13, 1836, Naundorff summoned the ex-King Charles X and the Duchess d'Angoulême to appear in the Civil Court of the Department of the Seine, to answer his claim to the Bourbon property in France. Two days later he was arrested by the police, his papers were confiscated and he was expelled from France by the decree of the Minister of the Interior. He went to live in London, where, on November 16, 1838, an attempt was made on his life, an occurrence which drew from the French Government the statement that Naundorff was a Jew from Prussian Poland, which that Government immediately denied. Naundorff, who wrote a book supporting his claim, lived in England until 1845, when he went to Holland where he died on August 10th, being described in the death certificate as 'Charles Louis de Bourbon, aged sixty, son of Louis XVI and Marie Antoinette'. To this day, Naundorff's descendants bring claim in the French Courts to establish their ancestor's identity. Their advocate in the nineteenth century, Julius Favre, who became a Cabinet Minister and as such had access to governmental archives, stated in his *Reminiscences* that he believed the genuineness of Naundorff's claim. Unfortunately Naundorff was denied the opportunity of fighting his claim in the French courts, and the treatment accorded him awakens the suspicion that he might have been able to prove it, given the opportunity.

The fate of the little Dauphin remains an enigma, perhaps the last great historical mystery and one that can never be solved. The theory of his escape from the Temple and his substitution by a mute and scrofulous boy may be no more than a delusion, one that was enhanced by the then prevailing belief in aristocratic and royal changelings and substitutions. Louis Charles, it was rumoured in Paris in 1792, had been sent for safety to Canada and the boy the Royal Family paraded was a substitute whom the absent-minded Louis XVI sometimes failed to recognize. Even the Duchesse d'Angoulême was believed to have been substituted, *en route* to Austria in 1795, for another girl, a theory that appeared to be supported after 1814 by her very different character to the poor Orphan of the Temple, and which was disclosed by the *Gazette de France*, which stated, shortly after Madame Royale's arrival in Vienna, that 'a young woman, an adventuress, or mad, declared that she was the French Princess, adding that the Princess who had recently arrived was a changeling'.

Whatever his fate may have been, and speculation is useless, Louis Charles fulfilled the Bourbon tradition by which, for seven generations, no son succeeded his father. Louis XIV was followed by his great-grandson, and Louis XV by his grandson, Louis XVI; of his sons, one died in infancy and the fate of Louis Charles is doubtful. Louis XVIII had no children and Charles X's two sons, Dukes of Angoulême and Berry, did not succeed him. Charles was followed on the throne by the 'Citizen King', Louis Philippe, the son of Philip Égalite, and his son was not called to the throne. If we include the King of Rome, Napoleon's son, and Louis Napoleon's son, the Prince Imperial, who was killed in Zululand in 1879, no ruler of France was succeeded by his son for a period of 160 years.

The Bourbon dynasty was in fact exhausted. Louis XVI, despite his attempt to bow to the Revolution, had his mind turned to the past. Behind him lay a thousand years of monarchical and hereditary rule. He could not forget it, and he intrigued weakly against the ferment of ideas that were released by the French Revolution. He died because he loved his people too greatly to kill them. Nor could Marie Antoinette overcome her monarchical heritage; at the moment of crisis, on August 10, 1792, she had not the courage to take command from her amiable and irresolute husband. Few men or women could have coped with the situation they faced. Napoleon Bonaparte could probably have done so, and he spoke the final epitaph to the Bourbons. On February 18, 1800, the new Director was conducted round his palace, the Tuileries, by the former Attorney General, Pierre Louis Roederer, who had miraculously survived the Terror. 'It all looks very sad, General,' murmured Roederer. 'Yes, very sad, this former grandeur,' replied the future conqueror of Europe, the ruthless man who benefited from the weaknesses of his predecessors, the Bourbons who had fought for principles, and the Revolutionaries who had striven to gain personal power.

CHRONOLOGY

1770		Marriage of Louis and Marie Antoinette
1774		Accession of Louis XVI
1778	December 19	Marie Thérèse (Madame Royale) born
1785	March 27	Louis Charles (the Dauphin) born
1789	July 14	Fall of the Bastille
1791	June 20	Flight to Varennes
1792	April 20	Declaration of War against Austria
	June 20	Mob invade the Tuileries
	August 10	Storming of the Tuileries
		King suspended
	September 2	Fall of Verdun and Massacres in Paris
	September 20	Battle of Valmy
	September 21	The National Convention
		Monarchy abolished
	November 6	Battle of Jemappes
1793	January 21	Execution of Louis XVI
	February 1	Declaration of War against Britain
	March 10	Revolutionary Tribunal
	March 18	Battle of Neerwinden
	April 6	Committee of Public Safety
	July 13	Marat murdered
	August 23	*Levée en masse*
	August 27	Surrender of Toulon to British
	September 17	Law of Suspects
	October 16	Execution of Marie Antoinette
		Battle of Wattignies
	December 19	Recapture of Toulon
1794	March 24	Execution of Chaumette, Hébert
	April 5	Execution of Danton
	July 27	9th Thermidor

	July 28	Execution of Robespierre
		The Directory
1795	June 8	Official death of the Dauphin
	December 18	Madame Royale leaves the Temple
1799	November 9	Napoleon's coup d'état

BIBLIOGRAPHY

(English titles where applicable)

ANGOULÊME, Duchesse d': *Relation du captivité*, London, 1823 and 1862

BEARN, Madame de (Pauline de Tourzel): *Souvenirs de quarante ans*

BEAUCOURT, Marquis de: *Captivité et derniers moments de Louis XVI. Récits originaux et documents officiels*, 2 vols., Paris, 1892

CAMPAN, M. A.: *Memories about the Private Life of Marie Antoinette*, 3 vols., London, 1887

CLÉRY, J. H.: *Diary of Events in the Tower of the Temple during the captivity of Louis XVI*, London, 1798

DAUDET, E.: *Madame Royale*, London, 1913

ENGLISH SPY: *Francis Drake to Lord Grenville. Fortescue Dropmore manuscripts*, vol. 2, 529, Historical Manuscripts Commission, 1894

FIRMONT, Abbé Edgeworth: *Memoires*, Paris, 1815

GORET, C.: *Mon témoignage sur le détention de Louis XVI et sa famille dans le Tour du Temple*, Paris, 1825

HUE, Françoise: *The Last Years of the Reign and Life of Louis XVI*, London, 1866

LA MORINERIE: *Papiers du Temple*, Nouvelle Revue, 1884

LAMORLIÈRE, Rosalie: *Account of Marie Antoinette's Captivity in the Conciergerie*, London, 1898

LENÔTRE, G.: *The Dauphin (Louis XVII)*, London, 1911

MALESHERBES, C. G. L.: *Vie*, Paris, 1802

MATHIEZ, A.: *The French Revolution*, London, 1928

MATHIEZ, A.: *Le dix août*, Paris, 1931

MORRIS, Gouveneur, *Diary and Letters*, 2 vols., New York, 1888

PANCKOUCK (Ed.): *Moniteur*

PINEL, Philippe: *Lettres*, Paris, 1859

PRUDHOMME, L.: *Histoire générale des crimes comise pendant le Révolution Français*, 6 vols., Paris, 1796

ROEDERER, P. L.: *Chronique des cinquante jours du 20 juin au 10 août*, Paris, 1832

ROCHEFOUCAULD, François de: *Souvenirs du 10 août et de l'armée Bourbon*

THOMPSON, J. H.: *English Witnesses of the French Revolution*, Oxford, 1938

TOURZEL, Duchesse de: *Memoires 1789–95*, 2 vols., Paris, 1883.

TUETY, A: *Repetoire V*, Paris, 1874

TURGY, F.: *Les quarte jours de la Terreur*, Paris, 1814

Note: The narratives of Dufour, Daujon, Turgy, Goret, Lepitre, Moelle, Lamorlière, Bault, Fouché, Magnin, Chaveau-Lagarde, Laviviere, Busne, Leger, Desfosses are printed by G. Lenôtre, *The Last Days of Marie Antoinette*, 1907.

INDEX